A RESEARCHER LEARNS TO

WRITE

Selected articles and monographs

A RESEARCHER LEARNS TO

W R I T E

Selected articles and monographs

DONALD H. GRAVES

EXETER

Heinemann Educational Books Inc.
4 Front Street, Exeter, New Hampshire 03833

LONDON EDINBURGH MELBOURNE AUCKLAND
HONG KONG SINGAPORE KUALA LUMPUR
NEW DELHI IBADAN NAIROBI JOHANNESBURG
KINGSTON PORT OF SPAIN

Clarke Irwin (1983) Inc. Toronto, Canada

Cover design by Ryan Cooper

Library of Congress Cataloging in Publication Data

Graves, Donald H.
  A researcher learns to write.

  1. English language—Composition and exercises—
Study and teaching—Addresses, essays, lectures.
2. Language arts—Addresses, essays, lectures. I. Title.
PE1404.G68 1984   808'.042'07   84-6525
ISBN 0-435-08213-2
ISBN 0-435-10270-2 (UK)

Printed in the United States of America

To Betty:

Who waited, then helped

Contents

Acknowledgements

Writers must learn to shut the door and write alone. But they must also learn to open the door and share their work with others. I wrote this book to show how I've changed as a writer over the last ten years. I also wrote it to show how to open the door and get help from other people. For this reason each article contains an introduction which shows how I wrote the piece, and how specific individuals helped me.

Some persons are not mentioned as their help was more generally supportive. They deserve to be mentioned here. First, our writer's group at the University of New Hampshire. Since the spring of 1976 a group of professor-writers has met weekly to share writing, readings, and talk about the place of writing and reading in their professional lives. Our group is diverse; arguments fly, but we still meet. Our differences polish the rough edges of thought. I am grateful for both the support and differences within the group.

Tom Newkirk, Associate Professor in the English Department, though not mentioned directly in the introductions, has always served as an excellent critic and supporter of writing process work. Jane Hansen has made valuable suggestions for many of the introductions compiled in this book.

Teachers helped. *None* of the research contained in this volume, nor the articles I composed, could have been done without the teachers who allowed me to enter their classrooms for long periods of time. These teachers uncovered the remarkable contributions children have to share with all of us.

Research costs money. The Education Professions Development Act, the Ford Foundation, the National Institute of Education, and the Research Foundation of the National Council of Teachers of English provided both direct and indirect support for most of the research reported here.

Philippa Stratton, my editor at Heinemann, has encouraged this venture from the beginning. Her gentle prodding, as well as expert assistance, shows an editor at work whose philosophy of editing is the same as that contained in most of my own writing.

Dori Farrell has been my secretary through this entire venture. More than typist, her cheery disposition and administrative help kept this book moving.

Finally, I owe my greatest thanks to my family and my wife, Betty, (to whom this book is dedicated). My first writing began in 1973 when we had five children at home. At this writing in 1984 only one child, Laura, herself a budding writer, is at home. Five grandchildren now joyfully interrupt my writing. Betty has heard me read just about every line aloud from both introductions and articles over the ten years. She is my first critic when I open the door to my study.

Sources of Original Publication

Many of the chapters in this book were first published as articles or reports. A complete reference list of these chapters follows. We are most grateful to all the organizations cited for permission to reprint the following:

2. "Sex Differences in Children's Writing," *Elementary English*, Vol. 50, No. 7, (October, 1973), pp. 1101–1106.
3. "The Child, the Writing Process, and the Role of the Professional," in *The Writing Processes of Students*, Patrick Finn and Walter Petty, editors, State University of New York at Buffalo, 1975, pp. 21–29.
4. "An Examination of the Writing Processes of Seven Year Old Children," *Research in the Teaching of English*, Vol. 9, No. 3, Winter 1975, pp. 227–241.
5. "Let's Get Rid of the Welfare Mess in the Teaching of Writing," *Language Arts*, Vol. 53 (September, 1976,) pp. 645–651.
6. "Language Arts Textbooks: A Writing Process Evaluation," *Language Arts*, Vol. 54, (April, 1977,) pp. 817–823.
7. "Balance the Basics: Let Them Write," (Ford Report), New York: Ford Foundation, February, 1978.
9. "We Can End the Energy Crisis," *Language Arts*, Vol. 55, October, 1978, pp. 795–796.
10. "Let Children Show Us How to Help Them Write," *Visible Language*, Vol. XIII, No. 1, pp. 16–28. (Special issue: "Teaching and Learning, the Craft of Handwriting")
11. "A New Look at Writing Research," in *Perspectives on Writing in Grades 1–8*, Shirley Haley-James, editor, NCTE, 1981, pp. 93–117.
13. "Questions for Teachers Who Wonder if Their Writers Change," *Language Arts*. Written with M.E. Giacobbe, Vol. 59, (May, 1982,) pp. 495–503.
14. "Write With the Children," *Writing: Teachers and Children At Work*, Chapter 5. Heinemann Educational Books, Inc., Exeter, N.H., 1983.
15. National Institute of Education Study. *A Case Study Observing the Development of Primary Children's Composing, Spelling, and Motor Behaviors During the Writing Process*. September 1978–August 1981.
16. "Don't Underestimate What Children Can Write." Presentation to the National Commission on Excellence in Education Hearings, Houston, Texas. April, 1982.
17. "Back to School." Editorial written for the Concord Monitor, Concord, New Hampshire, August 23, 1982.
18. "The Author's Chair," *Language Arts*. Written with Jane Hansen, Vol. 60, (February, 1982,) pp. 176–183.

1. It's Never Too Late

I published my first article when I was forty-three years old. That first publication came rather late in life and marked the beginning of my learning how to write. This introduction is a brief account of my experiences with writing from high school through yesterday, December 11, 1983. I give particular attention to the last ten years from first publication in 1973 and last writing in 1983.

I give this account to help others who wonder if writing can have a place in their lives. Most people I've met view writing, research, and publishing as mystical domains reserved for the talented and elite. My journey is ordinary and commonplace. Everyone has a voice and original thoughts that ought to be shared with others.

Mrs. Dower, my sophomore English teacher in high school gave me an inkling that I might be able to write. I had just completed reading Irving Stone's biography of Jack London, *A Sailor on Horseback*. I wanted to live London's life as an adventurer but most of all I wanted to be able to write like him. "What do you have to do in order to be a writer?" I asked her. She took my naive question seriously. "Write and rewrite," she replied. I worked at writing for only a brief time. But the notion never went away.

I went to college and majored in English. The writing dream was shattered. Worse, I was carefully taught that I couldn't write at all. I probably wasn't a very good writer, but I was willing to pay the price if someone would give me a hand.

English majors were required to write four long papers in their senior year, two in tragedy and two in comedy. I chose to write about the tragedy of Prince Andrew Bolkonsky, one of the key characters in *War and Peace*. I chose to write about the tragedy of Bolkonsky's life because one of my closest friends, Ted Davey, had just been killed in Korea while waiting to go into battle. Ted's situation was similar to Bolkonsky's: he never got to the fight. As I wrote the paper I was struggling with death and conscientious objection; I was due to be drafted the following June. I figured that literature was intended to wrestle with life's big issues. The paper came back with a D+ and the statement, "Please change your typewriter ribbon." The ribbon was bad but I nearly went haywire, failed three midsemester exams, and was placed on academic probation for my last semester in college.

After four years in the U.S. Coast Guard I started work on a master's degree in education at Bridgewater State College in Massachusetts. One of my last courses was one on educational research with Professor Jordan Fiore. I chose to write about Leo Tolstoy, whom I felt was a long-neglected educator. I lived at the Lamont library at Harvard University, wrote the paper, and was told by Professor Fiore that I ought to submit it for publication. I labeled his praise as misguided. Academic probates didn't publish. But six years after I completed my paper, Norman Weiner published his book, *Tolstoy and Education*. I wasn't ready to write a book but I did have a sense of what was right for publication. Maybe Fiore was right.

By the time I started to write for actual publication in 1973, fourteen years after Bridgewater and twenty-one years after college, I had gone through several careers. I had been a serviceman, a classroom teacher, a school principal, a director of education in a Presbyterian church, city director of English as a Second Language Reading bilingual programs, and a college administrator. Most of my work in all these careers involved administration. I avoided writing.

My career responsibilities also included much speaking, especially in the church, where I preached an average of once every six weeks for seven years. My work in the city and college required many public presentations. But writing, with the exception of proposals for funding, simply wasn't part of my repertoire.

Phase One: Doctoral Study and Dissertation Phase (1972–1976)

In 1970 I began doctoral study at the State University of New York at Buffalo. I wanted to learn more about language background and the solid information needed to understand the theories behind children's learning. At that time I was heavily involved in the field of reading as Director of Reading Programs for Lackawanna, New York. But the more I studied in the field of reading, the more I became disillusioned with clinical approaches to children's problems: All procedures seemed to point to what children couldn't do.

For about a year and a half I felt uneasy. Then, quite by accident I became interested in writing. I did an independent study with Professor Walter Petty in which I surveyed research in the writing field. I was surprised to see how little had been done. Most of the recommendations for writing research were not heeded. Walter Petty, Charles Cooper, David Honeycutt and Richard Salzer, my dissertation committee, allowed me to strike out on my own with a case-study approach to research. How fortunate I was to have a committee that would permit me such independence in pursuing a new research problem, and in such an unorthodox manner. Although Janet Emig preceded me with her research on the composing processes of twelfth-grade students, my committee was unaware of her work when I first started.

Writing about my research was a nightmare. No question, I had problems in writing, but my committee didn't know how to help me. Extensive corrections, with language supplied, just didn't work. I wrote and rewrote with some improvement but the message wasn't clear. Here I was writing about writing and I couldn't even write. My family watched me return from a conference on a chapter and studied my face to see if there was any promise of relief for me or them. I worked so hard to second-guess what was required that I threw out my *own* thoughts about language and clarity. The writing got worse, not better. I didn't compromise the data, and no one asked me to; I just couldn't say things clearly enough. I was so close to the data that I assumed my findings were clear to others. Besides, describing human behaviors as well as the environments in which they occurred was very difficult.

The dissertation was more abandoned than completed. The research was complete; the writing task was not. I finished my doctoral studies with very jaundiced views about ever writing again. Thus, the acceptance of my first article, "Sex Differences in Children's Writing," just before I completed my dissertation was surprising. Even more surprising was the letter I received in the mail almost a year to the day after I finished my dissertation informing me that my research had won the Promising Researcher Award from the National Council of Teachers of English.

I began teaching at the University of New Hampshire in the fall of 1973. I had to put the dissertation behind me. I put it behind me by writing about it. The study contained good findings and I wrote articles about them in order to get on to something new. But the dissertation syndrome plagued me for three years, from 1973 until 1976.

I struggled to find a new voice, even though my content was centered in my dissertation findings. Donald Murray, a master teacher of writing voice and colleague at the University of New Hampshire, helped me. We talked about research, writing, and what was needed in education. He listened and then asked tough questions about my writing, especially when I used jargon or shifted to the passive, apologetic voice . . . the voice so typical of doctoral students.

I published four articles about information in my dissertation:

"Sex Differences in Children's Writing"
"The Child, the Writing Process, and the Role of the Professional"
"An Examination of the Writing Processes of Seven-Year-Old Children"
"Let's Get Rid of the Welfare Mess in the Teaching of Writing"

Phase Two: Ford Foundation Study and Research Column, *Language Arts* (1976–1979)

In the spring of 1976 two events changed the course of my writing. They got me away from my dissertation and into new thinking about writing and research. In April I received a small grant from the Ford Foundation to study the status of writing and its relationship to reading. This was an "in-house" study to help Ford decide on future funding for the foundation. The other event was a letter from Julie Jensen, the new editor for *Language Arts*, who asked if I would do a research column for the journal. When I enthusiastically accepted I told her I wanted to write about research in such a way that the data would be more accessible to teachers. Although I wanted to help teachers, make no mistake, I was out to help myself as well. If I could write about research in such a way that teachers wanted to read it, I knew that my writing would also improve and a better voice would emerge.

There were times, however, when the dissertation voice reappeared, especially when I didn't understand my data, or when I felt a deadline too close upon me. Expediency led me back to what I knew, the dissertation way of writing about research. But the major rewrites of the Ford study plus the articles related to it in *Language Arts* gradually helped me as a writer to learn to use time better. I wrote more regularly and forced the information less. I began to learn to listen to my own data.

Speaking helped. By now I was traveling around the country more and needed my writing to serve as content for my speaking. But the speaking also served as a rehearsal for writing. When I speak I do not read or work directly from a text. Rather, I prepare twelve to fifteen outlines, write a lead and then an end. I'd guess that a good twenty percent, possibly more, of my talks are composed during the speech itself. Totally new content and metaphors occur to me during my talks, usually spawned by the various responses audiences give to my planned portions. The new content is almost always important information I'll use in my later writing.

Four selections from the Ford Study *Language Arts* phase are contained in this book:

"Language Arts Textbooks: No Change"
"Balance the Basics: Let Them Write"
"Sixty Minutes I and II"
"We Can End the Energy Crisis"

Phase Three: Research in Atkinson, New Hampshire (1978–1982)

In the spring of 1978 I received a grant from the National Institute of Education for a three-year study of the writing processes of young children. Ever since I had completed my study of seven-year-old children's writing for my dissertation in 1973, I had wanted to get back to more systematic observation of children's writing and this time I was determined to have more time to observe children. Above all, I wanted to show children as multi-dimensional human beings operating within actual classrooms, highly complex in their behaviors and decisions.

The writing had to be straightforward, simply telling what the children were doing and what order their behaviors followed. Our entire research team—Lucy McCormick Calkins, Susan Sowers and I—were committed to reporting our data in the articles which we published, mostly in *Language Arts*. We began writing these articles in the second month of the study and continued to write for the next three years. In all, twenty-six articles were published by the research team and teachers in Atkinson. All of the team plus Mary Ellen Giacobbe, first-grade teacher in the study, eventually traveled around the country speaking about the children and the writing process. This speaking was important to our writing since we constantly examined our data to give updates to other teachers and researchers.

As we drove the thirty miles to Atkinson Academy each day we planned what to observe. When we drove back to Durham from the research site we discussed the data and planned the articles we would write about our findings. There was much discussion and collaboration within the team in the early years. But as the study progressed, we didn't discuss our research as much as before. Our interests became more specialized. Nevertheless, these discussions were very important to me both in stimulating writing ideas and in refining our data.

But the Atkinson phase was also marked by another writing community, our weekly writers group at the University of New Hampshire. Donald Murray, Les Fisher, Tom Carnicelli, Ron Winslow, and Tom Newkirk from the English Department, our research team, plus visitors or persons on sabbatical met to share our writing (which ranged from fiction to nonfiction and research). We shared early drafts and final copy, but above all we encouraged each other as writers.

Writing was still a struggle in these years. How hard it was to report children's behaviors so that someone else would want to read about them! I was determined not to repeat the past mistakes of my dissertation. With the exception of the "off-the-top" writing in "Sixty Minutes I and II," all of the writing in these years was very painful for me. Of course, writing during data gathering is usually exceptionally difficult. Making sense of human behaviors using enough data to make judgments can lead to many deadends. As I wrote in "Sixty Minutes I," everything seems to be connected to everything else. An article can only be about one thing, but human behaviors never seem to be limited to one subject. Sometimes I got so frustrated I would try to end an article before it began.

I lived with the Atkinson data day and night for three and one-half years (September 1978 until March 1982). The shelf is still filled with notebooks on each child, and only half of the data are reported. We skimmed off the top. But the time comes when it is important to go on, to leave the past behind and look at children anew from different perspectives. I partially did this in the spring of 1981 when I started to write about how teachers should teach writing.

Articles contained in this book from the Atkinson phase are the following:

"Let Children Show Us How to Help Them Write"
"A New Look at Writing Research"
"Sixty Minutes I and II"
"Questions for Teachers Who Wonder if Their Writers Change"
"Write with the Children"
"Final Report—NIE"

Phase Four: Post-Atkinson Writing: Teachers and Children at Work (1981–1983)

The third and fourth phases overlap. When I started to write the sections in my book, *Writing: Teachers and Children at Work*, about what teachers ought to do when they taught writing, I was surprised to find that the writing went easily. The second chapter was written in four days, the third in six. With the exception of chapter seven, chapters two through nine were done in about six weeks. For the first time I wasn't describing detailed child behaviors. The writing was crisp and good. The editor made very few changes in the text. Phases three and four overlap because I still had to write the final report for the National Institute of Education. Back I went to struggling with child behaviors and study findings—and at the same time, to writing for the public.

In March of 1982 I was asked to testify before the President's Commission on Excellence in Houston, Texas. I had two weeks to compose a six-page presentation about our research in Atkinson plus my recommendations for future research in writing. Although I struggled, I found that the writing was much easier with the final research report for NIE behind me. I learned then that I write better when I only have one piece of writing going at one time.

This final phase also marks a new emphasis in my research, the study of reading and writing together. Jane Hansen and I had begun a study on the two processes in the fall of 1981. Back to difficult writing again. Describing child behaviors in two processes is near madness. Jane and I took a long time trying to chart behaviors—again charting them in such a way that they would be intelligible to others.

Finally, the first critiques of our work in the writing process movement have started to come in. They must increase as more and more people try the approach. Most of us working with the writing process have even stronger concerns than our toughest critics might voice about the movement. For this reason, I felt it imperative to write the final piece, "The Enemy is Orthodoxy."

The final selections from this fourth phase are:

"Don't Underestimate What Children Can Write"
"Back to School—An Editorial"
"The Author's Chair"
"The Enemy is Orthodoxy"

Final Reflection

Overall the writing is easier these days. I have learned how to maintain a regular schedule. Thirty minutes of writing a day for six days is better than twelve straight hours of writing. I have learned from the children that daily writing helps me to write even when I am not writing. I think about my writing when I am not writing. Ideas don't get neglected or grow stale; they evolve on a more systematic basis. I don't force the writing or try to end a piece before I know what the information dictates.

There will always be difficult pieces, and new research problems beckon like the Lorelei. But I've picked up a few tools along the way. The most important aid to my writing, however, is the plodding patience with which I put in my time each day on the computer waiting for something to emerge on the screen. I'm not in a hurry and I'm enjoying the trip much more than when I began to write about research in 1973.

2. Sex Differences in Children's Writing

Introduction

I remember picking up the morning mail at my home on 164 Union Street, Hamburg, New York, in June, 1973. In between the third and fourth class mail was an envelope from Iris Tiedt, editor of *Elementary English*. I broke the seal, pulled out the letter, and read that this article, "Sex Differences in Children's Writing," would be in the special October issue on Girls and Women.

I suppose everyone remembers the moment they received the acceptance of the first thing they ever published. I cried for more than joy: I cried out of relief. I was in the midst of writing my dissertation, and after the fourth return of copy for chapter four, I was convinced that I would never be able to complete it let alone ever publish anything. The acceptance of this article was at least confirmation that someone in this world thought I could write and had something worth saying.

The trail of this article began many months before. Janet Emig gave a lecture at the State University of New York at Buffalo, where I was studying. After her talk, Janet gave me a few minutes of her time in which I shared my preliminary findings on sex differences in children's writing. She urged me to write an article for the special issue on Girls and Women that she was coediting with Iris Tiedt. Probably neither Janet nor Iris realizes that they rescued me from the jaws of despair with their encouragement for this article.

The article contains a mixture of styles. It begins with an anecdotal, narrative account of how I got into the study, and then shifts to a more formal, research style. This is hardly surprising since I was torn between telling the story of the data and being the objective researcher. In the first part of the article I chatted along in the first person; then in the second part, I wrote: "After spending four months in the daily observation of behaviors of children and teachers, the researcher did not record one instance in which girls were exposed to the extended vocational roles of women." I have long since decided to use the first person in writing research reports, because I feel that the use of "I" demands careful documentation. The use of "I" affects the voice of the writer and the conviction with which he regards the data as well as the reader's comprehension of the material. It takes more courage, I feel, to say "I think that boys have a different pattern of using first person than girls" than to write "the researcher notes that boys use first person differently than girls."

Most of the data still stand, especially in classrooms where children do not have writing conferences or use a process approach to writing. On the other hand, new data from our three-year study in Atkinson show totally contrary findings.* Sex differences for use of person or territory could not be distinguished in children who

*The Atkinson study refers to the study of the writing process done in Atkinson, New Hampshire, in grades 1 to 4 by me, Lucy McCormick Calkins, and Susan Sowers from 1978 to 1980.

engaged in writing conferences and used a process approach to writing. I suspect that the reflective nature of the conference itself causes boys to gain distance on their thoughts about the topic they are working on. And the conference helps girls to become more adventurous in choosing topics beyond home and school.

This article suggests that sex differences are developmentally based. Now I am not so sure. The exacerbation of sex differences may simply be the result of the ways in which we respond to what children know. The writing conference does give children the courage to say more of what they feel. Thus, this very process may make them feel more comfortable with their sexuality. Topics that have heretofore been taboo along sex lines now become open means of expression for all writers.

In 1973 when this article was written, I had a different view of how writing should be taught. I trusted the children less than I do now. For example, instead of eliciting the boys' own words for saying how a character might feel, I said, "Here are some words you might use to tell how it felt. I have written them down so that you can use them if you feel they might be helpful in your writing." I know now that the child has the words without any help from me, if they are appropriate for what he wishes to say in his piece.

The day was a Saturday. Most of the boys remembered what they were doing that morning when a small plane taking off from Buffalo International Airport crashed in their neighborhood. Two homes were destroyed, the pilots killed, along with one of the house occupants.

At the time, I was researching the writing processes of seven year olds in a school building three blocks from the site of the crash. I noted with interest the effect of the plane crash on their behaviors when they arrived in school on Monday morning. The boys stood in clusters in their informal classroom as they shared recollection of the crash.

> Wow, you should have seen the smoke!
> There was junk all over the place!
> There was fire engines and police cars.
> My mother said I would'a gotten hit if I'd walked to confirmation class.

While the boys were discussing the event, a few girls were interested in the boys' excitement but did not seem to wish to discuss the crash.

In observing the behaviors of the two sexes in other classrooms the same reaction was present. Boys were excited and involved, with most girls distant bystanders.

This piqued my curiosity. Why would an occurrence of this magnitude produce such variance in behavior? Would the children behave similarly with other related events? Finally, if the interests of the sexes were different, would this not carry over into their thematic choices in writing? Although the issue was not the main focus of my research, I would be in a position to assess the issue from the data gathered. The subsequent assessment of these data explained the children's reactions to the aircrash incident and a number of developmental dilemmas encountered in the teaching of writing to young boys and girls.

The study (Graves, 1973) monitored the thematic choices of 69 children in unassigned writing. Unassigned writing was examined on the hypothesis that a more valid developmental profile of boys' and girls' writing interests would emerge without the interference of teacher assignments. From folders kept by each child over 40 teaching days, 860 unassigned papers were assessed to see what seven-year-olds would write about if no assignments were given. The children were in informal rooms in a blue-collar, middle-class school system. The rooms provide the children with wide choices in activity and self-direction. Because of this type of environment the children were composing throughout the day with 70% of their writings being done without assignment.

Boys and girls showed separate profiles in thematic choice. Boys wrote more about themes involving physical death, murder mysteries, war, fires, and the activities of men beyond the home and school. Characters in their writings were constantly moving, conquering opponents, and covering territory. On the other hand, girls wrote more about themes centering in the family, the classroom, and holidays. They were able to write more objectively about themselves. Characterizations in their writings were nuturant and far less aggressive than those in the boys' stories. Girls' themes involved limited and less expansive geographical territory.

As preliminary data indicated gross differences in the writing interests and behaviors of boys and girls, I could not help reflecting on my own inept experiences in assisting the writing of young children. My understanding of individual differences might relate instructionally to children three years apart in reading level, yet completely ignore the individuality and developmental needs of both boys and girls. For some reason, my understanding of individuality was projected in a kind of democratic, unisexual direction. Most of my assistance to writing was in the form of assigning stimulating themes that would inspire the children to write. The constant giving of these types of assignments, "my assignments," produced a myopic view of the developmental interests of each of the boys and girls. After all, my interests would naturally be their interests! My education was complete. There was an obvious need to begin to look at children differently, to view their behaviors without the control of teacher assignments, and to understand some of the developmental backgrounds behind their interests.

In order to understand the differences in the interests and behaviors of boys and girls, a review of developmental literature related to the subject is given. Finally, the literature and the seven-year-old study findings are related to instruction and suggested research directions.

Differences in the behaviors of boys and girls can be discerned at an early age according to Goldberg and Lewis (1969). At the age of thirteen months girls were found to be more dependent and less exploratory than boys in their play. The roots to the differences in behaviors could be traced to the responses of mothers to boys and girls in the first six months of life. Mothers talked to, held, and touched their daughters more than their sons. Later, daughters were found to touch and talk to their mothers more than did sons.

As boys and girls grow, parents make sharp distinctions in the behaviors permitted in each. Sears, Macoby, and Levin (1957) noted that parents allow boys more freedom in the expression of aggression within the family and with other children. Girls, on the other hand, get more praise for good behavior.

As aggression may be permitted with boys, dependency is encouraged with girls. Since it is a desirable trait for girls, dependency is usually associated with parental warmth, satisfaction and adjustment. The opposite is true with dependent boys. Their behaviors are associated with "coldness in the mother and a rejection of intimacy in the father" (Sears, 1969).

A number of sources contribute to the development of sex role consciousness in children. Children observe sex differences in body structure and the relative size and strength of the adult sexes by age five. These may be due to direct observations of adults, as well as the operation of cultural stereotypes. Observations of roles outside the family help children to learn about sex differences in societal responsibilities (Kohlberg, 1966). Mussen and Rutherford (1963) note that the sex-typed preferences of boys were not necessarily related to the masculinity-femininity scores of their fathers. Still, the like-sex parent does contribute substantially to a sex role consciousness. Finally, children are influenced by their peers (Rosenberg and Sutton-Smith, 1968).

Two behaviors, aggression and dependency, are manifest in the stories of young boys and girls. Pitcher and Prelinger (1963), in a study of the stories of 137 intellectually and socio-economically privileged children from two through five, observed the evolution of these themes by age and sex. Continuously evolving themes of space utilization, internal complexity and world expansion were seen as the children grew older.

Boys told about highly active characters who intruded farther into space than those of girls. Story content included more characters, occupational figures, objects, and wild animals. Themes centered in the self through aggression, death, hurt and misfortune. Pitcher and Prelinger observed:

> With the boys, aggression tends to be much more violent; one almost hears and feels the reverberation of crashing, shooting and pounding as general catastrophe reigns. They amplify descriptions and seem altogether fonder of the theme. They often use the word fight suggesting an adversary, and a definite concern as to who will win. At times the violent nature of the boys' aggression seems to leave the personal and become allied with the energy of nature.

The boys' stories rarely used names, and did not include girls.

Girls told stories reflecting greater socialization. Thematic content related to parents, morality, dress, and sociability. Their characters were more vividly and realistically portrayed than boys'. They expressed feelings, used names, and developed characters in greater detail. Pitcher and Prelinger observed, "The girl more often stays close to the here and now in her main interests which are the domestic and the familiar scene." Girls told more about small pets. If wild animals were described, their dispositions were not ferocious.

Thematic choices of boys and girls in the seven-year-old study (Graves, 1973) continued where the stories dictated by young children left off in the Pitcher and Prelinger (1963) study. Basic themes of aggression, territorial expansion were visible in the boys' writing. Themes of dependency and limited territory were noted in the girls'. To better understand their choices of writing themes, two developmental factors were examined, territorial range and use of first person.

Figure 2.1 shows the range of territorial writing in relation to the thematic choices of seven-year-old boys and girls. Primary territory covers the areas of

Figure 2.1

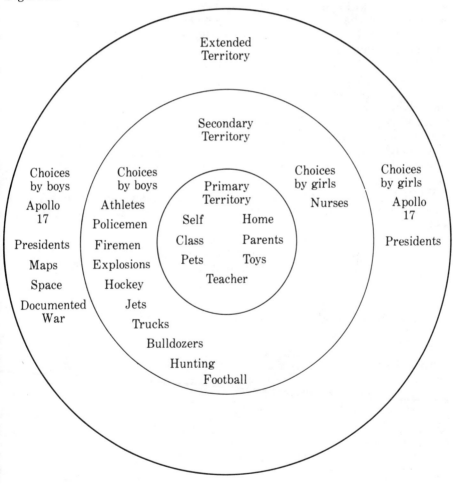

greatest child experience, namely, the home and school. Secondary territory expands to the metropolitan area around the child and includes transportation, adult vocations, professional athletics and community events. Extended territory refers to national and world events and persons identified with them.

The data in Table 2.1 show the distribution of the thematic choices of children in their unassigned writings. The distributions are reported in relation to the territorial areas covered in Figure 2.1. The data show that boys write more in secondary and extended territory whereas girls write more in primary territory.

The boys' writing content in the secondary territory was aggressive, violent, and was more about the omnipotence of persons and objects. Boys ignored the use of the first person, I, and projected themselves into a vicarious use of the third person. Their characters were always doing something, and seldom showed feeling. People in the stories were unnamed unless the boys were writing about the Buffalo Sabres, their favorite hockey team. In this situation high prestige was given to those boys who could spell the difficult French-Canadian names.

The incident of the plane crash would be classified as a theme belonging in the secondary territory. The lack of interest by the girls at the time of the crash is similarly evidenced in Table 2.1 in their apparent disinterest in the secondary territory. A few advanced girls ventured into this area to write about nurses or boats. This may suggest that the developmentally mature girl is ready to write more in the secondary territory at the age of seven.

Although girls increased their writing in extended territory, the boys still continued to write more. Once again, a few girls who exhibited other advanced maturational traits wrote in this sector.

While boys were more active in writing in secondary and extended territory, girls wrote more about themes in the primary area. Although terri-

Table 2.1.
Territorial distribution of thematic
choices in unassigned writing

Thematic Area	Boys N=36	Girls N=33
a. **Primary Territory:** Writing about self, home, school, personal toys, teachers and "I" stories.	52	95
b. **Secondary Territory:** 1. Metropolitan Community. Writing about objects, persons, and activities within the metropolitan community—e.g., jets, boats, police, firemen, crime, explosions, fires, bulldozers, nurses.	67	8
2. Sports. Writing about football, hockey, hunting, and baseball.	55	0
c. **Extended Territory:** Writing about current events on the national and world scene—e.g., presidents, Apollo 17, documented war, space.	55	17
Total	229	120

torially limited, their expressions of personal feelings, development of characters, and use of the first person, I, were much more developed than boys. Boys seldom used first person, whereas girls wrote objectively about themselves through the first person.

These preliminary findings show that sex does make a difference in both thematic choice and the types of characterizations in children's writing. There are developmental reasons for their behaviors that cause us to reevaluate the unique needs and strengths of both boys and girls in the classroom.

After spending four months in the daily observation of behaviors of children and teachers, the researcher did not record one instance where girls were exposed to the extended vocational roles of women. The primary world of writing about home and school was rarely expanded. Whereas boys were stimulated by contact with firemen, policemen, engineers, pilots and other male workers, girls had little exposure to the changing role of the adult woman. Moreover, textbooks, tests, language development kits dealing with occupations still fostered roles that ignored the expanded territorial occupations of women. In a recent review of a proposed state-wide reading test it was noted that almost all of the characters in the comprehension section were males active in sports, exploring, or space. Only one instance of female portrayal was seen in a woman who shared cookies with some boys. Comprehension may not have been affected, but the test, as with many other classroom materials, contributed to a concept of territorial limitation for women.

Many seven-year-old boys are ready for more sensitive involvement in developing characters in their writings, but are not receiving assistance. "Let them be boys!" is too easily said. As with advanced girls venturing into secondary territory, some advanced boys display great sensitivity and venture into effective uses of the first person. Many of these boys could extend these initial explorations through individual conferences. In this way it would be possible for teachers to ask questions about characters whom the boys already know as athletes or famous men. For example, in a personal conference a teacher might say: "Tell me about Perreault when he scored the winning goal. . . . How do you think he felt? Have you ever scored a goal in hockey? Tell me about it. Here are some words you might use to tell how it felt. I have written them down so that you can use them if you feel they might be helpful in your writing." Through working with the oral language of the child, his writings, as well as individual word lists, boys can be helped to expand expression in both third and first person.

Most writing assigned in American classrooms does not tap authentic feelings which boys are most familiar with. This bars many at a very early age from identifying the reflexive mode as a legitimate form of expression. For this reason, a prior step is needed before assisting boys to add depth to their characterizations. This step involves the controversial practice of allowing boys to express aggression in some rather brutal forms in writing as a legitimate form of high personal affect. In this case, boys *do* need to be boys! In the seven-year-old study boys moved into the secondary territory in writing because they were permitted wide latitude in using unassigned writing to their own ends. It is hypothesized that until boys have free flow in the secondary territory, greater personal depth in first or third person expression will not be possible.

In one classroom in the study, several formal assignments were given requiring children to write "All About Me" or to suppose they were objects or persons as "If I Were an Apple" or "If I Were an Ice Cream Cone." While the suitability of the theme might be debated for either sex, the use of first person or an abstract reflexiveness is most difficult for most seven-year-old boys. All of the girls but one were able to complete the assignment. Three advanced boys completed their work while the rest struggled to get off the ground.

Differences in the sexes transcend socio-economic divisions. Although both studies (Pitcher and Prelinger, 1963 and Graves, 1973) are exploratory, preliminary evidence suggests that the findings are consistent with children of both high socio-economic and blue-collar families. Differences in aggression, dependency, and territorial expansion were observed between the sexes in both samples.

The major differences in the sexes point to the need for a better understanding of the developmental sequences of both boys and girls. Developmental histories exist within each child having both sequence and significance. Within most elementary classrooms there are girls who need greater depth in primary territory before expanding into themes about the community and world. Still others need exposure to the changing roles of adult women. Their writing characterizations need to explore, travel, and deal with the broader world. On the other hand, some boys need to express aggression, omnipotence and the joys of physical contact. Others are ready for depth in characterizations, the expression of personal feelings, and the uses of conversation in their writings.

The teacher needs to draw on the knowledge of the young artist's developmental continuum. One of the first steps in the continuum is an understanding of the unique sequential, sexual development. At this point in time, the teacher has little research to draw upon to understand general developmental profiles. In children's writing there is even less assistance. The plea in writing research has been for longitudinal studies that give visibility to growth patterns for the young writer. No plea could be more plaintively addressed than that for exacting, longitudinal observations of children in their development as boys and girls through the writing process.

References

Goldberg, S. and Lewis, H. "Play Behavior in the Year Old Infant: Early Sex Differences," *Child Development*, 1969, 40, 21–31.

Graves, Donald H. "A Study of the Writing Processes of Seven Year Old Children," Unpublished Doctoral Dissertation, State University of New York at Buffalo, 1973.

Kohlberg, L. "A Cognitive-Developmental Analysis of Children's Sex-Role Concepts and Attitudes," In E.E. Maccoby (ed), *The Development of Sex Differences*, Stanford, California: Stanford University Press, 1966, pp. 82–173.

Mussen, P.H. and Rutherford, E. "Parent-Child Relations and Parental Personality in Relation to Young Children's Sex Role Preferences," *Child Development*, 1963, 34, pp. 589–607.

Pitcher, Evelyn G. and Prelinger, E. *Children Tell Stories*. New York: International Universities Press Inc., 1963.

Rosenberg, B.G., and Sutton-Smith, B. "Family Interaction Effects on Masculinity-Femininity," *Journal of Personal Social Psychology*, 1968, 8, pp. 117–120.

Sears, R.R. "Dependency Motivation," In M.R. Jones (ed), *Nebraska Symposium on Motivation*. Lincoln: University of Nebraska Press, 1963, pp. 25–64.

Sears, R.R.; Maccoby, E.E.; and Levin, H. *Patterns of Child Rearing*, Evanston, Illinois: Row, Peterson, 1957.

3. The Child, the Writing Process, and the Role of the Professional

Introduction

This article was started as preparation for a talk I gave to the first annual conference on language arts at the State University of New York at Buffalo in March, 1974. The actual writing was not completed until five months after the conference. The talk was the occasion for my first trip back to Buffalo since completing my dissertation in August, 1973. My writing was affected by the return to my dissertation site and by eminent conference participants like James Squire and Janet Emig, as well as by friends from the Buffalo area.

Speaking has always been rather easy for me; writing, especially at that time, was nearer to madness. Usually I don't write out my speeches beforehand. I merely make a list of the main points along with examples and data that show what I mean, and then constantly shuffle and reshuffle them for impact. The audience response usually shapes the final unity at the actual time of delivery.

The speech went well. The writing did not, and the text shows my audience's confusion. On the one hand, my lead is strong with an appeal to both teachers and researchers. But after this early involvement with my teacher audience I leave them to address my former dissertation committee. At this point in my writing career, I was not able to direct my writing to both audiences simultaneously. And I still had an urge to overinflate my vocabulary. After all, I was now Dr. Graves returning home. Such words as "modus operandi," "purported," "prototypes," "paradigm" could just as easily have been expressed in clearer language.

The speech and the article, however, were an important launching point for many of my ideas about writing in the seventies. This was my first opportunity to present a more systematic view of the implications for classroom teachers of my study of seven year olds. I stress the teacher's participation during the composing process: "Making rounds" becomes the more formal conference in later writing. I include the partial use of the child's own language through dictation. While I place greatest stress on the teacher's modeling of writing—as an example for the children as opposed to a later reference to the teacher actually writing with the children—I also give important attention to the need for a highly structured classroom environment. All of these basic features are still part of my emphasis on the teaching of writing.

How surprised I am in 1983 to find out how little many of my ideas have changed. I honestly thought writing these introductions would reveal great changes, especially in those articles I composed nine to ten years ago. But even the language in the ending of this piece could have been written yesterday:

There is something energizing about the discovery of a child's way of learning, or in sharing in the joy and confidence resulting from his growing sense of competence as a writer. It is this discovery that dissipates our fatigue and renews our vitality.

Although I would reedit this essay today to take out the -ing's, I would also revise the energy theme, with children as the source of energy, which is used so often as to be embarrassing. The information is correct; I just didn't realize how often I had used the idea.

I make much reference in this piece to developmental levels, especially as they are shaped by the reactive and reflective writer. Although there are developmental features in children's growth as writers, I do not refer to them at all today. It is more useful to look at writers as constantly changing rather than as fixed classifications. In this article I place great stress on precomposing, composing and postcomposing as linear components of the writing process. More recent research by me and many others shows that this simply is not the way children, or any other writers, compose. The writing process is a highly recursive event in which, for example, a second draft can be a rehearsal for the third draft, or in which reading and notetaking might come toward the final moments of composing. Composing and development are highly idiosyncratic processes that defy such simplistic categories as the reactive and reflective writers referred to here.

I have since found that the labels reactive and reflective are regressive. They don't help researchers or children. Rather, they are convenient ways of avoiding listening to children. Teachers and other educators have come up to me in workshops and said, "I've got about six of those reactive writers you've been talking about. They really are a problem, aren't they? Their backgrounds are quite limited." I hadn't said anything about background, but the label implied other behaviors that served to exclude the children from help with their writing.

I hope I have learned my lesson from this "reactive-reflective" mistake. Generalizations that classify behaviors are dangerous to children, to teachers, and to researchers.

I was startled by the sound of machine gun fire from the rear. Quickly I turned . . . and noted that seven-year-old Michael was writing again. He would gaze at his drawing of warfare between Germans and Americans at the top of his paper, reach up and crayon in a red explosion for emphasis, and with shooting noises escaping from his lips return to the written description of his private war. Although classified as a reader at the pre-primer level, Michael struggled with an average of three unassigned writings per day, yet apparently enjoyed the full process of writing.

Every day hundreds of thousands of Michaels wrestle, smile, laugh, curse and weep over their writings. Some, pondering new schemes for delightful fantasies, are in a constant state of rehearsal for writing. Others are repelled at the thought of writing one word because it means five to six redrafts of the spelling of a single word. Miracles of creation are occurring all around us, with some even contained in such short sentences as, "I gut a bik," or "My cat did." These sentences may hardly sound creative, yet on an individual basis, if the full context of developmental factors were understood, we would be impressed with these "simple" products. These miracles of process are occurring within our arm's reach from day to day.

Tragically these miracles within the process of writing escape us. For eighteen years I had wandered through hundreds of classrooms observing children and young people in the process of writing. These visits, however, only involved short observations of a child's word struggle, the rewriting of a phrase, or the answering of their question about topics for writing. For this reason my concept of the writing process was only made up of vague memories of collective vignettes about many Michaels.

Through the years I have bounced from one philosophy of teaching writing to another, none of which viewed writing as a process or accommodated for the child's learning strategies or sequences of development. At first I refrained from participating in any phase of the writing process. I decided to "teach" at the point of the finished product through a meticulous accounting of all errors. I embraced the domino theory of writing which considered the missing of one misspelling, grammatical error, or misplaced word as the beginning of the downfall of the young writer.

In time I began to have doubts about the success of my Salem witch hunt and changed from a vigilant conservatism to a permissive liberalism. It seemed that my proper role as a professional began before the child started to write. My task was now to "release" the child to write. Indeed, all that might be needed was the right "story starter" or the proper writing atmosphere. My oversimplification of both the writing process and the ranges of development in children led to a lottery philosophy that was suggestive of gimmickry and quick solutions. I was sure there was a magic creativity button existing within each child that begged for some ingenious teacher to come along and give it a push.

Both of these coercive and permissive approaches were contemptuous of children. In each case the teacher assumed a god-like role. In the coercive approach the teacher was kindly or reprimanding depending on the child's product. In the permissive approach the child was dependent on the teacher's preordained structure for his stimulation.

Through my ineffectual attempts to assist the writing of children with the beetle-browed look of a city editor, or the encouraging nods of a beneficent monk, I began to hope that research might offer some new avenue leading to an understanding of children and the writing process. A review of research did not add hope or precision to my concept of the writing process. Most studies in writing research dealt with broad investigations involving interventions with new materials, methodologies, or analysis of writing products. Up to the time of my own research survey just three studies involved a connection with the actual process of writing. Sawkins (1970) asked children to recount their writing habits and experiences after completing writing. Only Emig (1969) and Holstein (1970) were actually present when students were in the process of composing. Holstein's primary focus was on the use of metaphor rather than process, although a review of her data reveals a strong portrayal of variant composing habits. Emig's study with twelfth grade students was the most thorough investigation into the composing processes of young writers. Indeed, her study involving the actual viewing and recording of the composing of individuals dispelled many of the popular notions about how young writers arrived at their final products.

For too long we have *purported* to understand child behaviors in writing without an extensive bank of observations based on children actually engaged in the writing process. In the field of child development, for example, it would be unthinkable to attempt to draw conclusions about the nature of parallel play without at least first observing children in the process of play. However, statements continue to be made about the nature of the writing process by people who have never carefully observed children in the act of writing.

For years I had made pronouncements about children and the writing process, but not once had I observed a child's involvement in the writing process for more than a three to five minute period. After spending a year observing a small group of children engaged in classroom writing and other related activities, I feel better equipped to discuss the writing process, children and the teacher's role in this process.

Two Types of Writers: Reactive and Reflective

In the year's study of the writing processes of seven-year-old children, two distinctive types of writers emerge. These two types of writers are identified as a result of examining the various phases of the writing process in relation to certain developmental factors. The two types of writers are classified as *reactive* and *reflective*. The reactive child, for example, often used erratic problem-solving strategies, needed time and practice to rehearse what he would write, spoke out loud as he wrote and proofread only at the word unit level. The reflective writer, on the other hand, needed little rehearsal before writing, wrote rapidly and silently, and proofread in broader written units. The reactive writer is most often a boy and the reflective writer is most often a girl. The reactive and reflective writers, however, are each composite profiles of a general type of child. Identification of either the reactive or the reflective writer is not dependent on the observation of a single behavioral trait. Rather, the characteristics exist in varying degrees in all children, and can emerge under different types of writing conditions, but they gain greater visibility when viewed at the extreme high and low ends of a developmental continuum. These types of writers are specifically mentioned since they have great import for the discussion about the role of the professional.

Two prototypes of the reactive and reflective writer are now described to provide a sense of the components of the writing process and the developmental variables involved. This approach also provides a suitable backdrop for understanding significant points for teacher participation. The two prototypes, John, the reactive writer, and Laura, the reflective writer, are described within each of the three phases identified as important divisions of the writing process. These phases are prewriting, composing, and postwriting.

Three Phases of the Writing Process:
Prewriting, Composing and Postwriting

Prewriting

The prewriting phase immediately precedes the writing of the child. Within this phase it is possible to witness the rehearsal factor leading to the child's actual writing.

John usually rehearsed his writing through drawing. The drawing provided a means to find out what content might be contained in his writing. For example, if John were queried before drawing, "What will you be writing about when you finish drawing?" he would respond, "I don't know. I haven't drawn the picture yet."

As John drew, he made sound effects to simulate the appropriate action contained in the drawing. The order of drawing was in an action-reaction sequence. For example, he would first draw a gun and then the plane the gun was intended to shoot. He would then draw another coupled action on the other side of the paper that was unrelated to the first, yet generally related to the overall theme, war.

Laura apparently needed a less visible means of rehearsing for writing. For example, when Laura first picked up her paper for writing little more than a ten second delay elapsed before she was observed writing words on the paper. If queried before writing about the content, Laura would reply with a well-developed story which would subsequently emerge word-for-word in the composing phase. How was it possible for Laura to suddenly compose with no apparent prewriting phase in operation? It is hypothesized that this type child is in a constant state of rehearsal through daydreaming, story telling, reading, or listening to the stories of others.

Composing

The composing phase begins and ends with the actual writing of the message. Examples of factors observed in this phase are spelling, use of resources, the use of language expressed to accompany writing, pupil interactions with each other, proofreadings, rereadings, interruptions, erasures and teacher participation.

It appeared necessary for John to vocalize before writing words on his paper. If you were seated next to John's desk when he wrote you would hear him utter the exact words that would subsequently be written on paper. He would often struggle with three or four different spelling versions of the same word, reread to find his place, announce the next word, and write on. John wrote slowly, at approximately one and a half words per minute. It was not unusual for John to glance up at his drawing at the top of the paper for ideas, or should an area of high affect occur in the writing not contained in the drawing, he would draw in the missing event. Proofreading occurred almost exclusively at the word unit level. By the end of the year an occasional word within the phrase might be changed, but this was the extent of the adjustment.

When John was involved in unassigned writing (writing not required by the teacher) the content of his drawing and written message were filled with action. His characterizations were often extensions of his own desires to be a hockey player, pilot, bulldozer operator, or painter. Most of his writings were written in third person, excluded females, and involved a broad territorial range.

Laura wrote rapidly (fourteen words per minute) and silently. She would occasionally adjust a word at the phrase level, and gave no evidence of struggle with word selection or spelling.

Laura's unassigned writings were filled with fantasy about deeds of "long ago." "Once upon a time" was a familiar story beginning. Her characters were well developed and reflected on their feelings about events. If requested, she was capable of stating five to six sentences before they were written on the paper.

Postwriting

This phase refers to all behaviors following the actual completion of the child's first composing. Examples of these behaviors are product disposition, the child's solicitation of approval from others, proofreading, and contemplation of the finished product.

The Child's Evaluation of His Own Writing on His Own Criteria

John was asked, "What do you think a good writer needs to be able to do in order to write well?" John's response was, "You have to space your letters well, draw good, be neat, and spell all the words right." With the exception of drawing, John's chief concern was with the errors of writing. Other children in the study also stated that their points of struggle in writing were the desirable qualities needed in the good writer. In short, if a child could not spell, he felt the good writer needed to spell well.

Laura's response to the "good writer" question was more elaborate and reflective. She stressed the need for prethinking and having a good beginning and ending to the story. She also thought the good writer should use quotation marks, periods, capitals and have an understanding of where a sentence begins and ends. Finally, she stressed, "When you write about people you ought to tell how they feel."

Both the reflective and reactive writers were asked to evaluate their own papers, which were periodically collected in writing folders. John, when asked about his reasons for choosing his best paper would often reply, "I liked the picture. This was about hockey and hockey is my favorite sport." Laura, on the other hand, would respond, "It was good because it was long, and it had funny people in it, and it was about an unusual subject." Reactive persons tended to use simple, affective reasons whereas reflective writers were more elaborative in their judgments.

A paradigm for the writing process has been developed and described above as a three phase operation (prewriting, composing, and postwriting) identified in each phase. This paradigm can be useful with two differing writer's *modus operandi* in each phase. This model can be useful to the teacher who is striving to make his role in the writing process of his students as effective and productive as possible. The following suggestions are based on the model;

they relate to the three phases and they take into account the fact that in each phase there are two very different kinds of writer behaviors which must be accommodated.

Teacher as a Model

First the teacher should assess his own writing habits. The teacher who enjoys writing poetry, a personal journal, stories, or even carefully planned reports will tend to foster the desire to write in his students, and he will better understand the writing problems of his students. Furthermore, the teacher who writes can serve as a model for his class. Young students, or children of any age, see teachers and other adults engaged in speaking and reading, but they rarely observe adults in the act of writing. The teacher who seeks to enhance his students' propensity to write might ask himself: "How can I best begin to enjoy writing or continue to enjoy writing? How can my participation in the classroom serve as a model for writing to my students?"

Classroom Management

Following reflection on their own writing habits, professionals can begin to review the typical organization, direction, and management of classroom activities. A review of the two cases of John and Laura reminds us that writing is a highly individual act. Although it is possible to herd children into the position of having to write at the same time, the urge and need to write in a diversified environment can come at many points during a school day. Children's writing time and pace also need accommodation. Other questions for reflection are the following: "Can children write for varying lengths of time, especially where greater time is needed in the prewriting phase through drawing, discussion and other means of rehearsal? Is it possible for children to write throughout the day on a range of personal interests?"

Psychological and Physical Environment

Does the psychological environment in the classroom stimulate children to write freely when they want and about what they want? Does the physical environment stimulate ideas and suggest topics about which children may choose to write?

An example of a stimulating environment can be found in Laura's classroom. A high premium was placed on oral as well as written excellence. If interesting or stimulating phrases were stated by children, the teacher would record those sayings on a board entitled, *Class Quotes*. The name of the author would be placed beneath the quote.

Story telling, puppetry, reading and performing plays, and the opportunity to look at and read a large collection of library books provided imaginative and fanciful ideas and topics for writing. Building blocks, plants, animals, and science materials are among the concrete materials present which provide ideas, experiences, and topics for writing. In short, the environment stimulates language and the language produced is highly valued.

Value Placed on the Written Product

Another developmental trait needing scrutiny is permanence. Permanence is usually discussed within a perceptual context where a child recognizes the same object in different situations. This permanence is developed through the child's continued interaction with the object over a long period of time.

What attitude is a child likely to develop toward writing when his written products are quickly removed from sight, placed in a desk drawer, sent home the same day or simply buried in sheaves of dittoed exercises in arithmetic, social studies, etc.? Such treatment of children's written products certainly does not foster the idea in children that their writing is permanent and unique; nor does such treatment enable children to perceive progress in the ability to write over time.

A standard of excellence can be developed in each child through collections of his best work. Once the best writing has been determined for the individual child, he may have a personally bound book in which his writing is pasted or placed in a permanent collection of class writings. Other teachers have used bound journals in which the child writes on one page and the teacher responds on the opposite. With provisions for collecting writing the child may begin to sense his growth as a writer. He finds that he can read last month's paper again and again, thus taking advantage of the "instant replay" potential contained in print. Finally he may say, "Yes, these papers today are much better than the ones I wrote last October."

Teacher Involvement in the Writing Process of Students

Beyond providing an atmosphere conducive to writing, the teacher should be involved in all three phases of the writing process as they are engaged in by individual students. Since opportunities are provided for children to write throughout the day, the teacher must make the rounds at different hours. He or she cannot expect to have contact with each child every time the child writes, but over the course of a week or a month considerable interaction between the teacher and each child is possible while the child is actually engaged in the process of writing.

When making rounds the professional serves a wide range of functions depending on the phase the child is in. Children's awareness is so "now" oriented that the teacher can only provide services related to the stage where he finds the child at the time of contact. This is particularly true of the reactive writer whose awarenesses are based on moment to moment activity. Basically the professional should attempt to stimulate, extend, observe and diagnose the activity of the child. Through *stimulation* it is hoped that children will find new reasons for writing and become aware of new audiences to write for. Through questions and observation the professional seeks to find out the stage and *modus operandi* of the writer, in order to know best how to be a competent consultant to the child writer. What follows are examples of both the place and type of question that can be asked of the student actively engaged in writing.

Prewriting

Tell me about your picture, Bill. What are you going to be writing about when you finish? I notice you have some people swimming away from the sharks? Tell me about them.

Composing

What is going to happen next in your story? I notice that you are writing about a fashion show. What do you think are some words everyone ought to know to understand more about fashion? (child dictates, teacher writes the words). Would you like to use these words? Which sentence do you like best up to now? Which word was the most difficult to write? That seems to be a difficult word. Tell me all the places you can go to find out how to spell it. How is your story going to end? Do you think you know yet?

Postwriting

Would you read this out loud? Is there anything you would like to change now? Which part do you like best? Do you think this is one of your best? Why? Why not?

Teacher's Involvement After the Process is Complete

The final stage of teacher activity occurs when the child has completed all three phases of the writing process. Most of this activity occurs in the individual conference between child and teacher every five to six days. During the conference the child evaluates his work by selecting his own best papers. The teacher asks for the child's rationale with the intention of developing the child's ability to criticize his own writing. The task of the professional is to ask questions in such a way that the child will be able to discover standards for himself. Examples of such questions are the following:

You say that this paper about "horses" is your best and this one about "hockey" is not quite as good. Why do you feel the "hockey" paper is not as good? I agree. This paper about "horses" is excellent. Would you like to have it put in the class collection? (a permanently bound collection of class writings). OK, but I think there are some things needing changing to make it your very best. Where do you think you might begin?

You are making a fine point in this first sentence. Let's look at the next sentence. Read it out loud. Is that about the same subject in your first sentence?

Perreault has just scored a goal. How do you think he felt when he scored? (child dictates and teacher writes). Do you think others would like to know about how he felt? Would you like to use these words you have just dictated to me?

Summary

The teacher plays a vital role in the writing process of his students over a broad continuum of time. The teacher must evaluate a) his own writing activity and its effect on his students as an inspiration to write and as a model for writing, b) his management practices to determine whether there is time and space provided so that each child can write what he wants when he wants, c) the physical and psychological environment of his classroom to determine whether there is high value placed on good oral and written expression and whether there are materials present to encourage various forms of language expression and stimulate ideas, d) the value placed on written products to determine whether the "hidden curriculum" is teaching children to view their written products as permanent works where growth can be seen, or to view their written products as so much extra litter.

As children become involved in the three phases of the writing process, the professional seeks through observation and intervention to stimulate writing, extend it, as well as to diagnose at which developmental level the child may be functioning. Finally, a teacher's task in the facilitation of good writing is carried out in the writing conference where children are aided in both skills and their growing sense of excellence in communication.

This review of children, the writing process and the role of the teaching professional is concluded with a plea for greater involvement with young children. It is entirely possible to read about children, review research and textbooks about writing, "teach" them, yet still be unaware of their processes of learning and writing. Unless we actually structure our environments to free ourselves for process we are doomed to repeat the same teaching mistakes again and again. If we shield ourselves from a full involvement with students we lose out on a vital source of energy so needed in teaching in our time. There is something energizing about the discovery of a child's way of learning, or in sharing in the joy and confidence resulting from his growing sense of competence as a writer. It is this discovery that dissipates our fatigue and renews our vitality.

4. An Examination of the Writing Processes of Seven Year Old Children

Introduction

This article contains the main substance of my dissertation, completed at the State University of New York at Buffalo in 1973. I wrote it because as one of the four winners of the National Council of Teachers of English Promising Research Award, I was asked to submit an article on my work to *Research in the Teaching of English*.

This was my first postdissertation publication, and the dissertation style still afflicts the writing. One of the reviewers of the article penciled in the margin: "strong case of dissertationese." Although the article is still filled with jargon, it is much better than the draft I submitted. When writing it I was very much influenced by the audience I was to address—other researchers.

The task of selecting from a four-hundred-page dissertation to make a seventeen-page-article was formidable. Usually, such articles report heavily on findings with less proportionate attention to procedures and conclusions. Because my dissertation was a case study with one hundred and forty pages of findings, most of these data had to be ignored.

With the exception of Janet Emig's case-study work on twelfth-grade students, my research was the first to use the case study in the elementary years. I therefore decided to give extensive attention to the actual conduct of case-study research. I reasoned that future researchers using the case-study approach would benefit from the protocols, questions, and study design. I reported the findings, but in a condensed form as conclusions about the study.

I now have a different view of the case study than I did when I conducted this research in 1973. At that time, I stated that the case study was used when exploring virgin territory, that it was a means for discovering new variables when opening new avenues of research. But because of the intensive nature of the case study, especially where extensive, direct observation is involved, I now believe that findings reported as preliminary can be generalized to broader populations than has been previously thought. For example, the findings of Melas (1974) and Bodkin (1976), two dissertations with much larger numbers of children, upheld the work done in this case study.

Now that ten years have gone by since the completion of this study of seven-year-old children, I have a different view of the importance of certain of its findings. It is interesting to me that the case study, Michael, yielded the most lasting of the findings:

1. Rehearsal concept: Through Michael I was able to see for this study, and for our study in Atkinson, just how important behaviors prior to the act of composing were. At first, I saw only drawing as rehearsal. Later I added conversation, reading, previously composed topics, and inner thinking.

2. Participation of variables: As one of the conclusions of this study, I wrote: "Many variables contribute in unique ways at any given point in the process of writing." I tried to show this in the diagram of Michael's writing process included in the article. This finding was first cousin to the major finding of the National Institute of Education Study (see Chapter 15): "Writing is an idiosyncratic process that varies from day to day." This early observation showed me just how complex and idiosyncratic the writing process was for many young writers.

A further finding falls into the sex differences category. In this study of seven-year olds, I found significant differences between boys and girls in their use of person and territory in their writing topics.*

Melas, Dionysios D. "Differences of Themes in Assigned and Unassigned Creative Writing of Elementary School Children." Ph.D. diss., State University of New York at Buffalo, 1974.
Bodkin, Ann. "Observed Differences in the Written Expression of Boys and Girls." Ph.D. diss., State University of New York at Buffalo, 1976.

———————————◆·◆◆·◆————————————

The complexity of the writing process and the interrelationships of its components have been underestimated by researchers, teachers, and other educators, because writing is an organic process that frustrates approaches to explain its operation. Three major "Needs for Research" summaries in the last eleven years reflect specific concern for dealing with the issue of complexity (Braddock, 1963; Parke, 1960; Meckel, 1963). All three recommend extensive investigation of developmental issues, issues that focus much more on individual differences than on the "procedural-methodological" matters which have historically received research emphasis.

A review of research since the summaries indicates that most efforts have focused on correlative studies or the examination of the effects of single or multivariate interventions. The data from these separate studies make it difficult to produce a sound, organic understanding of what is even involved in the writing process. Furthermore, only two studies seem to have involved the actual observation of the behaviors of writers while they are in the process of writing. One of these studies (Emig, 1969) involved the composing processes of twelfth graders and the other (Holstein, 1970) was primarily concerned with the use of metaphor by fifth grade children.

This investigation was undertaken to explore the writing processes and related variables of a group of seven-year-old children. Through the gathering of data in a case study procedure, an analysis of broad samples of writing,

*See also the first article on "Sex Differences in Children's Writing."

and the naturalistic observation of children while writing in two types of classroom environments, formal and informal, the study sought to avoid both a fragmentary approach and teacher intervention. From this study a profile of writing in the early years emerges sufficient in depth and scope to make effective research hypotheses and recommendations.

In recent years new focus has come to the case study approach as a means to investigation of the variables involved in new areas of research. Indeed, the case study approach in the field of comparative research is most often recommended when entering virgin territory in which little has been investigated. Because of a lack of studies on the writing process or the actual observation of children while actually writing, the use of the case study to investigate the writing processes of children was considered as one of the appropriate methodologies.

The emphasis in this report of the study of the writing processes of seven year old children will be placed on a detailed description of the procedures used, and the conclusions and hypotheses formulated from the findings. This was done because the complexity and extent of the actual findings from case studies, small and large groups precluded their reporting in short space.

Procedure

The Sample

Two formal and two informal second level (second grade) classrooms in a middle class community were chosen for the principal focus for a five month investigation. The classrooms selected met specific criteria that identified them as being either formal or informal. These criteria concerned the degree to which children were able to function without specific directions from the teacher and the amount of choice children had in determining their learning activities.

Figure 4.1 depicts the makeup of the sample for the different phases of data gathering in the study. The First Phase involved ninety-four children (forty-eight boys and forty-six girls) with a mean age of seven years and six months at the beginning of the study. In Phase II fourteen seven year old children (eight boys and six girls) from each of the four rooms were observed while they were writing. In Phase III, seventeen seven year old children (nine boys and eight girls) from each of the four rooms were interviewed as to their views of their own writing and concepts of the "good writer." Finally, in Phase IV, eight children (six boys and two girls), two from each of the four classrooms, were chosen for case study investigation. The eight children selected were considered by teachers and administrators as representative of "normal" seven year old children; thus pupils of unusually high intellectual capacity and those with learning or emotional problems were excluded.

Data Collection Procedures

Throughout the data collection period from the first week of December, 1972, to the middle of April, 1973, the primary emphasis was placed on gathering case study data on two children in each of the four environments. Secondary emphasis was placed on gathering data from larger groups in the same four classrooms. Data were collected from: (1) the logging of five categories of information secured from the writing of ninety-four children; 1,635 writings were logged for theme, type of writing, number of words, use of accompanying art, and teacher comments; (2) the naturalistic observation of fourteen children while they were writing in their classrooms; (3) the interviewing in four different sessions of the eight case study children as to their views of their own writing and of seventeen children as to their concepts of "a good writer"; (4) the gathering of full case study data about eight children through parent interviews, testing, assembling of educational-developmental history, and observing the children in several environments. The purpose of this form of data gathering and reporting was to provide a range of cross-validation of data to support the findings and, thus, to add power to the research recommendations and instructional hypotheses posed. This approach

Figure 4.1. Study phases and procedures

Phase IV—Case Study
Michael
N-1

Phase III—Interviews
Interviews on children's views
of their own writing and concept
of the "good writer."
N-17

Phase II—The Writing Episode
The observation of fifty-three writing
episodes.
N-14

Phase I—The Writing Folder
1. Thematic choices of children
2. Writing frequency
3. Types of writing (assigned-unassigned)
N-94

Formal Classrooms   Informal Classrooms

Room A   Room B   Room C   Room E
N-24   N-25   N-24   N-21

made it possible to follow findings from the several larger settings to an individual case and, conversely, from the case and/or small group findings to all-class profiles and to the entire group of seven year old children studied.

Phase One—The Writing Folder

Writing folders were kept by all children in each of the four classrooms in the study. The purposes of having all children keep a writing folder were the following:

1. To reduce focus on the eight children chosen for case study work.
2. To provide background data of a total classroom nature in order to view the writing of the eight children with greater objectivity.
3. To assess the general writing habits of the children in terms of writing frequency, assigned-unassigned writing, use of illustrations accompanying writing, writing length, and the thematic interests of children.

The definition of writing that was employed to determine paper selection was as follows:

Any writing intended to be at least a sentence unit that was completely composed by the child.

Teachers distinguished between two types of writing—assigned or unassigned—when they reviewed the writing folders. Assigned was defined as writing that children were required to attempt and for which completion was expected. Unassigned writing was defined as unrequired writing. In this situation the child chose on his own initiative to write. There was no expectation by the teacher that specific work would be completed. Thus the child made choices as to mode, length of writing, and the disposition of the writing product.

Phase Two: Writing Process Observation (The Writing Episode).

In this stage of the investigation, fifty-three writing episodes of fourteen seven year old children (mean age—7:7), made up of eight boys and six girls from all of the four rooms were observed. Writing of the children in the episodes was observed within the classroom in order to gain a more valid view of their writing processes. Writing episodes were not structured by the researcher. Rather, recordings of the children's writing behaviors were made when they chose to initiate writing in assigned or unassigned work. For this reason, approximately 250 hours were spent observing children while waiting for them to enter into a writing episode.

Within each of the four environments two children were chosen as case studies. These eight children were the prime focus of classroom observation. Because these cases were not always engaged in writing, were absent, or were working with the teacher, it was possible to record some of the writings of other children in the rooms. Twelve of the fifty-three writing episodes recorded were from six children who were not case studies.

There is more to a writing episode than the children's act of composing and writing down words. The observation of writing at only one point in time limits an analysis of the writing process and may result in conclusions which overlook important variables. Therefore, a single writing episode was considered to consist of three phases of observation: prewriting, composing and postwriting. Definitions of these phases and the factors in each phase for which data were obtained are given.

Prewriting phase. This phase immediately precedes the writing of the child. Examples of factors related to writing observed in this phase were the contribution of room stimuli to thematic choice, art work behaviors, and discussions with other persons.

Composing phase. This phase begins and ends with the actual writing of the message. Examples of phase factors were spelling, resource use, accompanying language, pupil interactions, proofreadings, rereadings, interruptions, erasures, and teacher participation.

Postwriting phase. This phase refers to all behaviors recorded following the completion of writing the message.

Examples of these behaviors were product disposition, approval solicitation, material disposition, proofreading, and contemplation of the finished product.

Recording of the episode.

Whenever the researcher noted that a child was structuring materials for a writing episode, he moved close to the child and usually seated himself directly in front of his desk or table. Although the researcher was viewing the child's work in the upside-down position, it was the best location to record behaviors accompanying the writing episode. In this way the child's body posture, use of overt language, and rereading could be better observed.

For many children drawing was a major step in the prewriting phase. Michael, the case study chosen for reporting, apparently needed to draw before he was able to write in the composing phase. As he drew he would talk, often making appropriate sound effects to go along with the figure being drawn at the moment. While drawing the dinosaur referred to in Table 4.1, Michael made growling noises to simulate the dinosaur's presence. To aid the recording of such data the observer reproduced the drawing, at the same time numbered each operation to indicate the sequence in which the picture evolved. Notable behaviors that accompanied each step were also recorded.

As soon as Michael completed his drawing, he started to write about information contained in the picture. At this juncture he began the composing phase. The researcher immediately recorded the time in the center column (Table 4.1). When the child completed his writing the time was also recorded at the bottom of the column. In this way, the length of time the child was engaged in the composing phase could be computed.

The procedures for recording behaviors in the composing phase are contained in Table 4.1. The left column records exactly what Michael wrote. The sequence of the writing and significant acts are indicated by the numerals. Since specific behaviors were noted from time to time by the observer as the writing was done, reference is made to these by bold face numerals, with explanations of them given in the right column. For example, the bold face eleven in the left column is explained following the eleven in the right column. That is, as Michael wrote dinosaur, he copied the word from the dictionary. Other behaviors were recorded during the composing phase and

Table 4.1.
Example of a writing episode

A whale is eating the 　　1　2　　3　　4　　5 men. A　　　　　dinosaur is 6　7　8 **9** 10　　　**11**　　　12 triing to eat the whale. 　13　14 15 16　　17　　　　**18** 　A dinosaur is frowning **19 20**　　**21**　　22　23　**24** a tree at the lion. and 25 26 27 28 29 30 31 32 the cavman too.　the men 33　　34　　35 **36** 37 38 are killed.　The dinosaur 39　40 41　42　　43 killed the whale.　The 44　45　46 47　49 　　　　**48** cavmen live is the roks. 　50　　51 52 53　54 55　**56**	10:12 R IU R RR OV OV IS RR RR RR 10:20	**9**　Gets up to get dictionary. Has the 　　page with pictures of animals. **10**　Teacher announcement. **11**　Copies from dictionary and returns 　　book to side of room. **18**　Stops, rubs eyes. **19**　Rereads from 18 to 19. **20**　Voices as he writes. **21**　Still voicing. **24**　Gets up to sharpen pencil and returns **25**　Rereads from 20 to 25. **36**　Rereads to 36. Lost starting 　　point. **48**　Puts away paper, takes out 　　again. **56**　Rereads outloud from 49 to 56.

Key: 1, 2, 3, 4, Numerals indicate writing sequence. 4—Item explained on the right. ////—erasure o proofreading. T—Teacher involvement; IS—Interruption Solicited; IU—Interruption Unsolicited RR—Reread; PR—Proofread; DR—Works on drawing; R—Resource use. Accompanying Language OV—Overt; WH—Whispering; F—Forms letters and words; M—Murmuring; S—No overt language vis ible.

noted in the right-hand column. To assist the summary of these behaviors, lettered symbols were placed in the center column from the key below to indicate the classification of the child's behaviors in the episode. For example, in the center column opposite the numeral twenty in the right column, the symbol "OV" was recorded. This symbol indicates that in step twenty Michael voiced words as he was writing them.

In the key at the bottom of Table 4.1 the range of behaviors monitored when a child engaged in a writing episode were listed. Teacher involvement (T) was any form of teacher interaction with a child during his writing episode. Interruptions (IS-IU) were monitored for their effect on the continuance of the child's writing. Two other behaviors, rereadings and proofreadings (RR and PR) were important indices of other writing habits. Rereadings were the child's rescanning of writing composed prior to the current word being written whereas proofreading was defined as an adjustment of a previously composed writing operation. In a number of instances children would adjust a picture to go with a new idea in the text (DR). The use of resources to aid writing (R) such as word banks, phonic charts etc. were recorded during the observations. Finally, the range and type of language used to accompany the actual writing was recorded. This language behavior ranged from full voicing (overt—OV) to the absence of any visible or aural indication of accompanying language (covert—S).

From time to time the researcher would intervene and elicit information from the child when he was engaged in a writing episode. The purpose of this procedure was to gain understanding of the child's rationale for a previous operation or insight into his strategies for future operations. The type of intervention varied with the phase of the episode. Examples of interventions and their settings and objectives are shown in Table 4.2. Although there were many types of interventions they were infrequently employed to minimize the observer's effect on the child's writing.

Phase Three—Interviews

Two types of interviews were used to record children's views of their own writing and writing in general. The first included individual conversations

Table 4.2
Examples of interventions made by observers during writing episodes

Phase in Episode	Setting at Time of Intervention	Observer's Objective	Observer's Questions or Statements
Prewriting Phase	1. The child was about to start drawing his picture.	To determine how much the drawing contributes to the writing.	"Tell me what you are going to write about when you finish your drawing."
	2. The child has finished his drawing.	To determine how much the drawing contributes to the writing.	"Tell me what you are going to write about now that you have finished your drawing."
	3. The child has finished his drawing.	To determine in less direct fashion how the drawing contributes to the writing.	"Tell me about your drawing."
Composing Phase	1. The child is about to start writing.	To determine the range in writing ideas possessed before the child writes.	"Tell me what you are going to write about."
	2. The child attempts to spell a word.	To determine the child's understanding of the resources available for spelling help.	"That seems to be a hard one. How can you figure out how to spell it? Tell me all the ways you can figure out how to spell it."
	3. The child has written three to four sentences.	To determine the range of ideas possessed after the child has started writing.	"Tell me what you are going to write about next. Tell me how your story is going to end."

(continued)

Table 4.2 (continued)

Phase in Episode	Setting at Time of Intervention	Observer's Objective	Observer's Questions or Statements
Postwriting Phase	1. The child is starting to put his paper away.	To check the child's oral reading in relation to the actual words written by the child.	"Would you please read out loud what you have just written."
	2. The child is starting to put his paper away.	To check the child's feelings or value judgments about work that has been completed.	Question series: "Which sentence do you like best? Tell me about it. Is there anything you would change to make it better? Pick out two words that you felt were the most difficult to write."

with the eight case study children about the writing in their folders. The purpose in employing the writing folder interview was to gain a profile of the child's view of his own writing. This profile was constructed from the child's rating of papers from his folder, the rationales for such ratings, and his responses to other statements and questions about the papers. In the interview the child was asked to rate writings in his folder from best to poorest and to state a rationale for his choice of the best paper. The second interview consisted of asking questions as to the child's conception of what good writers needed to be able to do in order to write well. The questions were asked of seventeen children, seven of whom were the case study children.

Phase Four—Case Study (Michael)

At the conclusion of the data gathering, a decision was made to report only one case study, Michael, but to use all of the writing observations and interviews of the other cases, as well as the additional information gathered on other children in the four classrooms. The procedures used for gathering case study data involved all of those used in the first three phases, plus additional procedures unique to case study research. The additional procedures were the interviewing of parents throughout the study, the individual administration of test batteries in reading, intelligence, and language; the gathering of the child's educational-developmental history, and the extended observation of the child in areas other than writing at home and in school.

Conclusions

The findings in this study led to conclusions in five areas: learning environments, sex differences in writing, developmental factors and the writing process, the case study, Michael, and the procedures used in the study. These conclusions are reported below.

Learning Environments

Since the study distinguished two types of environments, conclusions relative to writing in each are possible. These are the following:

1. Informal environments give greater choice to children. When children can write what they want, or when they want, they write more and in greater length than when specific writing assignments are given.
2. Results of writing done in the informal environments demonstrate that children do not need motivation or supervision in order to write.
3. The formal environments seem to be more favorable to girls in that they write more, and to greater length, than do boys whether the writing is assigned or unassigned.
4. The informal environments seem to favor boys in that they write more than girls in assigned or unassigned work.
5. In either environment, formal or informal, unassigned writing is longer than assigned writing.
6. An environment that requires large amounts of assigned writing inhibits the range, content, and amount of writing done by children.
7. The writing developmental level of the child is the best predictor of writing process behaviors and therefore transcends the importance of environment, materials and methodologies in influence on children's writing.

Sex Differences in Writing

Differences in boys and girls were examined in three areas: writing frequency, thematic choice, and their concept of the "good writer." Warranted conclusions relative to these appear to be the following:

1. Girls write longer products than do boys in either formal or informal environments.
2. Boys from either learning environment write more unassigned writing than do girls. Unassigned writing seems to provide an incentive for boys to write about subjects not normally provided in teacher-assigned work. Teachers do not normally assign work that includes themes from secondary and extended territory, the areas most used by boys in unassigned writing.
   (Secondary territory is defined as the metropolitan area beyond the child's home and school. Extended territory is defined as the area beyond the secondary which would include current events, history and geography on a national and world scale.)
3. Boys seldom use the first person form in unassigned writing, especially the *I* form, unless they are developmentally advanced.
4. Boys write more about themes identified as in secondary and extended geographical territories than do girls. The only girls who write in these areas are those who are more developmentally advanced than others.
5. Girls write more about primary territory, which is related to the home and school, than do boys.
6. Boys are more concerned than are girls with the importance of spacing, formation of letters, and neatness in expressing their concept of "the good writer."
7. Girls stress more prethinking and organizational qualities, feelings in characterizations, and give more illustrations to support their judgments than do boys in expressing their concept of "the good writer."

Developmental Factors and the Writing Process

Such factors as a child's sex, the use of language, and problem solving behaviors, all of which have developmental roots, are involved as a child writes and interacts in various ways to produce two distinctive types of writers, identified by this study as *reactive* and *reflective*. These characteristics and behaviors are summarized in the following statements:

1. *Reactive*: Children who were identified as reactive showed erratic problem solving strategies, the use of overt language to accompany prewriting and composing phases, isolation that evolved in action-reaction couplets, proofreading at the word unit level, a need for immediate rehearsal in order to write, rare contemplation or reviewing of products, characterizations that exhibited general behaviors similar to their own, a lack of a sense of audience when writing, and an inability to use reasons beyond the affective domain in evaluating their writing.
2. *Reflective*: Children who were identified as reflective showed little rehearsal before writing, little overt language to accompany writing, periodic rereadings to adjust small units of writing at the word or phrase level, growing sense of audience connected with their writing, characterizations that exhibit general behaviors similar to their own in the expression of feelings, and the ability to give examples to support their reasons for evaluating writing.

The reactive writer was most often a boy and the reflective writer was most often a girl. The reactive and reflective writers, however, were each composite profiles of a general type of child. Identification of either the reactive or the reflective writer was not dependent on the observation of a single behavioral trait. Rather, the characteristics exist in varying degrees in all children, and emerge under different types of writing conditions, but they gain greater visibility when viewed at the extremes of the high and low ends of a developmental continuum. The identification of a cluster of traits over a period of time from any one behavioral type (reactive or reflective) can be useful in predicting other writing behaviors of children and thereby be of assistance to teachers in adjusting instruction to their needs.

The Case Study, Michael

The chief conclusion drawn from the case study of Michael was that many variables contribute in unique ways at any given point in the process of writing. Although the contributions of these variables were specific to each child, the identification of them appears to be transferable to the study of the writing of other children. Table 4.3 reports several factors identified as contributing to various components of Michael's writing and writing processes. Findings from the case study data made it possible to chart the influence of four main variables on factors identified as important in the process of writing. In Table 4.3 the influence of four main variables, family and home, teacher—room D, Michael's developmental characteristics, and a peer, Kevin, can be viewed in relation to their effect on such writing process factors as writing cause, thematic origin of writing, prewriting, composing, and postwriting. Each of these variables should be viewed in relation to its influence on the writing process. For example, in investigating what causes Michael to write, one can view specific contributions of a positive nature from the family and

Table 4.3
General contribution of specific variables to Michael's writing and writing processes

	Family and Home	Teacher Room D	Michael Developmental	Peers (Kevin)
Writing Cause	Family is generally supportive of his work.	Provides mostly positive feedback.	Writes in order to draw.	Boys write up a joint project.
	Gives Michael encouragement with his drawing.	Provides help with self-direction.	Writes in order to play.	Kevin makes suggestion to write.
	Provides Michael with extra materials for drawing and writing at home.	Provides freedom of choice, time, and activity.		
Thematic Origin	King Arthur, sports, ghosts and witches, camping and hunting, fires and explosions.	Apollo 17, groundhogs, whales	Secondary and extended territorial use.	Mutual interests: Kevin: "Let's write about fires."
			Use of third person male, no females.	
			Little use of first person.	Request for Michael to draw and write on a subject to help Kevin with ideas and drawing models.
			Need to express aggression.	

(continued)

Table 4.3 (continued)

	Family and Home	Teacher Room D	Michael Developmental	Peers (Kevin)
Writing Process— Prewriting Phase	Rehearses for ideas in family discussions.	Provides materials that permit art work before writing.	Needs to draw to rehearse ideas for writing.	Two boys discuss what they will draw.
	Provided materials and encouragement for drawing.	Provides freedom to discuss materials and content.	Interested primarily in drawing.	
			Exhibits action-reaction style of drawing ideas.	
			Demonstrates playing behaviors with sound effects.	
Writing Process— Composing Phase	Vocabulary backgrounds.	Teaching of: spelling reading punctuation proofreading	Generally reactive behaviors.	Minimal contribution to ideation.
	Speech interference problems.		Letter reversal problems.	Some spelling assistance.

Writing Process—Post-writing Phase	Unknown	Provision of resources: phonic charts dictionaries word banks	Speech interference problems.	Affects pace and structure by saying to Michael, "Hurry up, let's paint."
			Speech interference with spelling.	
			Speech interference with written syntax.	
		Attempts to teach proof-reading.	Quickly disposes of writing product by placing in folder or desk.	Kevin sometimes is in a hurry for Michael to do another activity and may subvert proofreading.

home, the teacher, the satisfaction of personal need, and the support of Kevin. Any one of these factors alone, or in combination with others could be the cause of Michael's choosing to draw and then write.

The influence of these variables on the thematic origin factor can be both direct and indirect. Examples of a direct factor in Table 4.3 is seen in the home's influence on Michael's writing about King Arthur, sports, ghosts and witches. An examples of a multiple and less direct origin is seen in Michael's drawing in the prewriting phase. Michael may draw because of Kevin's suggestion, extra time given by the teacher, a desire to express a favorite theme, or the need to prepare ideas for writing. Thus, the following conclusions appear to be significant concerning the case study.

1. At any given point in a writing episode, many variables, most of them unknown at the time of composing, contribute to the writing process.
2. Children write for unique reasons, employ highly individual coping strategies, and view writing in ways peculiar to their own person. In short, the writing process is as variable and unique as the individual's personality.

Procedures Used in the Study

Because the use of the case study combined with data gathering from both large and small groups produced particularly striking findings, a number of conclusions related to the procedure are warranted. First, the case study is an effective means of making visible those variables that contribute to a child's writing. Through the unity of one child's life, the constant focus in observation, interviewing, and testing makes it possible to hypothesize concerning the variables that contribute to the child's writing. In a broad interventive-type inquiry involving many children such speculation would not have been possible. Many of the variables discussed in larger group findings became apparent as a result of the intensive case study. In this sense case studies serve principally as surveying expeditions for identifying the writing territories needing further investigation. Some of the areas identified through case study and reported in larger group findings are the following:

1. The use of first and third person reported in thematic choices.
2. The identification of secondary and extended territoriality reported in thematic choices.
3. The identification of the prewriting, composing, and postwriting phases in the writing episode.
4. The identification of the components making up profiles for assessing developmental levels of children.

Whereas the case study contributed to the identification of variables in the larger group data gathering activities, large-group data provided a means for additional testing of the suitability of certain research hypotheses and directions. For example, large-group data were of assistance in analyzing the case study findings in the following areas:

1. Combining all of the fifty-three writing episodes made it possible to develop and hypothesize about the range and relationship of the developmental variables deemed significant to the writing process.

2. The larger group data confirmed the significance of assigned and unassigned writing and thereby contributed to the recognition of the need to pursue the area with the case study children.
3. The larger group data made it possible to view the differences in boys' and girls' writing shown in the case studies with greater objectivity. Writing frequencies, thematic choices, use of assigned and unassigned writing, and responses to the question on the "good writer" in larger groups are examples of these differences which were observed.

Questions to Be Researched

The main purpose of this study was to formulate instructional and research hypotheses concerning children's writing. The most significant of these hypotheses grouped into related categories appear to be the following:

Assigned and Unassigned Writing

1. If given the opportunity in an environment providing the freedom to exercise choice in activities, will children produce more writings on their own than if the teacher gives specific assigned tasks?
2. Will unassigned writing be longer than assigned writing, show greater thematic diversity, and be used more by boys than girls?
3. Will boys in comparison with girls exhibit distinctive choices with respect to the use of primary, secondary and extended territory as well as first, second, and third person in their writing?
4. Will a survey of teacher-assigned writing in the primary years show that girls are favored through the assigning of topics chiefly concerned with primary territory?.

Concepts of the "Good Writer"

5. Will distinctive responses to the "good writer" question be noted with respect to: boys and girls in general, those rated high and low developmentally, and specific writing strengths and limitations of the respondents?

Developmental Factors

6. Will two distinct groups of seven year old children be judged high and low developmentally as a result of the demonstration of consistent behaviors related to writing in the following categories: word writing rate, length of proofreading unit during writing, concept of an audience who may read their papers, spelling errors, rereadings, proofreading after writing, range and complexity of ideas expressed before writing, and in reasons expressed in rating their own writing?

General Factors

7. Will general behaviors exhibited by the child in his writing episodes be determined principally by his developmental level and be changed only slightly by the classroom environment?

Needed Research Directions

To date the need for developmental studies related to children's writing has been virtually ignored. Direct contact and extended observation of the children themselves are necessary to reach conclusions relating to developmental variables involving the behaviors of children. In fields such as psychiatry, child development, or anthropology, the investigation of behaviors would be unthinkable without the direct observation of the persons to be studied.

With the exception of a few studies, researchers have been removed from the direct observation of children at the time of their writing. Furthermore, the scope of even the direct observation of children at the time of writing needs to expand to include other behaviors in the environment. Such studies, however, cannot be conducted without the successful development of procedures that effectively record the full range of child behaviors in their natural environment.

In order to improve both procedures and study scope, future research in writing should continue to explore the feasibility of the case study method. Further studies are needed to investigate the developmental histories of different types of children in relation to writing and the writing process. In a profession where there is a basic commitment to the teaching and understanding of the individual child, it is ironic that research devoted to the full study of single individuals is so rare.

References

Braddock, Richard, Lloyd-Jones, Richard and Schoer, Lowell. *Research in Written Composition*. Champaign, Illinois, NCTE, 1963.

Emig, Janet A., "Components of the Composing Process Among Twelfth Grade Writers." Unpublished doctoral dissertation, Harvard University, 1969.

Holstein, Barbara I. "Use of Metaphor to Induce Innovative Thinking in Fourth Grade Children." Unpublished doctoral dissertation, Boston University, 1970.

Meckel, Henry C. "Research on Teaching Composition," *Handbook of Research on Teaching*, American Education Research Association, Chicago: Rand, McNally and Co., 1963.

Parke, Margaret B. "Composition in Primary Grades," *Children's Writing: Research in Composition and Related Skills*, Champaign, Illinois, National Council of Teachers of English, 1961.

5. Let's Get Rid of the Welfare Mess in the Teaching of Writing

Introduction

The welfare metaphor came to me in the midst of a talk on the writing process in Janet Emig's seminar at Rutgers in February, 1976. It struck me that most teaching of writing is set up to make the writer dependent on the teacher. I find that many metaphors come to me in the midst of talks and if I am lucky, I can remember to use them in my writing. In this instance, I had a talk to give a month later in Atlanta, Georgia, at the National Language Arts meeting of the National Council of Teachers of English. I used the metaphor when I wrote this article for the conference.

I have since been rightfully criticized about the metaphor. People have argued that welfare is a real assistance to people in trouble and that my usage has given it a negative connotation. I agree. Welfare is needed, but the way it is administered, it often leads to humiliation and dependency on the part of those who receive it. Children do need help with their writing, but given in such a way that their dignity and independence are maintained.

There are a number of firsts for me in this article. Although there is still a substantial amount of material from my dissertation (reactive-reflective writer, phases of the writing process) I developed some new areas. For the first time I mention writing conferences and the voices of teacher and writer.

I shall by eternally grateful to Donald Murray for his major contribution to my work on the writing conference. In writing my dissertation, I knew that teachers needed to participate during the writing process. Donald Murray, although working with writers at the university level, showed me how. The writing conference is used throughout the teaching of writing at the University of New Hampshire. People walking the corridors of Hamilton-Smith Hall will see long lists of student appointments on professors' doors, whether the subject is freshman writing, poetry, journalism, advanced fiction, or nonfiction. We estimate that an average week would see the accomplishment of two thousand such conferences. Donald Murray alone accounts for sixty conferences per week. We estimate that in sixteen years of teaching here, he has conducted thirty-seven thousand conferences. The conference is truly an art form in which the professional seeks to help the writer teach the listener about his subject. Murray's Pulitzer Prize background in journalism makes him a master listener and questioner. In this article, I seek to apply what I was first learning with Murray to my listening to two types of writers, reactive and reflective. I am pleased to say that this is the last article in which I use the reactive-reflective writer labels.

Although I used the term *voice* in this article, it was new to me and I used it here in the general sense of the writer speaking with authority, knowledge, and distance on his subject. One might say that my early use of voice applied to writers who spoke rather loudly about what they knew. But a good voice could just as well be quiet, persistent, and sure of its facts.

It is important to note that I first realized the connection between teachers' teaching voices and children's writing voices in this article. When teachers live in a highly dependent atmosphere in which their professional voices are silenced, their approaches to teaching have a tendency to rule out children's voices as well. Teachers are continually second-guessed by administrators and parents who are distant from the classroom. Buildings are often set up so that teachers have preset curricula, haphazard and uninformed supervision, as well as constant interruption during the day. Such practices thwart teacher voices, and cause them to listen to the "voice" above, rather than the children's voices in their own rooms.

I don't like welfare. Peter wouldn't like it either . . . if he knew he were on welfare, writer's welfare. Each day Peter waits in line in his second grade classroom to receive whatever praise may come his way on writing assignments about subjects that have been carefully chosen to stimulate him into "creativity." He writes for others, not for himself. He writes to communicate with one person, the teacher. He is dependent on the teacher for criticism, topic, writing time (always between 1:00 and 1:40 after lunch—when few professional writers can write). Opportunities for writing are carefully controlled and only come when the teacher makes writing assignments.

The writing welfare system makes children become dependent on the teacher in two ways. In the first the teacher controls all phases of the writing process from the decision that children need to write to the final correction of their papers. In the second children feel the pressure to make their voices correspond with the teacher's. That is, the authority and distance the child has in relation to his own writing is given over to the teacher. Eventually the only question remaining for children under these conditions is, "What do teachers want?"

Examination of teacher-made decisions throughout the writing process reveals the comprehensiveness of their control. Peter was dependent on his teacher's decision for:

1. His need to write.
2. When he would write.
3. What he would write.
4. To whom he would write.
5. How he would write.
6. How the paper would be judged.

When dependency was fostered on the first four points it was not surprising that Peter cared little about the last two points, how he would write, or how the paper would be judged.

As teachers we are seldom aware of our involvement in the writing welfare system. There are many subtle turns in the road when we encourage thinking similar to our own, and discourage divergent thought, thus denying the child's own voice. When children evidence interest in "hot wheels" we gently steer writing to subjects with which we are more familiar. The welfare syndrome leads us to steer topics to our own interests when the lonely prospect of correcting sheaves of papers is on the horizon.

Dependency is not fostered by individual teachers alone. In the current emphasis on accountability teachers themselves lose their sense of authority and objectivity in instruction, their own teaching voices. The hierarchy of administrative involvement in "accountability missions" fosters suspicion leading from the federal government to the child in the classroom. A California teacher spoke of her teaching situation in which children's writing was assessed by many levels of administration starting with the state department of education. In addition, her own superintendent of schools, feeling the brunt of public pressure for some data on the status of writing in the system, had asked for an objective panel review of composition. Her principal also wished to assess the status of spelling, capitalization, punctuation, and compare pupils in his building with national norms. Children from her room who were involved in the Title I writing project were given pre and post tests on writing skills. With all of the accountability pressure from above, the teacher in turn felt constrained to provide much higher grade placements in writing skills areas the following May. Under these circumstances many writing assignments were given with a strict accounting of all errors on each paper with the hope that there would be significant improvement in basic writing skills. Under these assessment circumstances instructional "short-cuts" are made leading to greater teacher control of the writing process and a stronger emphasis on the correspondence between pupil and teacher voice. Thus, development of the child's independence in the writing process voice, and the capacity for self-assessment are lost in the rush of expediency and the distrust of accountability.

If we look at writing from Peter's perspective, is it strange he believes that his writing, his language, or its evaluation is the property of those who control him? He has never been asked about his opinion or evaluation of his writing. He has never been asked about his interests, or the important events occurring in his life. It has never occurred to the teacher that his insights about his own writing are information that can be used to help him learn to write. Peter is in the second grade but the teaching practices that ignore the development of self-critical skills in the writing process will continue throughout his entire educational career, even if he receives advanced university degrees.

How can we help children retain control of their language and develop their powers to evaluate what has been written? How can this be developed from the beginning, from the child's first attempts to write? How can a foundation of self-criticism be developed that will be consistent with effective writing at any age? These are some of the questions that will be addressed as we examine the process of developing self-critical tools in the young writer.

A frontal assault on developing the young child's capacity to be critical of his own writing is not in order. The teacher needs to step back and look at the nature of the writing process and then view the different composing styles of children within that process. Child behaviors in three phases of the writing process provide guidelines and limits on how far we can go in helping the child to be self-critical. The ignoring of these two areas by most educators may be one of the reasons so little progress has been made in placing the evaluation of writing where it belongs, with the writer.

Children's views of their own writing as well as how they actually went about writing was a major part of a study completed on the writing processes of seven year old children in 1973 (Graves). It becomes clear from the study data that if we are to be of help to children we need to help them to be critical in each of three writing activities: precomposing, composing, and postcomposing. The definitions of these activities and some of the behaviors of interest to the teacher in each are the following:

Precomposing. This phase immediately precedes writing. Children prepare for the act of composing through art work, discussion with other children and the teacher, reading, or in reflecting on events that have occurred in their lives.

Composing. This phase begins and ends with the actual writing of the message. In this phase the observation of how children use language to accompany writing, reread, proofread, use resources, or react to outside interference are useful data to the teacher who would help a child to be self-critical.

Postcomposing. This phase refers to all behaviors observed following the completion of writing the message. Examples of these behaviors are product disposition, solicitation of approval from others, proofreading and contemplation of the finished product.

Different composing styles need to be viewed at different points in the writing process. Two traits, reflectiveness and reactiveness, describe two general types of writers who emerged in the study of seven year olds. Each writing type demands a different approach to the development of self-critical powers. For example, reactive writers do not wish to reexamine finished products. For them, the actual doing, getting the message down in rough form, is everything. Teachers who wish to help reactive children to become more self-critical have a difficult task since self-criticism is a reflective act which involves a *return* to something written. Reflective writers, on the other hand, enjoy the contemplation of their writing, the meaning of their message, and the development of their characters.

Both writers, reactive and reflective, are better understood through a more complete review of their behavior types in different phases of the writing process. The behaviors exhibited during the process give a cue to the depth and type of questions the teacher asks during writing conferences with the child. The following are behaviors exhibited by each type of beginning writer during their involvement in the writing process.

	Reactive Writer	*Reflective Writer*
Precomposing	Rehearses before writing through drawing or some form of construction; uses sound effects and converses with other children.	Does not visibly rehearse before composing. Child may rehearse through reading, television, daydreaming, etc.
Composing	Uses overt language to accompany act of writing; the word is heard before it is written down. Ideas follow in couplet form—e.g., "He hit 'em; he hit 'em back." Characterizations are similar to those of the writer; they react and are interested primarily in doing. When asked what will be written next, this writer does not know beyond the next sentence.	Uses no overt language to accompany act of writing. Ideas are elaborative and show the beginnings of paragraph construction. Characterizations are similar to those of the writer; they reflect, show feelings. When asked what will be written next, this writer will respond with a complete message, usually close to what is subsequently written on the paper.
Postcomposing	Puts work quickly away when the composing phase has been completed.	Occasionally studies the paper, rereads, or adjusts a phrase.

To further understand the needs of each type of writer, reactive and reflective, in developing self-critical skills, portions of interviews with each are reported. In each case the children were asked to rank papers in their writing folders from best to poorest and give a reason for selecting the best. Secondly, children were asked to tell what a "good writer needed to be able to do well in order to write well." Through each interview, the child's readiness for self-evaluation can be viewed.

The Reactive Child

Researcher: Would you look at these papers from your folder and choose the one you think is best, and the next best, . . . and then the next best?

Greg: (The child chose papers very rapidly with little apparent judgment being applied to the choice.)

Researcher: Why is this the best paper? (The child has chosen a paper about a hockey game. The paper had a picture of the hockey game at the top with the writing beneath.)

Greg: Like there is a fight. Like the goaldy . . . the hockey players
                and the referee.

Researcher: You seemed to choose this one because you liked the picture
                best.

Greg: (Nodded assent.)

Researcher: Why is this paper not as good as this one you thought
                was the best?

Greg: I goofed on the body.

In subsequent interviews, as well as in this one, the child's criteria for
choosing the best paper were based on the drawing. For this child, the
precomposing activity was much more interesting and important than the
composing phase. Later on Greg volunteered, "The teacher likes the words
not the pictures, but I like the pictures."

When queried as to what he thought a good writer needed to be able to do
well in order to write well, Greg replied, "The words . . . see they spelled right
draw good, and have the right spaces between the words." Other children
considered reactive in the study also focused on the first phase of the writing
process, the composing, and offered rationales that reflected the accidents of
discourse, those elements criticized on their papers, such as spelling, hand
writing, paper neatness, etc.

Although Greg, a reactive writer, shows little sensitivity to writing con
cepts, he did gain a greater sense of his own likes and dislikes about writing
themes. In subsequent interviews Greg shared more about his own experi
ences which the teacher could suggest as writing topics. In each interview
evidence was given by the child, which the interviewer, the teacher, could use
to assist him to be more critical. The teacher, through the questions used in
the interview, directed the child to think about his own work. The work was
not being compared with other children's writing. Rather, the child, even in
these very early stages of writing development and self-evaluation, is being
aided to develop his own criteria.

The Reflective Child

An example of an interview with a child who exhibits behaviors consistent
with the reflective writer can be seen in the following interview:

Researcher: Why did you pick this paper, "The Ant," as number one?

Lorna: Cuz I like poems and I liked this better than any other. I like
                the way the words go together.

Researcher: Would you choose your favorite line?

Lorna: "Some people think it is nothing at all."

Researcher: Why did you pick this as number two?

Lorna: I like drawing pictures of girls and gowns and things.

Researcher: Are there any here you would like to fix to make them better?

Lorna:	No.
Researcher:	How do you think a teacher decides which papers are the best?
Lorna:	Well, on the poetry she looks over the sentences and then she decides on the way it sounds and the way the words are put together.
Researcher:	Lorna, what does a good writer have to know or be able to do in order to write well?
Lorna:	You have to first think ahead before you write.

Read the story after they write it to see if they make any mistakes. They should have a little play in there and if it is long they should have one or two days. If you run out of things to tell, start another day.

You should tell how a person feels if he is in the story.

You have to know how to spell. If you don't, look it up. If you can't find the dictionary ask for help. I usually ask Jody. Remember capital letters, periods, and if someone talks, use quotation marks.

Write neat so people could read it and leave spaces between the words.

Lorna's interview, as well as her functioning within the entire writing process, are very different from Greg's. Lorna has a strong sense of the ingredients involved in the actual process of writing, as well as audience sense. Further interviews with Lorna can focus much more on style, a sense of what communicates with different audiences, as well as the development of a sense of authority with her writing voice.

The Writing Conference

The focal point for developing self-critical powers in the young writer is the writing conference. The conference, depending on the developmental level of the child, may be as often as every five days, or every ten days. The reactive writer needs more frequent interviews and is often helped best while he is actually engaged in the first two phases of the writing process. Sometimes the teacher may be able to be of assistance when the child has just finished writing through questions and reactions during the third phase, postcomposing. Conferences usually do not last more than five to ten minutes and are easily scheduled when children are engaged in other self-directed activities.

How are writing conferences conducted with children? The teacher seeks to elicit information from children rather than in issuing directives about errors on their papers. This is done for two reasons. First, children need to hear themselves offering opinions. They gain a sense of voice by first hearing themselves express ideas and opinions orally. This is particularly true if the teacher is a good listener who *actively* enables children to express their thoughts. Secondly, the teacher needs to gain a sense of children's logical thinking and interests. This can only come from the words of the children. Greg's statement, "The teacher likes the words, not the pictures, but I like the pictures," provided valuable insights into Greg's composing priorities.

What factors in the writing process need to be considered during conferences with the young writer? The following are examples of questions and
procedures used in child conferences:

Factor	*Conference Procedure*
Voice	"You seem to know a lot about fashion. How did you decide what outfit your doll would wear? . . . How was that made? I didn't know that you knew this much about clothes. Are there some clothes you especially like to wear for different times . . . like parties . . . going to school . . . to visit someone special?"
A Need for More Specifics	"What happened after the man won the race? Good. I would be interested in reading what happened."
	"You say he had an accident in the race. What happened to the car? What did the front fender and headlight look like after it hit the guard rail? Here are some words you just used in telling me about the accident. Would you like to use them?"
	"I am going to close my eyes. Can you tell me some words that will help me get a picture of what that racing car looks like?"
Language and Organization	"Which word do you like best? Do you have some words here you have never used before?"
	"Is there a sentence here that seems to say what you wanted to say more than any other?"
	"Do you think this sentence ought to come after this one? Read it out loud and tell me what you think."
	"You have two thoughts in this sentence. Read it out loud and tell me where the first one ends."
Progress and Change	"Let's look in your folder here. Do you see any change between this paper you wrote last December and the one you have just completed? Where do you feel you have improved? What are some of the things that haven't improved, yet you still wish they were better? Do you think your handwriting has improved?"
Audience Sense	"Which paper do you think is your best? I agree. Do you think it is good enough to go into the class collection? Do you want it to go there? Are there some things you would change in this paper, to make it your *very best*? Who are some of the people in this room who would be interested in reading this? Would you like to share it with them? Will they be able to read it?"

These questions will respond to a range of child differences to help both the
reactive and reflective writer. The teacher will need to be sensitive to the
degree of abstraction and amount of reflectiveness contained in each question, the children's interest in their own work, and sensitivity to their own
changes as writers. The questions are intended to develop children's senses of

authority and voice as well as to provide questions they will ask when writing alone.

When children are involved in individual conferences from the beginning, led to discover strengths and weaknesses in their own communication, it is not long before they begin to tell *us* what is needed to make their writing a stronger communication. When this point has been reached, we know the issue of dependency has been removed; indeed, the entire writing welfare issue has been put behind us. We know the writing process is where it belongs in the first place, in the hands of the child.

Reference

Graves, D.H. "Children's Writing: Research Directions and Hypotheses Based upon An Examination of the Writing Processes of Seven Year Old Children" (Doctoral Dissertation, SUNY at Buffalo, 1973). (University Microfilms No. 74-8375) (Also see the article, "An Examination of the Writing Processes of Seven Year Old Children," *Research in the Teaching of English*, 1975, *9*, 227–41.)

6. Language Arts Textbooks: A Writing Process Evaluation

Introduction

One of my many data-gathering expeditions for the Ford study ("Balance the Basics: Let Them Write") was a look at how language arts textbooks provided for writing. In the spring of 1976 my research colleague for the study, Becky Rule, analyzed the content of language arts textbooks, their philosophy of writing, and the proportion of each book devoted to the actual teaching of writing. We didn't expect to find much provision for writing, but we were surprised to find the manner in which the small amount of writing was taught. Fill-in-the-blank exercises, story starters, total textbook direction with little use of the writer's own information, were the typical approaches.

The data were clear, the question simple: "How do language arts texts provide for the teaching of writing?" The article was an easy one to write.

Part of the Ford study included interviews of editors and publishers of textbooks. Although I had little sympathy for the quality of textbook materials, I did begin to understand the precarious nature of the industry, particularly in the late seventies. At that time, work on the writing process was in its infancy. Textbook companies could not risk the inclusion of the new data on the writing process. Publishers were not yet ready to make the leap.

Writing process research has burgeoned since this piece was written in 1977. In addition, more and more teachers have become involved in writing themselves through the National Writing Project out of the University of California at Berkeley. In the spring of 1983 I asked my research colleague, Valjean Olenn, to take a quick look at current trends in the publishing of language arts textbooks to see if there had been any changes in the last seven years. The rhetoric of process had been included in some of the textbook introductions but the contents belied their intentions. Textbooks didn't provide any more opportunities to write than they had before. In some cases there was less attention to writing than in 1977. We chose four leading textbook companies for examination to get an index of trends. Note the numbers of pages in each book (number in parentheses) and the actual pages devoted to writing itself.

Total Pages Devoted to Writing

	Grade 2	Grade 5
Harcourt Brace Jovanovich (1983)	(209)−6	(407)−9
Laidlaw (1979)	(159)−4	(400)−6.5
Scott Foresman (1980)	(143)−8.5	(351)−8
Ginn & Company (1979)	(144)−17.5	(383)−7

The greatest provision for writing was by Ginn & Company in their grade two language arts textbook. Although textbook companies may consider that their books make more provision for writing than we do, it is important to note that we do not include the following exercises within our definition of writing:

- writing an ending to a sentence
- making lists
- recopying a paragraph or story, putting the sentences in the correct order
- outlining
- filling in blanks
- giving single sentence answers or responses

This pitiful provision for writing may be a blessing to the children. The few attempts to teach writing can only be described as horrendous. Books are still filled with story and picture starters. Topics are almost always given to children, thereby suggesting that children are without topics of their own. Writers should write about what they know. How can textbooks presume to know what individual children know? The Ginn series did suggest that fifth graders keep a journal for a week, one of the few times young writers were asked to draw on their own resources.

Writing process work in the hands of the capable teacher rules out use of any textbooks. The writing teacher who writes knows there is little need for drill or grammar exercises. These can be handled within the child's own writing which must provide the facts and present them clearly.

Publishers may argue that language arts textbooks are strictly for teachers who have had no experience in teaching writing at all. This is the publisher's market. But the textbooks hardly teach the neophyte teacher to *grow* as a teacher of writing. "We do the best we can under the circumstances," we can hear the publisher saying. But "the best we can" is *harmful*. Publishers make money, but children learn to hate writing, and taxpayers donate dollars to a lost cause.

Publishers ought to look at how the reading process is taught in their own reading manuals. Most of these manuals make me ill, but at least they attempt to take the child through a process, and as such, they are also instructive to teachers. Language textbooks are not. They are not responsive to children, they are unsystematic in their approach, and they do very little to teach teachers about writing or the writing process, whether it is 1977 or 1983.

Ninety-five percent of classroom instruction can be attributed to classroom materials. This is the claim of a new study by the Educational Products Information Exchange Institute, a nonprofit, consumer supported organization.

Although I have a hard time accepting the ninety-five percent figure, the power and place of textbooks in American classrooms cannot be overlooked. For this reason the content and approaches of textbooks ought to be reviewed more often.

A good place to begin is with the teaching of writing. Writing has received high focus in the last two years in both popular press and educational journals. At the same time writing process research has brought new information about what is involved in writing and how it ought to be taught. Since most classroom writing has origin in language arts textbooks, these books will be reviewed. They will be reviewed in the light of new information from interviews with publishers, teachers in the field, as well as research on the writing process.

Research and the Writing Process

Writing process advocates view writing as more than just the writing down of words. They take a time-expanded view of writing and study writers before, during, and after their composing. In fact, these close observations are usually conducted within an entire case study of the writer. These researchers believe that writing practice can only be described by viewing the writer over time. Janet Emig (1969) pioneered the work in this field and has been followed by many who have used the case study method for both students and professional writers to explain successful and unsuccessful writing practice.

Research on the writing process ought to lead to changes in teaching. The popular view of the teacher's role in writing is simply to stimulate student writing and then respond to it. Writing process research data show teacher roles ought to include response and preparation with children (grades 1–3) in the following ways:

Precomposing:	The provision of drawing, painting, informal drama, constructions, etc., as a means of rehearsing for writing. Questions and interviews with children on gathering information for writing. Plans for writing.
During Composing:	Observing word needs, questions of meaning, language clarification, plans for drafts.
After Composing:	Writing folder interviews—child evaluations of writing. Developing collections of "best work." Redrafting of best work.

With older students conferences are an essential part of teaching within the process. This method involves helping students at many points in their drafts through personal conferences—not the giving of topics and extensive corrections. The students write and the teacher responds in a manner appropriate to the stage in the process through which the writer is passing. The student is to discover what he or she knows and then is guided through many drafts until the topic is explained or clarified. The student spends as much time in gathering information from many sources to develop what he already knows. Unless there is information there is nothing to say. For this reason half of the two to three minute conferences with students may be spent on developing the student's authority as a writer through information. The conventions of language are taught through the final drafts—and taught through small groups on similar problems and within the final conferences themselves. Research data on the transfer of language conventions taught in isolation to actual student writing are bleak, and in many cases regressive.

Publishing and Writing

During the course of interviews with textbook publishers, one was frank to say:

> When writing is part of a reading series or much writing is required in any aspect of publishing, it (the materials) won't sell. Teachers want more labor saving devices, easier scoring, and if you have to respond to a lot of writing, there is more work involved. Some publishers have tried and they have been hurt by their ventures.

The investment that publishers make in a new language arts series is significant. The investment before manufacture runs to several million dollars. The amount of time it takes for a company to get a return on its investment is long, and with the recent fluctuation of the market, the risk is very high. Publishers must be careful; they publish to meet teacher desire and expectation; innovation is a risky business for them.

Publishers have another barrier. Teachers are poorly prepared for the teaching of writing. Textbooks are designed to fit the competency of most of the people who will use them. And teachers simply are not prepared for the teaching of writing. A random survey of 36 state universities preparing elementary teachers shows: 169 courses were offered in reading, 30 in children's literature, 21 in language arts, and only two on the teaching of writing. There is a knowledge base as well as a need to demonstrate the teaching of writing on site that is simply not provided in the preparation of most elementary teachers. A course may not be the way to help teachers, but many gaps are present that cannot be entirely covered by publisher's teaching manuals. In short, the means are simply not available to help teachers learn to teach writing.

Language Arts Texts

Eight language arts textbooks (both teacher and pupil editions) were examined at both the second and fifth grade levels. The objective was to determine how much and in what way writing was taught in language arts texts. The texts were examined in the light of new issues presented by writing process research data.

How Much Writing is Provided in Language Arts Textbooks?

The debate hasn't ended on what should be counted as the teaching of writing. Some believe the teaching of writing is equated with teaching mechanics, others only the actual composing with words, and some both mechanics and writing. James Squire (1975) tersely states his belief:

> Composing is not spelling. It is not grammar, not usage, not manuscript, not penmanship, not writing neat little snatches of perfectly formed sentences. It is neither writing with "two-inch margins," nor with perfect alignment. It is not rhetorical analysis of selected passages, nor is it completing a careful sequence of exercises on paragraph organization. Composing is none of these things.

Rather, teaching of composing or writing process involves teaching while the student is preparing for composing, actually composing, and reviewing a different draft.

For the sake of this study it is important to define those aspects of textbooks in which we have decided the teaching of mechanics and composing are included. They are the following:

Mechanics: Grammar and punctuation, literary conventions, spelling, sentence combining, proof-reading and editing unallied with the child's actual writing. Mechanics are usually taught independent of when the child composes on his own.

Composing: Writing stories, poetry, paragraphs, sentences, brainstorming story ideas, rewriting, proofreading and editing related to the child's own composing.

What are the findings? How much writing is provided in a language arts textbook? A review of Table 6.1 shows that 31% of all activities in grade two texts are devoted to teaching both composing and mechanics. Of the 31%, 17% is given to mechanics and 14% is given to the teaching of writing at the time the child writes. At the fifth grade level (Table 6.2), 51% of all activities are devoted to teaching both composing and mechanics. And of the 51%, 37% is given to mechanics and 14% to the teaching of composing. In short, the amount of attention given to composing is constant at both grade two and five, whereas activities in mechanics rise rapidly. Grammar and punctuation activities made up 72% of the mechanics in grade two and 76% in grade five.

What makes up the teaching of a child's composing? At the second grade level, 47% of the activities attend to the writing of sentences, 38% is longer prose (letters, descriptive writing, topics from story starters) and 14% is given to poetry. At the fifth grade level, the greatest emphasis (54%) is given to prose, with 14% to writing sentences and only 8% to poetry. Three new categories are added at this level: writing paragraphs, brainstorming story ideas and rewriting.

In summary, the teaching of writing is basically a situation where the teacher chooses the genre, the unit at which the student will write (paragraph, sentence), and the topic or story starter. The majority of the books attend to getting the writer going.

Teaching Practices in Texts

The book is the primary source of motivation for writing. This comes in the form of story starters and topics for teachers to suggest for children. More topics and starters are provided for second graders than for fifth graders.

Table 6.1
Activity Percentages in Language Arts Texts
Grade Two

	Percentage of Language Arts Texts Related to Writing: Mechanics and Composing Combined	Activities Devoted to Mechanics	Activities Devoted to Child's Own Writing	Percentage of Mechanics Devoted to Grammar and Punctuation
:ott, Foresman, *.nguage and How Use it*, 1969	19	8	11	80
olt, Rinehart and 'inston, *The Arts .d Skills of English*,)72	34	20	14	77
.arcourt Brace Jovan- ·ich, *Language for .aily Use*, 1973	39	21	18	90
. C. Heath, *.mmunicating*, 1973	21	11	10	53
.)llett Publishing .)., *The World of .nguage*, 1973	12	6	6	57
"ebster-McGraw Hill, .merican Language .)day*, 1974	43	25	18	68
.aidlaw, *Experiences . Language*, 1975	46	35	11	52
.arper & Row, *New .irections in English*,)73	35	9	26	100
Mean Score	31	17	14	72

Research data show (Graves, 1973) that second grade children, if given the chance, are rarely without topics they wish to write themselves. One of the benefits of second grade self-centeredness is in being sure of the rightness of a personal topic and the authority to write about that topic.

Writing is still dominated by the English-literature syndrome even in the early years (grades 2 and 5). This is shown by the fact that the primary use of writing is to write about literature. In none of the texts did writing apply to math, science, or social studies.

Writing process advocates have shown that collections of writing are valu-

Table 6.2
Activity Percentages in Language Arts Texts
Grade Five

	Percentage of Language Arts Texts Related to Writing: Mechanics and Composing Combined	Activities Devoted to Mechanics	Activities Devoted to Child's Own Writing	Percentage of Mechanics Devoted to Grammar and Punctuation
Scott, Foresman, *Language and How to Use It*, 1969	45	36	9	91
Holt, Rinehart and Winston, *The Arts and Skills of English*, 1972	55	41	14	52
Harcourt Brace Jovanovich, *Language for Daily Use*, 1973	62	46	16	88
D. C. Heath and Co. *Communicating*, 1973	41	38	3	66
Follett Publishing Co., *The World of Language*, 1973	26	15	11	68
Webster-McGraw Hill, *American Language Today*, 1974	40	30	10	62
Laidlaw, *Experiences in Language*, 1975	71	53	18	93
Harper & Row, *New Directions in English*, 1973	71	42	29	84
Mean Score	51	37	14	76

able for both children and teachers since they serve as a source for evaluation. Writing collections can also be used as permanently bound books of children's writing, or be used for circulation in classroom and school libraries. Four of the companies surveyed in this project recommended writing collections. The collections, however, were used as class magazines, a child's book of poetry, or a collection of class writings. Although these are valuable, in no teacher's edition were writing collections used for the purpose of helping a child to evaluate his writing in relation to his own work. One company did recommend that it would be useful to a school system to collect writings from year to year.

Very little help is recommended for writers while they are actively engaged in the writing process. Less than four percent of the recommendations for students or teachers involve activity *during* the writing process. When help does come, it is in the following forms:

1. Asking children questions to extend their writing, e.g., Where are you? What are you seeing? What are you doing?
2. Helping the child in mechanics and spelling while he is writing.
3. Reminding children of stylistic options such as combining sentences with and, who, or that.

What is not provided or recommended is an active role for the teacher or pupil in all three process phases. Little or none of the following are contained in any of the recommendations or activities for children.

1. *Precomposing*: A need to recognize that children have to rehearse (particularly young second grade children) before composing in writing. That is, drawing, painting, building or informal drama are rehearsal forms if the child knows he can write after he has finished. With older fifth grade children the development of gathering information from many sources—to have the facts for writing—is an essential step.
2. *Development of Voice*: This is an aspect of writing that is most important to process-oriented writers and teachers. This refers to developing the young writer's sense of authority in relation to personally known information. Over time, the editor or teacher seeks to develop the writer's authority and sense of accomplishment whether it be in writing fantasy or on specific informational topics. The same would be true in poetry. Both the writing folder and the writing conference are essential aspects of the development of voice. All three were lacking in teacher recommendations or student materials in the texts.
3. *Drafting-Revision Process*: Although only a few seven year old children are ready to revise, a much larger percentage of fifth graders should be ready to revise at points of information, language, organization, and conventions. Of the less than four percent attention given to revision, almost all of the revising would fall in the cosmetic department. That is, the second draft would merely clear up mechanical errors and look more neat than the first.

Conclusion

Publishing has a powerful influence on what happens in American classrooms. It has a strong grip on what actually occurs when a child is taught to write. Most writing instruction really isn't instruction at all. Rather, the teacher provides the appointment for writing through assignments and then responds to the mechanical errors contained in the child's writing after it is completed. The entire process area is left untouched by the texts. Neither prewriting, composing or postcomposing activities are suggested with strength or substance in either teacher or student texts. Nor is the learner's capacity for voice development or self-critical capability developed.

Teachers need help and they are not getting it. To conference with a child and respond to the specifics of the message, to develop a sense of voice and authority takes preparation, practice and skill. It is rare when a teacher has been prepared in these tools. Textbooks can do more, but they can't do it all. Until something is done for teachers, whether in preservice, inservice or advanced work at universities, the new research on the writing process will have little effect. Until teachers write and discover what the process means for themselves, they will not be able to help students.

References

Emig, Janet, "Components of the Composing Process Among Twelfth Grade Writers," Doctoral Dissertation, Harvard, 1969.

Graves, Donald H. "An Examination of the Writing Processes of Seven Year Old Children," *Research in the Teaching of English*, 9 (Winter, 1975) 227–241.

"National Survey and Assessment of Instruction," *Epiegram*, 4 (#14, April 15, 1976).

Squire, James R. "Composing—A New Emphasis for the Schools," in *The Writing Processes of Students*, W. Petty and P. Finn (eds), Buffalo: State University of New York, 1975.

7. Balance the Basics: Let them Write
(Ford Report)

Introduction

"Balance the Basics: Let Them Write" was commissioned by the Ford Foundation in April, 1976. The original intent of the review was to prepare an in-house paper on the status of reading and writing in the United States and abroad to be used as a guide for Ford Foundation policy in subsequent years. When the final paper was reviewed by the foundation in March 1977, the decision was made to use it as a monograph for the public. Mr. Donald Miller of the Ford Foundation (now at Oakland University, Michigan) was instrumental in commissioning the project and seeing it through to completion.

The time frame for gathering data proved almost impossible: from April 1976 through July of 1976 Rebecca Rule, my research associate, was instrumental in helping me gather data from many, many sources. From the outset, we wanted to look at reading and writing as two aspects of the larger communication habits of Americans in the broader culture, as well as the communication patterns within classrooms. We also wanted to do intensive interviews with people from all walks of life to get their views about how they read and wrote, as well as about current practice in the schools. This meant a great deal of interviewing with the post office, telephone company, CB radio personnel, publishers, school supply houses, and librarians. We also traveled extensively around the United States, Canada, and the United Kingdom. The result of all this work was an enormous fund of information. From all of this information, only one point could be made.

Even including my doctoral dissertation, I had never attempted a task as large as the Ford report. Up to this point, I had written only a few short articles. Furthermore, I had never ended up with such an enormous, diverse array of data. Worse, the time frame for working with all of the data was very short. I began writing the report the second week of July, after returning from interviews in the United Kingdom. After two weeks of writing, I had little to show for my efforts. I had wanted to have a full draft by the middle of August, and instead, I only had four or five pages of convoluted prose rewritten six times to show for my efforts. As usual, I went to my friend, Donald Murray, for expert advice.

Murray took one look at my writing and said, "This isn't you." He didn't need to tell me that the writing was terrible. (What Murray doesn't say is most eloquent.) He continued "I'd like to try something on you that I've never had the courage to try on myself." I said, "I don't care what it is, I'm desperate." Murray disappeared down his cellar stairs and returned with a cardboard box that would hold a ream of paper. With great ceremony, he cut a hole in the cover about nine inches wide. With equal ceremony and silence, he took masking tape and taped all around the edges of the box. "Now," he said, "you can't change anything when you write. When you come to the bottom of a page, you take the typewritten sheet and put it through this slot here and then go on to the next page. You can't use any notes from your data when you write. What you forget, your reader shouldn't have to suffer through."

It worked. The first day I wrote ten thousand words. At the end of the day I took the box to Murray for comment. He unsealed the masking tape, read the pages, and said, "This sounds like you. Keep writing because the writing is not all that bad." I kept on writing and within ten days, I had written one hundred and twenty pages. At last I had found my voice and the report began to make sense.

One hundred and twenty pages, of course, was much too long. If the report was to have any impact, it needed to be cut. In the cutting, whole chapters became single lines. For example, all the data that were gathered from school supply houses on the trends in paper consumption in the schools were merely reported: "Orders for lined paper, principally used for writing compositions, are going down." Also, an extensive review of textbooks from six publishers was condensed into two lines: "But only ten to fifteen percent of language arts textbooks for children are devoted to writing. Most of the texts are dominated by exercises in grammar, punctuation, spelling, listening skills, and vocabulary development."

Although the commission was to examine the relationship between reading and writing, from the outset it was clear that the main emphasis in schools was on the ability of children to receive information, not to send it. In fact, the entire culture places a major emphasis on the ability of persons to receive information. The one thing the report sought to address was the necessity of restoring a balance in communication in the schools, principally through writing.

People want to write. The desire to express is relentless. People want others to know what they hold to be truthful. They need the sense of authority that goes with authorship. They need to detach themselves from experience and examine it by writing. Then they need to share what they have discovered through writing.

Yet most of us are writing less and less. Americans are writing fewer personal letters, and the U.S. Postal Service estimates an even lower volume in the years ahead. Studies undertaken for this report show that people of many occupations and all educational levels turn to writing only as a last resort.

When we do write, we often write badly. The press continually reminds us that students can no longer punctuate, use proper grammar, spell correctly, or write legibly. But the crisis in writing goes well beyond these visible signs. People do not see themselves as writers because they believe they have nothing to say that is of value or interest to others. They feel incompetent at conveying information through writing. Real writing, they seem to think, is reserved for the professional.

For the rest of us, writing is perceived as a form of etiquette in which care is taken to arrange words on paper to avoid error rather than communicate with clarity and vigor. When writing, Americans too often feel like the man who has been invited to a party of distinguished guests. Being a person of modest station he attends with great reluctance and discomfort. He has but one aim—to be properly attired, demonstrate correct manners, say as little as possible, and leave early.

This view of writing was taught to us in school. In the classroom learners are viewed as receivers, not senders. A far greater premium is placed on students' ability to read and listen than on their ability to speak and write. In fact, writing is seldom encouraged and sometimes not permitted, from grade one through the university. Yet when students cannot write, they are robbed not only of a valuable tool for expression but of an important means of developing thinking and reading power as well.

The imbalance between sending and receiving should be anathema in a democracy. A democracy relies heavily on each individual's sense of voice, authority, and ability to communicate desires and information.

There is hope, however. Barriers to good writing are not as high or insurmountable as they seem. Students who write poorly can improve quickly with skilled, personal attention that concentrates on what they know and can tell others. Good teaching *does* produce good writing. There *are* schools where writing and expression are valued.

This study reports on several such schools and identifies one broad, flexible, and effective approach to the teaching of writing. It also addresses two central questions underlying the crisis of writing in America:

Is it important to write? And, if so, why don't we write?

Why Writing is Important

Writing is most important not as etiquette, not even as a tool, but as a contribution to the development of a person, no matter what that person's background and talents.

Writing contributes to intelligence. The work of psycholinguists and cognitive psychologists shows that writing is a highly complex act that demands the analysis and synthesis of many levels of thinking. Marcia, an eighth-grade student, has written a composition about handguns, a subject of her own choosing. She first became interested in the problems raised by handguns when a shooting occurred in the family of a friend. She knew the family, had seen the gun on an earlier occasion, had felt the shock of the incident, and had experienced with neighbors the emotions that surfaced in its aftermath.

To begin writing her composition, Marcia listed key words and details surrounding the incident: the expressions on the faces of her friends, the statements of neighbors, the appearance of the gun itself. As she set down these impressions she recalled details that otherwise would have escaped her. The process of writing heightened a remembered experience. It developed a way of seeing.

Later, Marcia found further material to add to her initial draft. She gathered general information on handguns, their use in robberies, their suitability for protection or for sport. She reviewed data on accidental shootings. Taking all this information, she analyzed and synthesized it through the process of writing.

In successive drafts, Marcia shaped her material into a structure that gave more meaning to the details. A sense of order and rightness came from the new arrangement. Through organization, the mass of data was simplified. This simplicity, in turn, made it possible for Marcia to stand back from her material to see new details and meanings, such as the evident concern of the police, the effect of the shooting on the family, and her own feelings.

What Marcia would have expressed orally at the time of the shooting was different from what she later developed on the page. Reflection and discovery through several drafts led to depths of perception not possible to reach through immediate conversation. Marcia now can say with authority why she has always opposed the sale of handguns. Through the successful analysis and synthesis of fact and feeling she has strengthened her cognitive abilities.

In addition to contributing to intelligence, writing develops initiative. In reading, everything is provided; the print waits on the page for the learner's action. In writing, the learner must supply everything: the right relationship between sounds and letters, the order of the letters and their form on the page, the topic of the writing, information, questions, answers, order.

Writing develops courage. Writers leave the shelter of anonymity and offer to public scrutiny their interior language, feelings, and thoughts. As one writer phrased it, "A writer is a person with his skin off."

There lie both the appeal and the threat of writing. Any writer can be deeply hurt. At no point is the learner more vulnerable than in writing. When a child writes, "My sister was hit by a terck yesterday" and the teacher's response is a red-circled "terck" with no further comment, educational standards may have been upheld, but the child will think twice before entering the writing process again. Inane and apathetic writing is often the writer's only means of self-protection.

On the other hand, writing, more than any other subject, can be the means to personal breakthrough in learning(1). "I was astounded," a student reports, "when the teacher read one of my paragraphs in class. Until then I had no idea I could write or have anything to say. I began to think I could do something right for a change." Another says, "Writing for the school newspaper turned me around. Other people started reading my stuff and saying, 'Did you really write that?'" This kind of discovery doesn't always happen in an English class. Another student observes, "I learned to write in a chemistry course in high school. The chemistry teacher was a stickler for accuracy and economy. Writing up lab reports was really disciplined writing. I began to see things differently."

Writing can contribute to reading from the first day a child enters school. Donald Durrell, a pioneer in the reading field and an authority for fifty years, strongly advocates the use of writing as a help to reading. "Writing is active; it involves the child; and doing is important," Durrell says. "Teachers make learning too passive. We have known for years the child's first urge is to write and not read and we haven't taken advantage of this fact. We have underestimated the power of the output languages like speaking and writing."(2).

Writing also contributes to reading because writing is the making of reading. When a child writes she has to know the sound-symbol relations inherent in reading. Auditory, visual, and kinesthetic systems are all at work when the child writes, and all contribute to greater skill in reading.

As children grow older, writing contributes strongly to reading comprehension. Students who do not write beyond the primary years lose an important tool for reading more difficult material(3). Research has tied reading comprehension to the ability of students to combine sentences in writing. The ability to revise writing for greater power and economy is one of the higher forms of reading. Reading is even more active when a writer has to read and adjust his own ideas.

It is just beginning to be recognized that writing also contributes to learning in the field of mathematics. A great number of mathematics students consistently fail to solve problems at the point of reading. Seldom are these students in the position of writing problems, or creating the reading of mathematics. Until they work "on the other side," at the point of formulating examples, they will not fully understand the reading contained in mathematics.

Why Don't We Write?

Five-year-old Paul writes. Children want to write before they want to read. They are more fascinated by their own marks than by the marks of others. Young children leave their messages on refrigerators, wallpaper, moist windowpanes, sidewalks, and even on paper.

Six-year-old Paul doesn't write. He has gone to school to learn to read. Now that he is in school, the message is, "Read and listen; writing and expression can wait." Paul may wait a lifetime. The odds are that he will never be truly encouraged to express himself in writing.

Paul will wait and wait to write because a higher premium is placed on his ability to receive messages than on his ability to send them. Individual expression, particularly personal messages in writing, will not be valued as highly as the accurate repetition of the ideas of others, expressed in *their* writing. Since Paul will write so little, by the time he graduates from high school he will think of himself as a poor writer and will have a lowered sense of self-esteem as a learner. He will have lost an important means of thinking and will not have developed his ability to read critically. Worse, as a citizen, employee, and parent, he will tend to leave the formulation and expression of complicated ideas to others. And the "others" will be an ever decreasing group.

The recent national attention given to the weaknesses of American elementary education has not improved Paul's prospects. All signs point to less writing, not more. The so-called return to basics vaults over writing to the skills of penmanship, vocabulary, spelling, and usage that are thought necessary to precede composition. So much time is devoted to blocking and tackling drills that there is often no time to play the real game, writing.

The emphasis on before-writing skills may have the matter backward. When children write early, their experiments with sounds and symbols produce spellings that may not be entirely accurate, but research shows that if these children continue to have ample opportunity to write they gradually increase in spelling power(4). Moreover, it has been shown, the freedom to experiment with spelling (as with other aspects of writing) is important to the development of fluency and confidence.

Another reason that there will be less writing is that too often our schools show little concern for the individual development of the learners themselves or the important ideas they may have to share. Our distrust of children is most evident when we insist that they always be receivers rather than senders. If our approach to writing is to change, that change must be born of a confidence that what students have to say is worth saying. Writing is a matter of personal initiative. Teachers and parents must have confidence in that initiative or there will be little real writing.

The teaching of writing also suffers because reading dominates elementary education in America today. Nowhere else in the world does reading maintain such a hold on early learning. Although reading is valued in other countries, it is viewed more in the perspective of total communication.

Our anxiety about reading is a national neurosis. Where else in the world are children scrutinized for potential failure in a subject area in the first two months of school—or even before they enter school? And our worst worries are fulfilled. Children fail.

Concern about reading is today such a political, economic, and social force in American education that an imbalance in forms of communication is guaranteed from the start of a child's schooling. The momentum of this force is such that a public reexamination of early education is urgently needed. As we have seen, when writing is neglected, reading suffers. Neglect of a child's expression in writing limits the understanding the child gains from reading.

A review of public educational investment at all levels shows that for every dollar spent on teaching writing a hundred or more are spent on teaching reading. Of exemplary programs in language chosen for recognition by the U.S. Office of Education in 1976, forty-six were in reading, only seven included any writing objectives at all, and only one was designed for the specific development of writing abilities (5).

Research on writing is decades behind that on reading. Research on all aspects of writing has produced only about as many studies as has research on the topic of reading readiness alone. A National Institute of Education analysis of research in basic skills does not even include writing in that category, mentioning only "reading and mathematical skills" as being required "for adequate functioning in society" (6).

Of research articles in education published in 1969, 5 percent were on reading; articles on writing were included in a category labeled "other," which constituted less than 1 percent (7). The U.S. Office of Education has published numerous studies to show the effectiveness of compensatory reading programs. Not one study has been published on writing programs.

Teacher-certification requirements also assure a continuing imbalance between reading and writing. Most states require one course in teaching reading, many require two, and some are attempting to raise the requirement to three. A survey of superintendents of schools in a New England state asked, "What should be the minimum standards or criteria used when interviewing candidates for a vacant position in the elementary years?"(8) Seventy-eight percent of the superintendents thought that teachers should have had a minimum of three courses in the teaching of reading. No comparable criterion relating to the teaching of writing was felt necessary.

Publishers' investments in new language series have followed the research dollars and the wishes of school systems. Their textbook lists directly reflect the one-sided emphasis on reading. More than 90 percent of instruction in the classroom is governed by textbooks and workbooks(9). But only 10 to 15 percent of language-arts textbooks for children are devoted to writing. Most of the texts are dominated by exercises in grammar, punctuation, spelling, listening skills, and vocabulary development.

One textbook editor spoke for his profession when he said, "When writing is part of a reading series or when much writing is required, the materials won't sell. Teachers want more labor-saving devices, like easier scoring. If you have to respond to a lot of writing, there is more work involved. Some publishers have tried, and they have been hurt by their ventures"(10).

Even a casual survey of elementary-school workbooks shows that pupils are customarily required to circle, underline, or draw a line to identify correct answers. Rarely are they asked to respond in full sentences. In secondary schools and universities, students are asked more and more only to fill in squares with pencils for computer analysis. Examination essays are disappearing.

Thus, although writing is frequently extolled, worried over, and cited as a public priority, it is seldom practiced in schools. Orders for lined paper, principally used for writing compositions, are going down(11).

In a recent survey a large sample of seventeen-year-olds were asked how much writing they had done in all their courses in the previous six weeks. The results: 50 percent had written only two or three pages, 12 percent had written only one short paper, and 13 percent had done no writing at all(12). Thus only a quarter of the students had written anything more often than once every two weeks.

Even in school systems reputed to stress writing as a major concern, there is often little writing. A survey of three such systems discovered that children from the second through the sixth grade on the average wrote only three pieces over a three-month period(13). Even less writing was asked for at the secondary level. Yet if writing is taken seriously, three months should produce at least seventy-five pages of drafts by students in the high-school years.

The current emphasis on testing and documenting pupil progress makes writing a stumbling block. Writing resists quantitative testing. A sixth-grade teacher says, "I know why writing isn't emphasized more; it can't be tested. We are so hung up on reporting measured gains to the community on nationally normed tests that we ignore teaching those areas where it can't be done. How do you say, 'Susie has improved six months in the quality of her writing'? We test them to death in reading and math and do some assessing on language conventions, but that's all."

The demand for other evaluation of writing is also a deterrent to the teaching of writing. Evaluation is hard work. Most English teachers who take home a hundred compositions to mark feel they must meticulously review each word, make comments, and wrestle with a grade. Such work is exhausting, and not many English teachers have as few as a hundred students. This work is different from that of colleagues who score multiple-choice tests or run down the answer column on the right-hand side of a mathematics paper. Many teachers, knowing its importance, would like to offer more writing, but just don't have the time to correct papers as thoroughly as they think necessary. Research data now show, however, that scrupulous accounting for all errors in a student paper is actually harmful to good writing development (a point returned to in the next section).

As we have seen, few adults write. Teachers are no exception; they do not write either. Teachers report that they do not write because they don't like writing, feel they are poor writers, do not have time to write because of teaching demands, or do not believe it necessary to practice writing in order to teach it(14).

Seldom do people teach well what they do not practice themselves. It would be unheard of for teachers of music or art not to practice their craft. For some reason, the craft of writing is seen as an exception. What is not valued by teachers in their personal lives will not be introduced into the lives of children. It is therefore little wonder that writing is taught, if at all, as an afterthought, even when it is spoken of approvingly in public.

Most elementary-school teachers have not been prepared to teach writing. Even for teachers who want to get help, adequate courses in the teaching of writing are simply not available. A recent survey of education courses in 36 universities shows that 169 courses were offered in reading, 30 in children's literature, 21 in language arts, and only 2 in the teaching of writing(15). Teachers do not teach a subject in which they feel unprepared, even when the subject is mandated by the school curriculum. Writing is such a subject.

The situation of teachers in secondary schools is no improvement. Those who were English majors in college are not trained for the teaching of writing. In colleges there is little formal attempt to teach writing beyond freshman English courses, although even in them the emphasis is on literature. There is little writing. Indeed, writing is given low priority in most English departments, and the teaching of it is often relegated entirely to graduate students and junior faculty members. At one large state university, the contract offered teaching assistants recommends that student assignments in the English writing course be limited to 7,500 words per semester, or about two typewritten pages weekly(16). With this kind of university background, it is not surprising that most high-school English teachers would much rather teach literature than have anything to do with writing. The writing achievements of high-school students reflect this attitude.

Writing models thus do not exist for most children, in school or out. Children may see adults read and certainly hear them speak, but rarely do they see adults write. And it is even less likely that they will actually observe how an adult composes. We know of the importance of models in reading and speaking. Although we have no good research data on how adult models affect children's writing, clear inferences can be drawn as warnings about the future of writing in America. Children begin to lose their natural urge to put their messages down in writing as soon as they begin to have a sense of audience, at eight or nine years of age. It is as this point that adults begin to have a strong influence as models. It is also the time when teachers' comments on children's papers begin to have an impact. This impact affects children for the rest of their lives.

Collages of haunting memories dominate the thinking of people from all walks of life as they recount learning experiences in writing: "There was something dark or sinister about it." "Be neat and tidy or you flunk." These are typical memories of children and housewives, businessmen and engineers, garage mechanics and laborers, teachers and politicians who were interviewed in the preparation of this report. For most people, the way in which they were taught has determined their view of writing and the degree to which they practice it.

Writing is a form of discipline, in the best sense of that word, that has been turned into a form of punishment. A castor-oil syndrome plagues writing from the first grade through the university: "It's good for you." Punishments in the form of compositions and mechanical writing exercises are still not uncommon in the classroom. "Write a hundred times, 'I will not chew gum in school.'" "Write a three-hundred-word composition on how you will try to improve your attitude." School discipline, grammar, and spelling are often mentioned together as a single package containing what is most needed in education today.

In speaking criticallly of his early school experiences, a businessman says, "There was no emphasis on content in writing—they worried about grammar and spelling but not about what was said." The same person, asked about what is needed in education today, replies, "Today there is too much emphasis on whether or not the kids have a good time. When I was in school we were physically punished. It was a form of discipline. That's the biggest difference today—no discipline and not as much teaching of mechanics."

Parents often reflect this view that the mechanics of writing are more important than its content. In one suburban community, it was found, parents regularly checked their children's papers to make sure that teachers had identified all errors(17).

Teachers' impressions of what constitutes effective teaching of writing are similar to those of the general public. As we have seen, neither the teachers of college courses nor their advanced professional training have aided them in teaching writing in any other way. They therefore teach as they were taught.

And so the links in the chain are forged. Seven-year-old children were asked, "What do you think a good writer needs to do in order to write well?" Children who had a difficult time with writing responded, "To be neat, space letters, spell good, and know words." Children who were more advanced in writing added, "Have a good title and a good ending." Children were also asked, "How does your teacher decide which papers are the good ones?" The following criteria were commonly cited by children of all ability levels: "It has to be long, not be messy, and have no mistakes(18). In both cases, the children's impressions of what good writing demanded were connected with their teachers' corrections on their papers. And clearly, teachers did not tend to call attention to the content of the papers. Not once did children speak of good writing as providing information of interest to others.

We persist in seeing writing as a method of moral development, not as an essential mode of communication. The eradication of error is more important than the encouragement of expression. Clearly underlying this attitude toward the teaching of writing is the belief that most people, and particularly students, have nothing of their own to say. And therefore, why should they write?

How Writing Can Be Taught

A way of teaching writing called the process-conference approach is a proven, workable way to reverse the decline of writing in our schools.

Teachers using this method help students by initiating brief individual conferences *during* the process of writing, rather than by assigning topics in advance of writing and making extensive corrections after the writing is finished. Emphasis is given to the student's reasons for writing a particular composition. The teacher works with the student through a series of drafts, giving guidance appropriate to the stage through which the writer is passing. By putting ideas on paper the student first discovers what he or she knows and then is guided through repeated drafts that amplify and clarify until the topic is fully expressed. A single completed paper may require six or more conferences of from one to five minutes each.

The process-conference approach in a seventh-grade classroom might follow a script such as the following one. Notice that the teacher doesn't even review a draft until the fourth conference.

Conference 1

Jerry:	I want to write about sharks but I have a hard time getting started. I'm not much of a writer.
Ms. Putnam:	Well, have you had any experiences with sharks, Jerry? How did you get interested in the subject?
Jerry:	Yeah, me and my dad were trolling for stripers and all of a sudden this fin pops up just when I got a hit. That was it. No more fishing that day. Can they move! I got to talking with the guys down at the dock; they said we've got more than usual this year. Blue sharks they were.
Ms. Putnam:	You have a good start with what you have just told me. Many people talk about sharks but few have actually seen them. What else do people at the dock have to say about sharks? Any old-timers who might have had run-ins with them? You say the sharks moved quickly. Well, how fast can sharks swim?

Conference 2

Jerry:	Hey, listen to this. Charley Robbins, the old lobsterman, saw a thirteen-foot blue, nudged his boat—didn't know whether he just got bumped or the shark intended to get him. Said he'd hit the bastard with a boat hook the next time he saw him.

Ms. Putnam:	Well, do sharks attack or not? Have there ever been any shark attacks in this area? Do you think this is important information? Where can you find out?

Conference 3

Jerry:	I asked at the newspaper and they didn't know of any shark attacks over the last five years. So, I asked them who might know. They said I ought to call the Coast Guard station. They said, no attacks but lots of sightings; they were more worried about people doing stupid things in their boats with this shark craze that's around.
Ms. Putnam:	What do you mean, doing stupid things?
Jerry:	Well, now when a beach gets closed, people stop swimming, but these crazy kids go out in small boats to harpoon them. They could get killed. Sharks really don't harm people, but if you start poking them, who knows what will happen?
Ms. Putnam:	Jerry, you certainly have good information about sharks. I suspect that very few people know what the Coast Guard is up against. And what do you think will happen if some eighteen-year-old has to prove he's a man?

Conference 4

Jerry:	Well, here's the first shot. What do you think?
Ms. Putnam:	You have a good start, Jerry. Look at these first four paragraphs. Tell me which one makes you feel as if you were there.
Jerry:	This one here, the fourth one, where I tell about two kids who are trying to harpoon a shark.
Ms. Putnam:	Don't you think this is the one that will interest readers most? Start right off with it. Hit 'em hard. This is an actual incident.

Conference 5

Jerry:	I've got so much stuff on sharks I don't know what to do with it all. All those interviews and these books.
Ms. Putnam:	You can't use it all, can you? I want you to put down the five most important things you want to leave your audience with. Don't look at your notes; just write them down off the top of your head. You know so much you don't have to look any more.

Conference 6

Jerry:	Well, I took those five points. I feel better now. But look at all this stuff I haven't used.
Ms. Putnam:	That's the way it is when you know a lot about a subject. Over here on the third page you get a little abstract about people's fear of sharks. Can you give some more examples? Did you get some in your interviews? What needs to be done before this becomes your final copy?
Jerry:	Put in those examples of fear—I have plenty of those. I have plenty of weird spellings—guess I'd better check those out—never could punctuate very well.
Ms. Putnam:	I think you have information here the newspaper or the Coast Guard might be interested in. Had you thought about that? Let me know what you want to do with this.

Most of Jerry's time was spent in gathering information from many sources to develop what he already knew. Without information a student has nothing to write about. This is why in three of the six conferences Jerry's teacher worked on developing information and strengthening the authority of the writer. Until students feel they have information to convey, it is difficult for them to care about writing or to feel they can speak directly and with authority. From the first wave of information a rough draft emerges. Succeeding drafts include more information, more precise language, and changes in organization.

Teachers who use the process-conference approach do not see a composition as something that can be "wrong." It can only be unfinished. The teacher leads the writer to discover new combinations of personal thought, to develop the sense of knowing and authority so valuable to any learner. Indeed, the main task of the teacher is to help students know what they know.

In a city school in upper New York state, children make reading for themselves and others. Each child maintains a folder in which writings are kept over a ten-day period. At the end of this period, the children are helped to evaluate their progress in writing. Sometimes a child and the teacher may agree that a very good piece of writing belongs in the class collection. Sometimes the children put their own writings into books that they construct themselves(19).

When children are able to see their own writing used by others, their concepts of themselves as writers are heightened. When writing is not just a context between the child and the teacher but serves a broader audience, the teacher does not have to attend continually to correcting technical errors, but can concentrate on other matters essential to good writing.

As with older students, writing conferences are essential to the young child's growth as a writer. With younger children, perhaps 90 percent of the conferences are only a minute in length, occurring throughout the day. A roving teacher in a second-grade classroom might teach like this: "And what are you writing now, Sandra? Oh, you're telling about prehistoric animals. Are there some words you will need for your word page? Some of those names are hard to spell. Now this is interesting, Derek. Which sentence do you think tells best about what racing cars look like?" Throughout, the teacher's questions are related to the message first and to the mechanics and finer points second.

The same method of teaching can apply with equal effectiveness to other kinds of classroom work: "What do you like best about the picture you're painting, Martha? Perhaps we could find the best part with these cropping Ls. What do you think?"

This teacher in this classroom was not dealing with either the initiation of compositions or their final evaluation. Rather, she was participating at points within the process where help counted most. With Sandra she was trying to find out how far her pupil was thinking ahead in the writing process. She asked Derek himself to choose the line that had the best imagery, at the same time letting him know she cared about his interests in cars. Although Martha was not writing, the teacher's attention to her composing with water colors was another way of helping the learner develop critical powers basic to both writing and painting—of finding a way of seeing and a way of looking for the best parts in a whole.

In a rural school in Connecticut where writing conferences were the norm, I asked Rebecca, a second-grade child who was about to write, "What does a good writer need to do well in order to write well?" Rebecca replied, "Details. You have to have details. For example if I walked down the street in the rain, I wouldn't say, 'I walked down the street and it was raining.' I would say, 'As I walked down the street in the rain, I sloshed through the puddles and the mud splattered to make black polka dots on my white socks.' "

In this instance Rebecca demonstrated one of the important contributions of writing: heightened experience. Writing is a kind of photography with words. We take mental pictures of scenes when we're out walking but don't really know what we have seen until we develop the words on the page through writing. Rebecca noticed what happened when she walked through puddles with white socks on. Having written down what she saw, she will notice even more details the next time she walks in the rain.

In our conversation, Rebecca went on to show me in a book how another writer had used words to give the reader more details. Because of this child's confidence in her own writing voice, she could read the writing of others with a critical eye.

One of the common complaints of reading teachers is that children fail in the higher forms of comprehension: inferential and critical questions. It is difficult for many readers to separate their own thinking from that of the author, to stand far enough back from the material to see the author's point of view as distinct from their own. On the other hand, children who are used to writing for others achieve more easily the necessary objectivity for reading the work of others.

I wouldn't have expected to find process-conference teaching when I first looked in on a primary school in Scotland in which the rooms were formally arranged with neat rows of desks and chairs. However, teachers there were clearly well versed in the individual strengths of each child, even though there were thirty-five children to each room. It was obvious that high standards were set. I asked a child how he managed to write so well. His reply: "I am from Aberdeen, and this is the way we do it." Indeed, this spirit prevailed throughout the school. Children had a sense of voice and expressed themselves with confidence, both orally and in writing, as if it were their birthright.

Teachers in the Aberdeen school felt it was the children's responsibility to proofread their work. Few marks were seen on papers. A teacher would merely say, "But you're not finished yet, Matthew. You must be having an off day. Perhaps Margaret will look it over with you."

The process-conference approach flourishes in schools where administrators, teachers, and children trust one another. Such teaching cannot occur otherwise. Writing is affected by school climates. The stance of the school system as a whole shows quickly in the way writing is taught. A California teacher reported that her children were given four different tests for language skill. Four levels in the educational hierarchy—the federal granting agency, the state department of education, an independent community committee commissioned by the local board of education, and the school principal—all wished to know how her children compared with other children nationally. Although this program of testing took up valuable time, its other effects were greater: it created suspicion and fear that some children might lower the class scores, that other teachers' classes might do better, and that the test scores might be misused by administrators. Under these conditions the teachers inevitably became more concerned with the measurable surface elements of writing and less able to respond to the content of the writing of individual children. The teaching of writing was severely hampered.

School systems don't have to work this way. In a New Hampshire system, the teaching of writing turned around after the superintendent of schools enrolled, almost by accident, in a writing course given as an elective in an advanced program in school administration.

In the course, the teaching of writing was approached through the process of writing, not through reading about writing. As the superintendent gradually saw improvement in his own writing, he saw what might be possible for teachers and students in his own system. He made arrangements for a cooperative venture in writing instruction between his school system and the local university. The university would work with teachers on the process-conference approach, and the school system would aid in the development of new procedures for the assessment of writing.

Working in the schools, university faculty members sought to help teachers discover the power of their own writing. The writing process itself was studied, as well as the use of the process-conference approach with students. Thirty teachers from grades one through twelve took part in the training sessions. And the professors, the superintendent and other administrators, and the teachers all wrote and shared their writing.

Once the teachers began to understand the writing process and their own powers as writers, they could develop an effective approach to assessing student writing. Together, a teacher and a student would choose the student's four best papers for assessment. Thus students were assessed at their points of strength, as they wrote on topics of their own choosing in a variety of genres.

In a school whose teachers follow the process-conference approach in teaching children to write, a teacher might think, "Jennifer is ready for quotation marks in her writing now." In a school that teaches to meet predetermined test-oriented standards for correct writing, a teacher would be more likely to think, "Paul had better get going on quotation marks or he'll pull us down in the next city-wide achievement test."

Jennifer will meet quotation marks when dealing with the conversation of characters in the story she is writing. She will also look at models from literature: "See, this is how this author shows that people are talking. You put your marks here and here. There, now you can show that this is your knight talking." Jennifer masters the conventions of language in the process of conveying information.

Paul is more likely to struggle with quotation marks as an isolated phenomenon. He will punctuate sentences provided for him in a workbook. He will not see himself as a sender of information, a writer.

Paul wanted to write before he went to school. He is less eager to write now.

Paul should write because it will develop his self-concept as a learner and his powers as a thinker. Writing will strengthen his work in other subjects. If he writes throughout his school years, he will later make more effective contributions as a citizen, parent, and worker.

Writing is the basic stuff of education. It has been sorely neglected in our schools. We have substituted the passive reception of information for the active expression of facts, ideas, and feelings. We now need to right the balance between sending and receiving. We need to let them write.

Notes

1   Data for this were taken from the interview responses about educational background and experiences. Although people cited writing most often as the personal breakthrough in learning, another group cited it as a negative, punishing experience. There seemed to be little middle ground in referring to writing experiences.

2   Although Durrell has stated this same point in recent writings, this is a quotation from an interview with him.

3   This kind of research is in its infancy, yet early data returns are more than promising. These studies, as well as the Stotsky article, are important beginnings in portraying the contribution of writing to reading.

Combs, Warren E. "The Influence of Sentence-Combining Practice on Reading Ability." Unpublished doctoral dissertation, University of Minnesota, 1975.

Obenshain, Anne. "Effectiveness of the Precise Essay Question in Programming the Sequential Development of Written Composition Skills and the Simultaneous Development of Critical Reading Skills." Master's Thesis, George Washington University, 1971.

Smith, William. "The Effect of Transformed Syntactic Structures on Reading." Paper presented at the International Reading Association Conference, May, 1970.

Stotsky, Sandra L. "Sentence Combining as a Curricular Activity: Its Effect on Written Language Development and Reading Comprehension," *Research in the Teaching of English*, 9(Spring, 1975) 30–70.

4   Chomsky, Carol. "Beginning Reading Through Invented Spelling," *Selected Papers from the 1973 New England Kindergarten Conference*, Cambridge, Massachusetts, Lesley College, 1973.

Chomsky, Carol. "Write First, Read Later," *Childhood Education*, 1971, 47(No. 6), 296–299.

Paul, Rhea. "Invented Spelling in Kindergarten," *Young Children*, March, 1976, (No. 3), 195–200.

5   *Educational Programs That Work*, U.S. Office of Education (U.S. Government Printing Office: Washington, D.C.) 1976.

6   *1976 DATABOOK—The status of Education Research and Development in the United States*. (The National Institute of Education: Washington, D.C.) 1976.

7   Persell, Carolyn, *The Quality of Research on Education*. (New York: Columbia University, Bureau of Applied Social Research) 1971.

8 *A Survey of Current Instructional Practices in and Approaches to the Teaching of Reading/Language Arts in New Hampshire.* (Division of Instruction: State Dept. of Education, Concord, N. H.) 1976.

9 "National Survey and Assessment of Instruction," *Epiegram*, 4(April 15, 1976). (Published by Educational Products Information Exchange, New York City, New York).

10 Interviews with both publishers and writers spoke of the risks of publishing. A number of publishers have gone back to publishing texts of ten to twenty years ago because of their stress on the basics, and the basics do not include *actual writing*.

11 Our surveys of school supply companies and the purchasing of paper by school districts show a decline in the use of lined paper. There is also an accelerated purchase of ditto paper, which is rarely used for writing.

12 These data were cited by Rex Brown, Education Commission of the States, Denver, Colorado at the National Council of Teachers of English, Secondary School English Conference, Boston, Massachusetts, April, 1976.

13 As part of this study three systems in rural, suburban, and urban communities in three different states were examined. All three were *making efforts* to improve student writing.

14 Teachers from grade one through the university were interviewed. Individual writing was a universal problem.

15 Our own survey of the catalog offerings in departments of education in 36 universities. Most of the universities were state schools engaged in teacher preparation. In the 1960s the United States made an effort, through the National Defense Education Act, to better prepare teachers to teach writing. Since that time, however, the effort has languished.

16 This was a contract recently agreed upon at a Big Ten university in freshman composition.

17 This was a common concern of teachers surveyed in a suburban school system near Boston, Massachusetts.

18 Graves, Donald H. "Children's Writing: Research Directions and Hypotheses Based Upon an Examination of the Writing Processes of Seven-Year-Old Children." Unpublished doctoral dissertation, SUNY at Buffalo, 1973.

19 The examples that follow in this section were from schools in four regions of the U.S. These schools were visited to provide contrast and perspective on the status of writing in the U.S. As mentioned earlier schools were also visited in England and Scotland.

8. Titles for the Ford Report

The titles of articles, books, and reports are essentially to help readers by providing advanced organizers for their reading as well as a unifying statement of the main emphasis of the content. For this reason, I thought it would be interesting for readers to see how the final title for the Ford Report evolved from first to last attempt. The following is the list of titles:

1. Back To Real Basics: Children with a Voice
2. Let's Get Back to the Real Basics: Children
3. New Voices Needed: Children Who Can Write
4. New Voices Needed—Let Children Write
5. Let Them Write: New Voices Needed
6. Let Them Write—Back to Real Basics
7. The Real Learning: Let Them Write
8. Poor Writers Make Poor Readers
9. Today's Children: Toward a Nation of Mutes
10. If We Want to Get Back to Basics, Let Them Write
11. If We Want to Get Back to Basics, Let the Writer Say Something
12. Back to Real Basics; Helping the Writer to Say Something
13. Real Basics: Writers Having Their Say
14. Let Them Write: The Real Basic
15. Don't Lose the Real Basic, Let Them Write
16. Don't Lose the Real Basic: Help the Writer to Say Something
17. Balancing the Basics: Let Them Write
18. Balance the Basics and Let Them Write
19. Balance the Basics: Let Them Write

The process of composing titles seems to be one of juxtaposing sound and sense. From the beginning, key words entered the sequence. Some stayed and some didn't. For example, the word "basics" appeared right away. In 1977, "Back to Basics" was quickly becoming a catch-phrase in education. I wanted to capture the public's attention with the word, yet to use "basics" as a means to steer the movement in a new direction.

The word *basics* is therefore the one word that appears in the first title and goes all the way through to the final title. The next combination of words actually appears first in line 5, with the cluster, "Let Them Write." At line 5, I had realized that the word *children*, which had appeared in lines 1 to 4, needed to be changed to the less definite pronoun, *them* and I realized that everyone needed to write. I could have used "everyone," but the word is too long for a title. From lines 5 through 7, I tried several combinations of "Let Them Write," even to the point of using the colons which would appear in the final title. I felt from the outset that children's or writers' voices were not being heard in the schools. For the longest time I struggled with the "voice" notion, starting with line 1. This notion appears literally as voice in "Say

Something", and in a backhanded way in line 9, "Today's Children: Toward a Nation of Mutes."

There are two instances, in lines 8 and 9, where strong titles appear, neither of which contains any words that appear in the final title. These titles are really titles to other articles that probably need to be written:

8. Poor Writers Make Poor Readers
9. Today's Children: Toward a Nation of Mutes

Many words had to be tried and then abandoned. Notice how short-lived the following words, listed with all the lines in which they appear, are:

```
children:  1,  2,  3,  4,  9
    back:  1,  2,  6, 10, 11, 12
   voice:  1,  3,  4,  5
  writer:  8, 11, 12, 13, 16
    real:  1,  2,  6,  7, 12, 13, 14, 15, 16
```

The actual breakthrough for the title came in line 17. It was clear to me at line 16 that things were getting worse, not better. I went and chatted with my wife, Betty, telling her that I had neither the sound nor the sense of what I wanted. I told her that I thought there was an imbalance between sending and receiving in school classrooms. She suggested using the word "balance." From that moment, I could smell the end. Balance and basics would go together. I first tried "balancing" but "=ing" words do not belong in titles. They slow the thinking down. The final step was to remove "and" and replace it with a colon.

9. We Can End the Energy Crisis

Introduction

Julie Jensen, editor of *Language Arts*, contacted me early in 1978 to write a lead piece on writing for the October issue. As usual, Julie was efficient and well-organized, giving plenty of notice for her expectations. The piece was to be short, about five hundred words, and I thought when I first received her letter that two days ought to take care of it. However, I seem to have the gift of making short tasks into long ones. I drafted and redrafted this piece over a two-month period.

It takes me about three to four hours to prepare for an hour address. A ten-minute talk takes about ten hours of preparation. I think the same principle must have been at work with this article, which had the ironic title, "We Can End the Energy Crisis." I worried about the piece all through June and July of 1978.

The notion that I should focus on energy came early. Even the title came within the first week. Since the Ford study, I had been impressed with the amount of energy in the lives of teachers who were responsive to children's writing. They seemed to receive energy from the children and pass it on to other members of the staff.

I wanted to convey the information through a narrative about a composite teacher, Ms. Page. When I show details through specific cases, especially in narrative, I find I can convey much more information than through exposition. Narrative provides more context, and with more context I can raise the information level in a very short space. The hard part was to encapsulate all the content I wanted to include about writing issues into the story of one teacher. At the time I was writing this piece I was also participating as a faculty member in the Vermont Writing Project at the University of Vermont under the direction of Paul Eschholz. Every day in class I would encounter a new issue that I thought ought to be contained in the piece. Soon, my narrative was so clogged with issues that I simply couldn't write. The teachers in the Vermont Writing Project wrote in the morning and studied the teaching of writing in the afternoon. Ms. Page's experience was that of several hundred teachers over the course of four years' participation in the program. Each year, teachers would return to the program and recount how listening to students and conducting writing conferences with them had changed their lives as teachers. It may be that I had difficulty with the piece because I was bombarded daily by so many success stories.

This very short piece contains a summary of many of the beliefs that I held up to that summer of 1978. The following is a list of the dos and don'ts in the teaching of writing contained in it:

1. Writing takes energy for the student writer.
2. Teachers expend large amounts of energy correcting papers.
3. The term *creative writing* is often used when children write about subjects they know nothing about.

4. Children do have interests but they seldom have a chance to write about them.
5. Teachers do extensive corrections because this is often the only methodological option in their teaching repertoire.
6. Schools, in their heavy emphasis on skills at the expense of information, demand extensive corrections.
7. Most tests of writing only look at skills, not at the quality of information.
8. Teachers need help with their own writing.
9. Teachers learn about the writing process by learning how to write themselves.
10. Teachers who write themselves look at children's papers differently.
11. Teachers teach best by helping children to teach them about their subjects.
12. Teachers need to be genuinely interested in what their children know.
13. Teachers should share their writing with the children.
14. Children are the source of energy for teaching if they write about what they know.

Writing demands energy. Students' legs and arms become spaghetti before the terror of the blank page. Teachers' eyes close to half mast before a sheaf of uncorrected compositions. Writing demands energy from the writer producer and the teacher responder.

What takes energy? Ask John. Today John writes on the topic, "If I Were an Ice Cream Cone," his teacher's favorite topic for "creative writing." John's teacher, Ms. Page, doesn't believe John can write well and John knows it. Besides, John is not interested in turning himself into an oozing, sticky mass, an ice cream cone. John has never been an ice cream cone and doesn't want to be one. So John will write about a subject he dislikes to an audience of one, a teacher.

Moments ago he was energetically reading about "hot wheels." Now he slumps in front of his blank page. Ms. Page watches him. "Another energy crisis," she sighs.

That night she faces John's paper on being an ice cream cone amidst twenty-eight similar compositions. Ms. Page yawns and gets out her red pen to correct mistakes which shouldn't exist at her grade level. She feels new pressure to correct because her superintendent of schools, not to be out of step with national trends, has ordained a heavy emphasis on writing. Her students will be assessed on their knowledge of language conventions on a system-wide examination at the end of the year. Ms. Page has never liked to teach writing, and wearily teaches as she knows best—assigns topics and marks papers with the red pencil. Ms. Page makes a pot of coffee and attacks the papers.

The next summer Ms. Page learned to teach writing. She attended a workshop where she took John's place and became a student. But she had an experienced writing teacher. Slowly, in conference and workshop sessions, the instructor drew out of her an account of her experiences on an Indian reservation. Ms. Page found she had something worth saying and a voice worth hearing. She was surprised to find that her city-bred instructor genuinely wanted to learn about her reservation experience. Before she believed writing was only for the professional; now she realizes writing is also a worthwhile activity for her and the children.

Today Ms. Page has the courage to write with her children. She takes energy from their interests. John's younger brother, Alex, illustrates a small booklet on racing cars. Ms. Page cares little about such greasy-loud sport, and knows even less. Her first instinct is to save the next generation from poor energy consumption and the needless burning of tire rubber. But she remembers how the instructor in the writing workshop elicited her story about the reservation. The instructor let Ms. Page teach her about the subject, while she taught her how to write about it.

Now she learns about racing cars from Alex. Alex learns how to write about something of importance to him for a teacher who wants to know it. With a burst of carburetors, distributors, spark plugs, timing and fuel pumps Alex pours forth on the relative power efficiency of different engines. For the first time Alex shares information from his territory and Ms. Page learns more about what her children already know. That same day Ms. Page shares the many drafts of her piece on the Indian reservation.

We can end our profession's energy crisis today. When teachers learn from their children about their real, non-ice-cream world, they create energy rather than drain it away, and the children see their teachers as fellow writers. Let's write together tomorrow.

10. Let Children Show Us How to Help Them Write

Introduction

This article was written during our study of young children's writing in Atkinson, New Hampshire. Lucy Calkins, Susan Sowers, and I decided early on in the study to write about what we were finding. The study, funded by the National Institute of Education, began in September, 1978, and would continue in the school until June, 1980. Analysis of the data is still going on in 1983.

I was asked by *Visible Language* to write an article on handwriting. Since handwriting was one of the areas of investigation in the study, I accepted the assignment. Two years before, I had written an article for *Language Arts* entitled "Handwriting is for Writing." That article focused on the need to see handwriting as a vehicle for communicating information. It also analyzed the basic motor components in helping writers to write. The original title of this new article for *Visible Language* was "Handwriting in Context." The title was a carry-over from my old belief, which I still held; but something new was needed.

Children had already taught us so much in this new study that the title, "Let Children Show Us How to Help Them Write," was an instructional maxim as well as a description of our own situation in learning from the children. This new article for *Visible Language* showed particularly the reflection of oral discourse on how young children wrote. Because we had videotapes of children actually composing, we could see how the child's voice was reflected on the page.

On January 21, 1979, I began the article. This opening paragraph in my first draft (long since discarded) shows the early thinking that would underlie the entire article:

When children speak, they fill the air with words, spraying them toward the listener like water from a garden hose. When children write they fill test tubes with sulphuric acid. Eye and hand work closely together to fill space with just the right proportion of the printed ingredient.

The language is a bit strong to say the least, but that is typical of my early drafts. I try many voices, some of them quite strong, before I find the right tone for the message. What probably happens is that I discover more clearly what I want to say, and the tone follows the data. The above paragraph was later embedded in the opening paragraph to the piece:

Six year olds Toni and Jennifer paint side by side as they stand at their easels. "I'm goin' to fill this one all in with red," says Toni, as she points to the outline of a house with the tip of her brush. When Toni speaks, she sprays her words in many directions as she paints and glances around the room at the same time. She knows that Jennifer can hear and understand her words without sending them in a specific direction.

From the beginning, I struggled with what the piece was about. One particular paragraph shows the nature of the struggle. In session 1 on January 22 I kept typing incomplete sentences. I was able to put them together in a paragraph the next day in session 2.

.

Writing is more than handwriting. Composing is certainly more than the mere writing down of words at one point in time. Indeed, any aspect of the writing process

Since writing is such an act of precision,

Handwriting, though apparently a mere motor act, reflects

Since handwriting is such an act of precision, changes in its flow and structure reflect the effects of various contexts to the writing act

The act of placing words in sequence on paper is a highly sophisticated venture, especially or the young child. As such, it is subject to a wide range of contextual inf

Writing is a sophisticated act, especially for the young child.

t is therefore the meeting point of many contextual forces of

t is the meeting point of a wide range of forces

As it scrawls, gains precision, moves up and down on a line, blackens,

lows down, speeds up,

ightens, the action of a wide range of forces is made manifest

A wide range of forces show themselves as

..

Handwriting is a sophisticated act, especially for the young child. Many forces show hemselves when a child scrawls, gains precision with letters, writes over the same letter hree to four times, slows down, −speeds up, blackens and lightens a xxxx word, lines out, rases, or adds in words. These forces xxxxxxxxxxxxxxxxxxxx show How these forces nanifest themselves is dependent on the child's course of development within the writing process. As such handwriting is more than the mere information of letters on a page at one noment in time. It is caught up in a broad climax It is influenced by all phases of the writing
children
rocess, transitions from oral to written discourse, and the problems a child needs to solve t particular times in stages in their development.

Actual Published Text Using Above Information

When children are given control of the writing process, teachers need information to know what they see, to sense the significance of different child struggles. Children's handwriting is ne place where the struggle shows. But the handwriting is only one component of the writing process. Handwriting is more than the mere formation of letters on a page at one noment in time. It is influenced by all phases of the writing process, children's changes from peaking to writing, and problems unique to different stages of a writer's development.

The lead to the piece, which went as far as the heading *Drawing*, was rewritten nany times. As I continued to work on the main sections of the chapter, I kept discovering new information which in turn demanded a new lead. When the lead was finally established, I was able to smooth out the text in the rest of the piece.

Six-year-olds Toni and Jennifer paint side by side as they stand at their easels "I'm goin' to fill this one all in with red," says Toni, as she points to the outline of a house with the tip of her brush. When Toni speaks, she sprays her words in many directions as she paints and glances around the room at the same time. She knows that Jennifer can hear and understand her words without sending them in a specific direction.

Fifteen minutes later Toni is seated in the writing area. She writes:

AND
I
KISS
h M
I Love sopp owl

Words can go up, down, or across for beginning writers like Toni. Toni has been writing for two weeks and does not know yet that written words, unlike spoken words, must conform to space, have a set direction, and have specific beginnings and endings.

Toni wants to write about "super owl." Even though she is just learning how to control the pencil and use space on the paper, it is the urge to tell that makes her write from 250 to 300 words per week without specific assignment. Toni writes this much because she controls the topic, spelling, and the process of discovering how to get her message down on paper.

When we let children like Toni show us their process of writing, we let them show us how to teach them. Best of all, they show us the energy source that made them write in the first place. When children do the pushing, they have control. Child control in this study is defined as child initiative. Children choose their topics, language inventions, discover space on the paper; and teachers follow, observing, solving problems with them, in order to steer their craft into greater clarity.

When children are given control of the writing process, teachers need information to know what they see, to sense the significance of different child struggles. Children's handwriting is one place where the struggle shows. But the handwriting is only one component of the writing process. Handwriting is more than the mere formation of letters on a page at one moment in time. It is influenced by all phases of the writing process, children's changes from speaking to writing, and problems unique to different stages of a writer's development.

This chapter will take a broad view of handwriting. It will seek to explain handwriting performance in the midst of child development and the writing process. The information has come from preliminary findings in our study, "A Two Year Case Study Observing the Development of Primary Children's Composing, Spelling and Motor Behaviors During the Writing Process," funded by the National Institute of Education.

Through this grant from NIE, we follow twenty children over a two year period. Each day three full-time researchers are with the children, carefully recording data as the children compose. Composing is broadly viewed, from the child's painting, drawing, working with crayons, pens, pencils, to the composing of first, second, and third drafts. The data come from collections of all forms of composing, direct observation of the child writing, and video tapes made during the composing process.

This in-depth study of children's composing is not a controlled design. Rather, it is a case study of twenty children—in grades one and three—who were chosen because of their *differences* on a pre-selected developmental composing scale. The study seeks to describe in detail the "what" of composing in order to explain the "why" of child behaviors during the writing process.

Children have a strong urge to write. They like to see their own scratches and marks everywhere: hearths, bedroom mouldings, bathroom walls, moist windowpanes, paper bags, old envelopes and sidewalks. They want to be seen and heard.

Speech comes before writing. Since they are both communications, and speech comes first, it is only natural that writing should bear the imprint of speech. Children try to make writing like speech, but early attempts to make them the same lead to crude messages and script that is often unintelligible to both writer and reader. Speech and writing simply are not the same. Only advanced writers can make writing sound like speech.

Children do not need to be aware of the process of crossing over from speech to print. They don't need to be aware of the steps in learning to write any more than they needed to be aware of learning to speak. Children are so delightfully self-centered that their high assumptions about message quality provide a natural cloak of protection for both problem solving and experimentation. Remove this cloak and the child suddenly becomes unnaturally aware of the rigors and demands of the writing process. Their urge to write is relentless enough for parents and teachers to just let it happen. Their role is to sense the child's intentions, note what aspects of transition stand in the way, and then provide help.

The data in this chapter show children's changes from speech to print. The data are reported in four sections starting with drawing, since drawing and writing are much the same for children. Next come child discoveries of word order, separation, and page placement. Then, when redrafting appears, new uses of space and handwriting are reviewed. Finally, the significance of child use of prosodics in speech and print are discussed. In each section, examples of child behavior have been chosen from a large body of data to illustrate common child practices.

Drawing

Toni drew before she wrote, "I love super owl and I kiss him." When Toni drew, she chose the subject and gained control of the information as she sketched in the figure of a flying owl. As Toni drew she supplied the energy and information for her teacher to help her with the writing. Drawing is the driving force behind much of Toni's writing. It serves as a rehearsal for the text as well as an important bridge from speech to print.

Toni needed to draw because the drawing helped her know what to write. Teachers will see beginning writers like Toni draw before they write if they give them the right paper. The right paper has a large space at the top where children can draw, or at least is plain, unlined paper with large enough space to permit both drawing and writing.

Teachers can find out for themselves what drawing does for writing. Ask children before they draw, "Tell me, what will you write after you finish drawing?" If drawing is important, they do not usually know what they will write until they draw. On the other hand, when the drawing is completed and the teacher says, "Now tell me what you will write," she will get a more specific statement about what the child will write.

Drawing helps children change from speech to print. When John is seated next to Fred in a sandbox pushing mounds of sand with his bulldozer to make a fort, Fred knows what John means when he says, "This is gonna keep out the bad guys." Fred can see what John means because the situation tells him. But when John writes, he must supply words to describe the situation in which the message will fall. If John can draw before he writes, he creates the setting for his print, thus helping both himself and the child who will read his paper.

When children control their subjects, they write more, gain greater practice in writing, and ultimately care much more about the appearance of their letters on the page. For the beginning writer, drawing is one important means of maintaining that control.

When Toni first drew figures of people, they were large, turned on their sides, and occupied different parts of the paper. She was learning proportion, control of the instrument, and how to use space contained in the paper. Toni continues to discover space when she writes. Note again Toni's message about "super owl":

Space

In this instance, words flow from left to right (1–4) as well as from the top down (5–8). On other occasions, Toni will send a column up from the right hand side of the page, just as in this instance, she came down from the top on the left side. Toni generally understands that words go from left to right as shown in steps 1–4. But she has a dilemma. Step 4 falls on the lower right hand side of the paper. She has run out of space. It is hard for children to predict with accuracy where the full message will end. Since there is a drawing on the page, the message needs to go with the illustration. She solves the problem by coming down to the line on the left side. Adults may consider this a major problem. It is not to Toni. She knows the meaning of the message; at this point in her development, she is satisfied with just the placement of message ingredients on the paper. She assumes that if she knows the message, others will know as well, regardless of a lack of left to right order.

Toni writes as she speaks when words run together in steps one to four. Words run together without spaces in between. When Toni read this selection, her voice rose and fell just as the words undulated across the page. Toni's intention to simulate speech seemed almost deliberate since her addition of steps five through eight show her knowledge of word units.

Six year old John wrote, "Ste fosd," for Steve Austin. John was trying to tell where one word ended and the other began. For John, words in speech flow together like "hamaneggs." All children at some stage in their writing must go through the process of separating words from speech into discrete units.

Further Adjustments to Space Problems

About the time young children develop good letter formation, with a left to right flow and spaces between words, new problems of space arise. The problems are caused by new information, the beginning of redrafting. The discovery of new information without any place to put it can come as early as six years of age. Six year old Chris had just read a book about prehistoric animals and was composing one of his own to share with the children. Chris and his teacher had this dialogue:

Teacher: I see that you were able to put in the word "may" to show that "Brontosaurus' may travel in families." (Chris had been able to sandwich in the small word without erasing.) But you didn't say why they travel in families.

Chris: They travel in families to protect the young.

Teacher: Do you think that is important information?

Chris: Yes, but there isn't any place to put it. (The writing goes from left to right over to the right hand margin at the bottom of the paper. Above this writing is a picture of a brontosaurus.)

Teacher: Look the paper over and show me where you could write it in.

Chris: There isn't any. (voice rising)

Teacher: Look the *entire* paper over and put your hand on any space where there isn't writing or drawing. (There is space above the drawing.)

Chris: Well, I could put it up here (motions to top of paper) but it would look stupid. The other part is down here.

Teacher: How could you show they were connected?

Chris: I could put an arrow down here pointing to the part that's at the top.
Teacher: Good, but you'll need to connect the arrow with the top. This is what
          writers do when they are getting their books ready for the publisher.

Chris knew additional information would create a mess. His usual approach was to erase words to put new ones in. Now his teacher has shown him how to control new information when there is a problem of space. She has also shown him that this draft is temporary, that a rewriting is necessary. Young writers need to learn a whole repertoire for messing up their paper to deal with new information, organizations and adjustments. This also adds to the importance of crafting the letters in the final draft. If children have controlled the process and know their information is good, the quality of their handwriting improves.

Just as children learn the appropriate use of language within the family, the playground or school, they need to learn the context of various kinds of handwriting and different uses of space. Most handwriting texts do not deal with the appropriateness of handwriting in context. Rough draft handwriting is not the same as handwriting in final draft form. Children who are preoccupied with word shape or correct spelling in an early draft, lose control of the draft and their information suffers.

Children show us in their handwriting when they take on the draft concept. Eight year old Andrea, like many writers, hoped her first draft would be her last. About the sixth word into this selection, her handwriting shows that she decided another draft would follow:

> Learning to fly
> Once when I was very little I got a hank to fly so I tryed jumping of things and tryed to float up and across I tryed and tryed til my father made me and my sister big cardboard butterfly... wings.

Later, Andrea went on to draw arrows and cross out lines until the message was shaped to her liking. Handwriting, in final draft, properly dealt with the aesthetics and etiquette necessary for good communication.

Prosodic Features Show Us Children Are in Control

Eight year old Scott did not like to write. He wrote at four words per minute with no spacing and over 45 percent of his words were misspelled. Letters were of various sizes, ran together, and were poorly formed. In October Scott's writing looked like this:

> I uosDivnin the SeRwoLanoLasan
> to caRS cRashing anI omstcRashingRotinto
> themButI tuRnedoUay andthanI tuRned.

Since October Scott has been required to write but with this difference; he controls the topic, information and language. He also gets help from two audiences, the teacher and other children. Help comes principally at the point of clarifying Scott's understanding of the information and the appropriateness of the meaning he wants. Help comes in early drafts, then Scott rewrites for final copy. Two months later Scott's writing looks like this:

> I was going down the Stairs and I took two steps and!! Then I slipped and fell down fifteen steps on my back. Ow yikes then on the last step I went bam!! I was aching and I was in pain. Then I said I am never going to go down those stairs unless I have to. And my brother said, "Well if you had on your shoes wouldn't have happened". And I said Shut up.

Scott showed that he had re-entered the writing process on his own terms through speech features marked in the written text. Children try to "speak" through their texts when they feel they have control. The elements that show this kind of involvement are called prosodic features. The use of these features puts sound, stress, pause and intonation back into writing. Toni showed her use of prosodic features when she made important words large and her words undulated across the page as in the rise and fall of speech patterns.

Scott, along with other children striving for "sound," shows early voice through:

Use of capitals
Important words, especially nouns that carry major meaning, are written in capital letters. Other words may have a single capital letter at the beginning.

Rewritten words
Words or letters that mark key points will be run over several times with the pen or pencil. Words blackened more than others show points of emphasis from speech.

Exclamation points and interjections also put sound back into written language. When children first discover them their delight in simulating sound leads to the excessive use of these prosodic features. For example, sentences of minor importance receive one exclamation point, whereas those of greater importance receive from two to four. The loudest and breathiest of all receives a large, blackened exclamation point that takes up two lines on the vertical.

Six year old Jenny needs to produce sound as she writes. It is her method of developing a voice, staying oriented in space, producing the right sound and symbol, as well as in maintaining control of the writing process. Through a very sensitive microphone tied in with a video recorder, the data show that Jenny's writing contains a high ratio of sound to written symbol, thus marking more clearly how much oral language must accompany writing for her to make an effective transition from speech to print. A sample of the data in Figure 10.1 show a typical ratio for both Jenny and other writers at this stage of development. Track I shows Jenny's sound and Track II shows at what point the letter was written in relation to the sound on Track I. For example, in line 1, Jenny sounded an "l," said "all" and wrote an L.

Figure 10.1

Jenny's message is, "all of the reindeer loved them."
                        Loll ave the riendrer lov em
Line 1: Track I: *l* all, all, of, all of the, the, the, all of the reindeer
          (sounded) s

          Track II: L oll ave   the
          (written)

Line 2: Track I: rein, *ruh*, rein loved them, all, of, them, the, *muh*, *muh*
          (sounded)   S   S   S

          Track II: R   iendeer   love e   m
          (written)

Children hear themselves say what they mean and go on. Therefore, they speak along with the writing and the speaking is an essential part in the composing. Transcriptions from other beginning writers show a wide range of voicing types. Thus far we have classified these voicing patterns:

Type of Language	Example
1. Says the message *before* it is written.	"The boy will go."
2. Says the word *before* it is written.	"boy"
3. Says the word *after* it is written.	"boy"
4. Rereads message *after* it is written.	"The boy will go."
5. Makes sounds of letter components.	"buh, buh, oi, oi"
6. Says letter names for spelling	"b-o-y"
7. Procedural statements:	"I haven't got any more room."
8. Statements to other children.	"This boy is goin' to blow the bad guys up."

With the exception of statements to other children, voicing is only intended for the child who is composing. A person standing nearby is unaware of most of the sounding, since only the sensitive microphone can pick up these data.

Summary

Children need to control their own writing. But they can't do it alone. Teachers need to help them maintain control because when they are successful, children see themselves as important learners with things to say. Furthermore, when children control the writing process, they write far beyond traditional expectations, spell better, and take pride in the craft of handwriting.

It isn't easy to help children control their own writing. Teachers need information to know when and how to help. Preliminary research from this study of children's composing shows that handwriting is a critical index for showing where to begin to help children.

When children first write, they treat writing as speech. They draw to supply context for the subject, run words together, spell words as they sound, let words run around the page, speak out loud when they write, blacken in letters, use capitals and exclamation points liberally.

Redrafting demands a new view of space and aesthetics. Just when the child has solved early problems of space, new information demands different help from the teacher. But this new step is a boon to good handwriting. When the craft of handwriting follows the crafting of the child's *own information*, a greater level of excellence in final copy is achieved.

Today Toni isn't bothered when her words run together or down the side of the page. Tomorrow she will be. She will need to see another way to handle the problem. Her teacher will need to know how to help Toni. Good teachers see these disturbances, and ask timely questions to show children how to solve problems for themselves. They ask good questions because they know how children learn to write.

11. A New Look at Writing Research

Introduction

This article is a chapter in *Perspectives on Writing in Grades 1–8,* edited by Shirley Haley-James and published by the National Council of Teachers of English. Walter Petty, a professor at the State University of New York at Buffalo and the original chair of the committee to investigate the status of composition in the elementary years, had asked me as far back as 1977 to do a piece on the status of research in the teaching of writing. I had been collecting extensive information on the teaching of writing over the last twenty-five years. I began to classify the types of research along with the methodologies used to conduct them. It wasn't long before I took my findings from these classifications and formulated questions for the needed research. That was the easy part.

The difficult part was in writing a survey of the research that teachers would want to read. One of my main points was that in the eighties, teachers needed to conduct their own research. How could my points have effect if teachers could not see themselves in the text? Just how difficult this task was is shown in the next two pieces, "Sixty Minutes I and II," (Chapter 12.)

First, the bad news. Only 156 studies of writing in the elementary grades, or an average of six annually, have been done in the United States in the last twenty-five years. Writing research was in such low esteem from 1955–1972 that 84% of all studies were done by dissertation alone. It wasn't important enough for most doctoral advisors to consider writing research for themselves. Rather, it was an exercise for students to apply courses in statistics to their dissertations. Eight-one percent (81%) of all dissertation research in this period involved experimental designs seeking to find "good methods" in the teaching of writing.

These sad figures came at a time in American education when most school money was spent on developing children's reading skills. For every $3000 spent on children's ability to receive information $1.00 was spent on their power to send it in writing. The funds for writing research came to less than one-tenth of one percent of all research funds for education.

From 1955–1972, sixty-eight percent (68%) of all research was concerned with what the teacher was doing in the classroom. We were so preoccupied with ourselves as teachers that only twelve percent (12%) of the studies were concerned with a look at what children did when they wrote. The research on best methods for teachers was of the worst type. We took the science model of research and attempted to remove certain variables from their context to explain two crafts, teaching and writing, by dismissing environments through statistical means. We tried to explain complex wholes and processes through "hard data" about insignificant variables removed from context.

We complained that teachers would not pay attention to research. But so far the teachers have been right . . . most of the research wasn't worth reading. It couldn't help them in the classroom. They could not see their schools, classrooms, or children in the data. Context had been ignored.

Context needs to be explained. When six-year-old Janet writes "reindrer" in the midst of the sentence, "All of the *reindrer* lovd him," the word falls in more than the context of a written syntactical unit. Janet sings, speaks, rereads, listens to her text as she composes this selection for the Christmas holidays. She draws after she writes, chats with other children about expectations of Christmas gifts, interviews with the teacher. She writes in a room that encourages child publication, mutual child help, the importance of personal voice and information. Within the context of Janet's own development, she has gone through three stages of invented spelling, first sounding letters, then writing consonants in initial and final positions, now borrowing from the visual memory systems contributed by reading. In the broader ethnographic context, Janet's mother writes letters, is college educated and interested in her child's progress, and lives in a suburban-rural town of 8500 in New England. Janet's teacher writes for publication. In Janet's school, the principal speaks, writes, and listens to teachers. In turn, teachers know their ideas will be heard.

Now for some good news. More than half of all research on children's writing in the last twenty-five years was done in the last seven, and only forty-two percent of it by dissertation. Research has broadened to include advisors of research and other professionals. Interest in descriptive studies of children's activity rose from twelve to forty-eight percent of all studies. The context of writing was beginning to be described, though very crudely. Studies of what teachers did through experimental design dropped to forty percent of the total.

A new kind of research entered that broadened the context of investigation through Janet Emig's case study of the "Composing Processes of Twelfth Grade Students" in 1969. Her research and the research of Graves (1975), and Graves, Calkins, Sowers (1978–80), focused on what writers did *during* the composing process. Descriptions were also given of the contexts in which the data were gathered. Although this is a new research area in terms of a history of writing research, there is growing interest by both researchers and teachers on the data coming from the studies. Most case study research is still being done with older students, notably the work of Hayes-Flowers (1979–80), Sommer (1980), and Perl (1979). Far more needs to be done with younger children. We need more information on child behaviors and decisions *during* the process, rather than through speculation on child activity during writing from writing products alone.

Time, money and personnel investments in writing have changed within the last three years. Great inbalances in attending to communication skills still exist, but there is more interest in the teaching of writing. Some of this has come through response to state-mandated testing which has been invoked or is on the drawing boards in almost all of the fifty states.

There is more interest in writing because teachers get more help with their own writing process. No longer are teachers lectured about the writing process, discussing the skill out of context, unallied with an involvement with writing itself. Such programs as the Bay Area Writing Project and the Vermont Writing Program, have had national effects through attention to the teacher's own writing. Teachers have begun to understand the nature and context of the writing process through their own writing. They now can view what children do within the framework of practicing the craft themselves.

These efforts have also spurred greater interest in research, but research that relates to teachers' new understandings of the context of the writing process. That is, they now know the meaning of rehearsal (prewriting), redrafting, the development of skills toward publication. They want to know more about research that provides information in which they can "see" the students and classrooms in which they teach.

Teachers want to become involved in research themselves. Those who write themselves, who have become interested in what children do when they write, want to know how they can participate in gathering their own information.

Financial commitments to the improvement of writing are still woefully low. The National Institute of Education allocated funds for research in writing for the first time in 1977. Requests for proposals for research in writing were also instituted two years later. We have gone from nothing to barely something in the provision of research funds. Far more funds have been expended on the assessment of writing. Educational Testing Service, the National Commission on Education in the States, and most State Departments have allocated funds to find out how students are achieving.

This is still a time of hope and optimism for the 80's. Research in writing has such a short history that it is not yet weighed down by many of the traditions that plague most research in education. Research in education has attempted to make a science of predicting human behavior from one setting to another through statistically controlled experiments. From the outset this review of research in writing reflected the experimental approach but only recently has begun to break away through process-observational studies and a broadened context to include the study of child growth. It is just beginning to provide information that teachers in the classroom can use.

A Necessary Pattern of Development

We may lament that time has been wasted on experimental designs, a preoccupation with self (what teachers ought to do) but I believe this pattern of development was necessary, important, unavoidable. Children, teachers, researchers, develop in similar patterns. I went through the same process in learning to teach.

The first day I ever taught I could only hear the sound of my own voice. I stood back and listened with terror as I searched for the right words. My seventh grade class was an audience that barely existed. My chief questions at that point were, "What do I say? What do I do?" I could scarcely hear children's responses to my questions. Plans written days before determined my actions, regardless of children's responses. Answers fit my questions on a 1–1 basis, or they were not worthwhile. I hardly knew what was coming from the blur of faces in front of me.

In time the faces became more distinctive. I even began to notice what children did after I asked questions, or directed them to an activity. But my main concern was to crank up the machinery of learning, set the children on a course and hope they would reach some worthwhile port of acquiring knowledge. Like the young learners in my room, I was only concerned with the beginning and end of learning. Not much existed in between. "How do I get started? What do I do when the papers are completed?"

Children develop along similar lines: They hear and write the initial consonants of words, then final consonants. The interior portions of words hardly exist. In reading, information at the end and beginning of selections is the most easily recalled. In Piaget's simple directive to children to draw all the steps showing a pencil falling from a vertical to a horizontal position, the children can only draw the initial (vertical) and final (horizontal) positions, with none of the intermediary stages sketched in. When children, adults, researchers, first initiate activity, there are no middles, only beginnings and endings. In short, they have a very limited space-time understanding of the universe, not unlike my first days of teaching. Furthermore, they are so absorbed in the rightness of their own acts, they find it difficult to empathize with the points of others.

It wasn't until much later in my teaching career that I was able to focus on what children were doing, in order to adjust my own teaching style. I found that I could not afford to be without the information that told me where they were. As a result, I began to participate in the "middle" of the process of their learning. For example, I asked questions while they were in the middle of observing the travel patterns of turtles. I responded to their initial observation notes, asking more questions. And back they went to add, delete, revise their earlier observations.

It is encouraging to note similar development in research patterns over the past twenty-five years. We have moved from a preoccupation with self in teaching to more studies of children, and now the middle ground, the process of writing itself. The space-time factors of research have been expanded. Such trends must continue for the 80's. But we must continue to be wary of studies that reduce the context of investigation.

Further Research Backgrounds

We look at recent history of research in writing that we might not repeat past mistakes. We review this history to take stock, learn, and forge on. We have been slow to take heed of the warnings of significant researchers. Since the early twenties, one researcher after another has warned of the danger of research in children's writing. Writing is an organic process that defies fragmentary approaches to explain its meaning notes Braddock (1968):

> Anyone who has read a considerable portion of the research in the teaching and learning of English composition knows how much it leaves to be desired. In the first major summary and critical analysis of the research, Lyman (1929) wrote that "a complex phenomenon such as composition quality seems to defy careful analysis into constituent parts" and noted that the pioneer studies he reviewed "measure pupil products and assume that by so doing they are evaluating the manifold intangible processes of the mind by which those products were attained."

Meckel (1963), Park (1960) and Braddock (1963) called for research that focused more on learners than teachers. They called for studies on the writing process that involved longitudinal research. Such research was difficult, too time consuming for doctoral students, and certainly defiant of conventional statistical interventions.

Problems With Experimental Design

Persons using experimental designs with writing research have contributed least to the classroom teacher, even though they purport to give direct help. They respond to questions teachers ask most, "How do I get the students to write? What will stimulate, motivate them into writing action? What is the best way to correct papers?" Typically the research model will try three different stimuli to "activate" students into better writing. One group will receive "no treatment." If one method, usually the favorite method of the researcher, should receive better marks, that is, show with 95−1 odds or better that the good results in student writing from the chosen method were not due to chance, then the approach is purported as valid for other children and teachers. This is an attempt to show via scientific means that an exportable method for teaching children to write has been found. Independent of the philosophical issues involved with this approach to teaching writing, the basic context remains.

We have tried to borrow science from other fields in order to apply it to the study of human behavior. In the field of agriculture, chemistry, medicine, practitioners cannot afford to be without the latest findings. Better strands of hybrid corn increase food production for millions, miracle drugs are synthesized and save lives. New processes for using chemicals are developed, saving millions of dollars for industry. Research in science delivers.

Research in education is not a science. We cannot transfer science procedures to social events and processes. We are not speaking of corn, pills or chemicals when we speak of what people do when they write. Elliott Mishler, in one of the most telling articles written on research in context, observes the domination of research by experimentation in the social sciences:

> Despite the philosophical critique of this traditional model of science, its application to human affairs has remained triumphant. Researcher methods based on this model, which can be referred to collectively as context-stripping procedures, are taught to us in our graduate schools and we become properly certified as educational researchers, psychologists, or sociologists when we can demonstrate our competent use of them in our dissertations.

Research about writing must be suspect when it ignores context or process. Unless researchers describe in detail the full context of data gathering and the processes of learning and teaching, the data cannot be exported from room to room.

Devoid of context, the data become sterile. One of the reasons teachers have rejected research information for so long is that they have been unable to transfer faceless data to the alive, inquiring faces of the children they teach each morning. Furthermore, the language used to convey these data has the same voiceless tone that goes with the projections of faceless information. The research is not written to be read. It is written for other researchers, promotions, or dusty archives in a language guaranteed for self-extinction.

Writing process research can help the classroom teacher with writing. It's just that this research cannot pretend to be science. This does not mean that research procedures cease to be rigorous when describing the full context of human behavior and environment. The human faces do not take away objectivity when the data are reported. The face emerges from enormous amounts of time spent in observing, recording, and analyzing the data. When the face emerges in the reporting, it comes from tough selection of the incident that represents a host of incidents in context.

Studies that expand the context of writing are expensive. Thousands of hours are required to gather the full data. Personnel costs are high. For this reason, better procedures need to be developed.

We can never forget that if information from one study is to be used in another teaching site, with other children, the most thorough description of contextual factors must be given. When the process and context are described in simple, straightforward language, teachers will be ready consumers of the information.

Teachers who read such information often want to try informal research projects of their own. Since the procedures were conducted in classrooms, they see themselves in the midst of the data along with the children. They begin to keep daily records of skills advancement along with collected writings of the children. Charts of daily child conferences, reading and writing growth patterns are observed and recorded. Much of these data are one step away from formal research studies.

Research For the 80's—What Do We Need?

Writing research must involve the fullest possible contexts in the 80's. We can no longer have experimental or retrospective studies that move in with treatments of short duration, or that speculate on child growth and behaviors through a mere examination of written products alone. Contexts must be broadened to include closer and longer looks at children while they are writing. These contexts must be described in greater detail.

In this section on research needed for the 80's, a more detailed description of context will be given, then a listing of research questions about children, teachers and writing environments, followed by a discussion of new research designs and procedures. The description of context is given within the confines of print, which is linear and segmented, word following word. The use of words is weak since it cannot portray the many systems and variables that operate *simultaneously* as children write. For example, as Chad writes we observe and infer the following *simultaneous* actions in a *four second interval*:

1. Voices "shhh—t—n" (shooting).
2. Hears own voice.
3. Leans toward page.
4. Grips pencil between thumb and forefinger.
5. Glances at drawing at top of paper and observes pencil operate between lines.
6. Holds paper with left hand with paper slightly turned to the right of midline.
7. Sits on edge of chair.
8. Tips shoulder as if to feel action of gun (inferred).
9. May hear voice over intercom asking teacher a question.
10. Produces mental imagery of man shooting (inferred).
11. Produces mental imagery of word, shooting (inferred).
12. Feels friction of paper on paper surface.

Another Look at Context

The meaning of any situation is contained in the context of the act. A fourteen month old child reaches several times for a ball beyond his grasp. In frustration he utters, "Ba." The mother turns, notices his outstretched hand and shouts to her husband, "John, Andy just said, 'Ball,' isn't it wonderful!" If the parent had heard the utterance without observing the context, she would probably have had a different interpretation of the sounds. The full understanding of Andy's act is contained in expanding the time and space frame of investigation to reviewing the child's previous utterances, uses of language with his parents, parent responses, the child's use of symbols, activities in shops, at grandparents', in clinics, or the broader communities in which such utterances develop. Even this brief expansion of contextual understanding is a simplification of many more complex ways of observing single acts. Studies of the growth and development of preschool children's oral language have paid far more attention to contexts than studies of children's growth in writing.

The understanding of any single written word demands similar expansion of the time-space frame of investigation. It is this time-space expansion that helps us understand the act of writing, as well as the designs and procedures needed to understand written acts. A simplified description of what is meant by "context" of writing is given in three different contextual categories: (1) The Writing Episode, (2) The Life of the Child Who Writes, (3) The Social-Ethnographic Context of the Episode. Each of these sections will be discussed through the life of one case, Chad. Following each section, questions will be raised for further study in the 80's.

Writing Episode

Chad is a six year old first grade child who has been writing for only two weeks. When Chad writes "the grts," (the good guys), the message is barely decipherable, yet it contains a major breakthrough for him, since in this instance it is the first time he is able to read back his message. This is but a small part of Chad's writing episode. In this chapter, a writing episode is defined as encompassing all that a child does before, during, and after a single writing. In the example below, some of Chad's activity on the first line is shown in the following:

Line 1: Writing		the	g		r	t		s
Line 2: Oral Language	the	the *guh*	guy	gut		t	"the gut guys"
							rereads	

The first line shows what letter the child actually wrote in relation to the second line, the language and sound supplied by the child as he wrote. Simultaneous to the writing, Chad supplies facial gestures and varying distances to the papers. He also changes his work as he goes. As a beginning writer he changes mostly at the points of sound-letter correspondence and the shapes of letters. He does not yet edit for syntactical semantical fit. Chad also reads as he writes, another important contextual feature in the process. And, he listens to what he hears in reading out loud to see if he is where he thinks he ought to be in the message. Writing for Chad is more complex than it seems.

The context of Chad's composing is understood further by going back to what he was doing just before he started to write. In this instance he rehearsed (not consciously) for the written act by drawing warfare between the "good guys" and the "bad guys" at the top of his paper. A series of action-reaction battles in the drawing were fought with eventual total destruction of everyone on the paper. When Chad was asked, "Tell me what you are going to write after you finish the drawing," he replied, "Wait and see." Broadening this context still further, data show that Chad answers with more complete information in the middle of drawing about what he will write. "Wait and see," is probably a staying action, the same as, "I don't know."

Moving ahead in time from the composing act, Chad rushes to the teacher when he finishes composing. Data from other episodes show that rushing to the teacher is an important sharing time for him. Chad stands next to the teacher where she is seated at the round table in the back of the classroom. His left arm presses against hers as he leans, points to the paper, speaks to her with his face eighteen inches from hers as he explains the episode on the paper. He can read some of the words, but the crude spellings of several have led to an evaporation of meaning. Still, he can at least get help from the drawing to communicate the main action of his writing.

A simple review of Chad's written product would have given a very limited explanation of what had occurred in the writing episode. The functions of various acts, the trials, would not have been understood in the same way as the direct observation of the composing of the episode itself.

More needs to be learned about what occurs within the writing episode in the 80's. We are just beginning to get a sense of the ingredients in the process, but far more data are needed to explain how children function. We particularly need the data to begin to develop a theory of writing as called for by Martha King (1979). Ten questions are posed for research investigation in the 80's.

1. What is the nature and function of oral language as it accompanies the writing process? How does this change within individual cases? Who are the children who do not use language to accompany the writing process?
2. How does rehearsal change as children grow older? What is the nature of different rehearsals within a single child, across many children?
3. What is the nature of syntactical and semantical decisions *within* child revisions? How do these decisions change with subsequent revisions of the same selection? How do these decisions change over a series of years within one child, across children of different ages?
4. How do children use other children or the teacher to help them in their writing? How does this vary with different kinds of writers and in different environments?
5. What is the context in the episode in which children change spellings? When do spellings become stabilized into a final form?
6. Under what circumstances do children reread their writing? What is the nature of the reading act in writing, especially the reading act in relation to revision?
7. How do children learn to use space on their paper when first writing or when doing advanced revisions? What are the changing spatial demands of writing?
8. Under what circumstances do children use conventions, change them and grow with them over the years? Are there certain ways in which children use information that demand a broader repertoire of conventions?
9. What types of hesitation, delay phenomena, are observed that might be connected with a concept of "listening" to the text?
10. What types of left-right brain activity are indicated in the child's functioning in the writing process?

The Broader Context of One Episode in a Life

One writing episode does not explain Chad's behavior. Other episodes are reviewed in relation to the one completed. The analysis of episodes reveal sequences of development over time. A simple example of a sequence is contained in children's general use of drawing in relation to writing. For most children, drawing first precedes writing since the child needs to see and hear meaning through drawing. Later, as children know better what they will write, they illustrate *after* writing. In time they do not need to draw at all. There are exceptions based on intra-differences and different functions for the drawing.

Other contextual data are needed from Chad's own background to better understand what he does in the writing episode. For example, interviews with Chad's parents and teachers show that Chad did not speak understandable messages until he was approximately four years of age. For many months Chad could not write. He did not understand the relationship between sound and symbol. He could not read his first attempts to write. There were too few cues to read them the next day. Still, his drawings were filled with information. He spoke at length with other children about the content of his drawings.

Other contextual information from Chad's life, gathered over time, is as follows: Changing concept of good writing, function of writing, sense and use of audiences, range and type of topics chosen, use of person, characterizations, territorial involvement of content, problem-solving strategies in such areas as blocks, science, mathematics etc. Sequences of development in each of these informational areas have their own context—What came before? What will follow? The sequence and interrelationship of each scheme provides more context for explaining behaviors in any one aspect of the composing process. Much of these data come from product analysis, child, parent and teacher interviews, and the analysis of writing episodes.

Far more needs to be done in these important areas in the 80's. Changing child concepts of the writing process are particularly difficult to gather from interviews and ultimately depend on data from child functioning within the writing process itself, as well as from extensive analysis of the writing product. The following questions for research in the 80's are related to background information needed to understand a child's writing process:

Research Questions for the 80's on Issues Related to Writing Episodes

1. What is the relationship between children's concepts of the writing process and what they *do* during their writing?
2. What is the relationship between children's oral language and what they *do* during the writing process?
3. What is the relationship between children's processes of reading and how they read and revise their own texts?
4. What is the writer's topical range and use of genre over time?
5. How does the child use language to discuss the writing process? How does this change? How is this related to what the child does in the writing process?
6. What is the writer's process of composing in different content areas?
7. What is the *actual* audience range within the child's classroom, school, home? How does this relate to the child's concept of audience, use of audience?
8. How much autonomy does the child exercise in the writing process?
9. How do children change in making the transition from oral to written discourse?
10. What is the relationship between a child's influence on the writing of other children (topic, skill, text, aid) and the child's own performance within the writing process?

Ethnographic Context

Chad's writing is not done in a vacuum. He is part of a social context in which children, teachers, administrators, parents, and a community carry out their values about writing. These values and practices affect what Chad does when he writes. They affect topic choice, interactions with other children and the teacher, his style of solving problems. It is difficult to know what aspects of the broader context affect the composing process and the child's voice in the process. This is one of the least explored areas in writing research.

Examples of ethnographic research conducted in Chris' writing situation are the following:

1. *Communication Patterns*: Examine the contexts of Chad's writing by collecting and tracing written and oral communication along these routes—

> Community
> Board of Education
> Superintendent of Schools
> Middle Management

	Principal	
Teacher	Teacher	Teacher
	Chad	
	Chad's Parents	

The contents, and values expressed in patterns would be classified, assessed, and the effects of those messages would be studied. They would also be assessed for open (answers solicited) vs. closed (directives without explanation or answers expected).

2. *Literacy Values*: How do adults in the same levels and routes mentioned in no. 1 (Communication Patterns) practice and value their composing? What is the nature of the composing? What past experience in teaching has each had with learning to write? What, in fact, is the volume and type of their written communications?

Research Questions for Teachers

The teaching of writing needs major focus for the 80's. But we can no longer afford the errors of the past when experimental designs were used to study specific teaching methodologies. Our preoccupation with the correct stimulus for writing, correcting and grading final products, or with exercises to increase sentence complexity need to be abandoned. So much more is now known about the nature of the process itself, children's development as writers, and the importance of the context of writing, that a new focus is needed on the teacher. Even though much of our research has focused on teachers in the past, we have never actually studied the process of teaching writing. We have never studied even one teacher to know what ingredients are involved in teaching writing. Whereas the case study was the gateway to understanding the writing process and the ingredients involved in it, the same approach is now needed for the teaching process.

We are not starting from scratch. Extensive case studies of children now puts us ahead of where we were with the first case studies of children in 1973. Over the last two years a research team from the University of New Hampshire has been observing the daily writing activity of young children. Because of the detailed focus on children through video and hand recording, there is an entirely different view of the importance and place of teaching. The situation is not unlike the artist who intently paints a landscape and becomes more acutely aware of the effect of weather on the emerging scene. The detailed observation of children is the beginning of understanding teaching, since teacher effects are seen more clearly in the context of child data. These kinds of data are also more easily reported to teachers since descriptions of the classroom, teacher activity, as well as the details of child activity before, during and after composing are given.

The emphasis of the New Hampshire study, however, is on the child, with some data on teacher activity. The child still remains in context. Next studies need to focus on the teacher with peripheral data on the children. Extensive child data with transcripts of meetings with teachers suggest a host of questions that need to be researched in the 80's. None of these questions can be considered without extensive time spent in the classroom, data gathered on both teachers and children, with full consideration given to what happens in the child's process of writing. Since more context is needed for understand-

ng the research questions posed for teaching, a two column format is presented here with the research question in the first column, and discussion of
hypotheses and preliminary data in the second.

	Question	Discussion and Background
1.	What do teachers do when they confer with children about their writing?	We need to describe in detail what is contained in the writing conference with good teachers of writing. Also, teachers who are just starting to teach writing should be chosen so that their changing patterns of conferring with children can be recorded over time. We are speaking of case studies of specific teachers in a variety of settings.
2.	How do teachers attend to children's papers in the writing conference?	Research conducted on this question will also respond to a host of other questions: 1. How specific is the writing conference? 2. How much did the teacher learn from the child in the conference . . . skills, information? 3. How does the teacher give responsibility to the child, or take it away during the writing conference? 4. What is the relationship between the content of the writing conference and the child's subsequent activity in writing? These questions have been formulated from at least one of two hundred recorded conferences from the University of New Hampshire study of the writing processes of young children.
3.	What is the number, frequency, and type of conference conducted in the classroom—daily, weekly, monthly, yearly?	We have very little knowledge about the patterns of teacher conferences with children. From our present study we see conferences of from thirty seconds to twenty minutes dura- tion. Conference patterns change, but what are those pat- terns?
4.	How do teachers change what they attend to in the writing conference over a half year, one year, two years?	We need to carefully monitor teacher changes with both experienced and inexperienced teachers (as in question 1). Teacher changes need to be monitored with different kinds of children. This question will make inroads on issues of match between teaching styles and child learning styles. Also, it may get at the question of match between teacher and child composing styles.
5.	How does the teacher help children to help each other with their writing?	Another preliminary finding from the New Hampshire study is that teachers who enable children to help each other provide not only an important service in immediate child help, but a unique chance to learn more about writing by helping another person. Children in this situation are able to use language to talk about writing more specifically. Children who conference with the teacher in these types of rooms come to the conference already primed to take more responsibility for their own writing content. The pro- cedures that teachers use to help children to gradually take on more responsibility for self-help needs systematic study.

Question	Discussion and Background
6. How does the teacher change the organization of the classroom to aid the writing of children?	There are many organizational plans that evolve as teachers gain experience in helping children to take more responsibility for their writing. The more choice and flexibility children have during the time for writing, the more structure and organization is needed. The process of providing a structure—first visible, then more invisible, needs more systematic study.
7. What types of writing does the teacher provide for children?	Children need to read the writing of others, and from the standpoint of their own authorship. This type of question examines the diet provided for children. The researcher questions: Is the writing the teacher's own? Other children's? Writers from children's literature? Child's own writing?
8. How much time does the teacher provide for writing?	The amount of time in relation to children's own writing episodes and patterns needs to be studied. What are the time provisions—daily, weekly, monthly, yearly?
9. How does the teacher use writing across the curriculum and in different genres?	Writing cannot be contained by the personal narrative alone. Since it exists to clarify meaning, it applies across the curriculum. The breadth of genres and content need to be examined in relation to time provided for writing, conference patterns, different types of children in the study.
10. How does the teacher provide for the permanency of writing?	Much writing should last . . . for the sake of the child, other children, parents and the teacher. This question seeks to examine ways in which teachers provide for writing permanency through publication, collections of writing, writing folders, charts etc.

Since so little data has ever been gathered on any of these questions, or on the process of teaching writing, they ought to be considered within the framework of case studies of competent teachers, those experienced with teaching writing, those willing to become involved in it for the first time. Detailed data gathering through video tapes, audio tapes, direct observations, teacher and child interviews, needs to be done. One of the best ways to gather the teacher case data is to do simultaneous case studies on children in the same environment. In this way the basic ingredients in teacher-child transactions can be examined more closely.

Research Designs and Procedures for the 80's

Researchers in the 80's need to draw from many fields if they are to broaden the contexts of their investigations. Procedures from linguistics, anthropology, developmental psychology, need to work their way into the territories needing investigation. Educators ought to acquire more background in these fields. Similarly, educators need to invite specialists to become more acquainted with the process of education in public institutions.

Research teams ought to be more interdisciplinary. A review of research of the last 25 years shows how insular writing research has become. In the past, the only persons to serve on doctoral committees outside of education departments were statisticians and linguists.

I am not advocating that writing research be turned over to outside specialists. The locus of research control must still remain with the educator who knows the context of the public school setting.

Design and Procedures

Depth needs to be added through different uses of case, experimental, and ethnographic procedures *within the same study*. In short, the space-time dimensions of research must be expanded to include procedures in the same study that in the past have been used solely for one type of study alone. An example of such a study is contained in the following design:

Figure 11.1

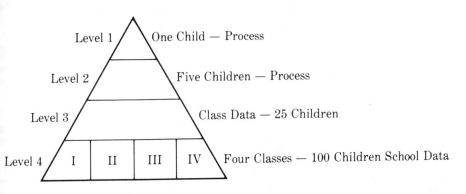

In such a design, data are gathered simultaneously at four levels of investigation: Intensive process data through direct observation of the child at levels 1 and 2 over at least a year's time, and the full context of writing episodes are gathered from before a child writes until the child has had a response to his product. The child in level 1 is a writer who gives more than the usual amount of information, involves a broader spectrum of development, and therefore merits more time from the researcher. Level 3 data come from the entire class in which level 1 and 2 children reside. Some informal observations are taken from them but all of their products are classified or duplicated for examination. Finally, product analysis is given to four classes within the same school building, but also including each of the first three levels of the study. In this way product analyses of larger groups can be further investigated for their process implications in the case study data. Similarly, case data variables that appear to be pivotal can be examined through interventions or product analyses at levels 3 and 4. To date, three studies have been done in this manner, Graves (1975), Graves, Calkins, Sowers (1978–80), and Calkins (1980).

Depth must also be added through more intensive case studies with intra-differences explained through one case. One child's behavior is described within the context of at least one to three years. In this way the pattern of development within one variable or across variables can be examined and explained over a much longer period of time. Too often research contributes to a lottery philosophy of educating. That is, we look for similarities across children, ways of generalizing one child's behavior to aid other children. There is a value in this, but there is also a grave, potential weakness. We will look too quickly to see why the child before us is *the same* as other children rather than look at how the child is different. Or, if the difference is located, we seek to extinguish it in order to integrate the child into a homogeneous mass for more convenient instruction.

In short, we will overlook the one thing that makes the child before us different, unique. We will overlook the voice—the one experience or knowledge area the child knows well. Good teachers have responded to this uniqueness on an intuitive basis for years. Research needs to document intra-differences of the components that make children unique. Glenda Bissex's (1979) study of Paul over a five year period, is this type of study. Also, the child in level 1 (Figure 11.1) is a potential type for study of intra-differences. Data gathered in such depth usually point the way to discovering new variables not seen in the larger data gathering. We cannot afford to be without such studies.

How Will Writing Research Have Influence in the 80's?

In the past teachers have been excluded from the process of writing research. If this practice continues, then every recommendation written in this chapter won't make any difference. The base of research involvement must be broadened to include an active role by the public school teacher. When teachers become involved in research, researchers not only gather better data, but the context of research, the public school classroom, is enriched by the study itself. Teachers and researchers ought to know each other better for the sake of the research and the children.

Dispel the mystique of research. For too long it has been maintained through irrelevant, context-stripping designs, and a language intended for the closed shop of other researchers. It is even doubtful if the intended audience of professionals understands the language any better than the perplexed classroom teacher.

Teachers need to write. They not only need to write in order to understand the process they teach, but they also need to put into print their thoughts about the teaching of writing. Teachers who do this become different consumers of research information.

Even with the work of the Bay Area Writing Project where great stress is placed on the development of the teacher's own writing, there is scant opportunity for teachers to develop their own skills in the process. People who teach a craft must practice it. It would be unheard of for a teacher of piano never to play, or a ceramicist to say to a class, "Here is the wheel, throw the clay," without first demonstrating what the teacher practices daily. Teachers don't need to become professional, publishing writers, but they do need to be acquainted with the craft at a personal, practical level.

Researchers in Residence—A Case Study

In the fall of 1978 three researchers began to observe children in the elementary schools of Atkinson, New Hampshire. They were there to observe "How and in What Order Children Developed as Writers." The two year grant from the National Institute of Education focused on children, not teachers. The team resisted requests for formal writing workshops with the staff. The researchers would answer teacher questions about their children or the writing process.

The researchers had all been teachers and were published writers. Over coffee, at lunch, at breaks when gym, art and music were taught, teachers asked questions about their children and the relation of the data to their teaching. The teachers controlled the questions and used the answers to help children write in their classrooms. The researchers did not have a writing program.

In a short time the mystique of "research and researcher" was removed. Researchers were just as perplexed as teachers about certain children. From the beginning, the researchers wrote, shared findings with the teachers, and published. Teachers could see that they often knew more about their own children than the researchers. Nevertheless, both teachers and researchers learned from the children.

Teachers began to write. They demanded an in-service course in both writing and the teaching of writing. An outside consultant worked with the teachers. Two of the teachers took formal courses in writing. Gradually most of the staff of fourteen teachers worked on their own writing. More importantly, the teachers began to collect their own information about the children. Researchers kept charts of data about the children, and shared them with the teachers. Teachers, in turn, began to keep their own charts, their own data systems, and from these data to write articles of their own.

Most of the teachers keep extensive records, the base of good data for their own research. One teacher records the contents of each writing conference, the patterns of spelling as children change throughout the year; another records the changing strategies of a child who has great difficulty in writing. They write about their information in such a way that they *show* other teachers what they do, as well as the data on which their judgments are based. Some of these recordings and methods are contained in Marion Caroselli's chapter on "Exemplary Teaching Practice."

The status of these teachers has changed. They have become a community since they have shown through their own writing what is the nature of that community. They share stories about their own children, orally and in writing; they teach each other just as their children teach them, and they teach their administrator as well.

In a time when there is a shortage of teaching energy, these teachers even find the energy to write about it. They can do this because they have placed the responsibility for writing where it belongs, with the children. They believe that it is the child's responsibility to teach them about what they know. They help the child through extensive listening, confirmation and questioning to share personal experiences, stories the child wishes to share.

When the children lead, and teachers listen, not only is there a new professionalism with the child, but the teacher (with the child speaking and supplying the energy) has time to write down the information children share. When children must assume a greater responsibility for information, drafting, and proofing, teachers in turn have the energy to publish and to review the data they have from conferences. Once teachers begin this approach to gathering information, they soon learn they cannot do without it.

When these teachers listen, gather data, write about it, share it with other teachers, travel to other communities for workshops, they read research with a different voice. Doers of research, whether it be informal data gathering, small action projects, or year-long classifications of children's writing themes, are critical, active consumers of what happens in the field. They are interested in what is happening in their territory since they are part of the territory. Furthermore, since they observe children and their own actions in relation to them, they have a different view of theory. They realize that basic research on children's writing and development, and the theories of writing that emanate from the data are grounded in real children, can be of help to them in their work with children, not ten years from now, but tomorrow.

Not every system can have full-time researchers in its midst. There are few grants given by the National Institute of Education. But there is a middle ground that researchers, teachers and administrators can examine together, that will give a new focus to the teaching of children and research for the 80's.

Professors of education need to spend more time in the only true laboratories, public school classrooms, to understand the role of teacher, the processes of learning. Perhaps the reason we researchers have neglected issues of context of learning in research for so long, is that we have spent so little time on the sites where experimental data have been gathered. We have gathered research in absentia whether we were doctoral students, psychologists, or professors of education.

There are several options that local school systems and universities can consider together. The success of the proposed ventures is dependent on both professors and teachers learning from children together. It is only the information they have in common about the children, the writing they do together, that will determine the development of a research community.

1. Professors of education need to take more sabbaticals on site with teachers and children. Joint research projects can benefit teachers, professors, and the local school system.
2. Teachers can gather their own data during writing conferences, or review data patterns from children's writing collections. Many teachers have data that are very close to full research studies.
3. Teachers can spell each other to observe children during breaks. These are breaks that make a professional difference. They supply a different kind of energy.
4. School systems can hire resident writing professionals whose main task will be to "live in" selected classrooms to provide data about responding to children's writing. The resident professional must be both writer and researcher. This person will not only work with the staff on their own writing, but share data on the writing processes of children as they aid the teacher whom they serve.

Final Reflection

In the past, research has been done at too rapid a pace. We can no longer zoom in on a research site, emerge like green berets from a helicopter, beat the bushes for data, and retire to our ivy-covered sanctuaries. Sadly, an increasing number of school systems have marked their schools as "off limits" to researchers. With good reason. Researchers, like poor campers, have not left their sites more improved than when they arrived. Pre and post test data have been gathered, a six week intervention introduced with the final data not reported to the school system. Administrators and boards express their feelings directly, "I don't want any researchers experimenting on our kids." Research that ignores context tends to be in a hurry, to avoid the human issues of the persons involved in the study.

Research that broadens the base of context is automatically slower. Rarely is the study less than a full year. Although there are interventions included in the data gathering, much time is spent in describing children, teachers, the research site. Researchers spend months in advance of data gathering becoming acquainted with staff and in making it possible for the staff to get to know them. If researchers are to be guests in the classroom home of the teachers, and rent free, the teachers had better know the guest's values and habits. No one wants a landlord with free lodging.

Our experience in the New Hampshire study indicates that persistent, thorough, yet slow-paced data gathering, has influence on the pace of teaching in the classroom. The teacher slows down and listens to the children, responds differently to the child's drafts. Full descriptions of context of child, family and school make them aware of many other processes operating on the child's behalf. Finally, teachers are able to focus far more on what children *can do*. Researchers and teachers alike share in the amazement of child potential. Perhaps the focus of research in the 80's ought to be: slow down, look at the full context of writing, get to know the real potential of both children and teachers.

12. Sixty Minutes I and II

Introduction

To date, "A New Look At Writing Research" is the most difficult writing I have done. Just why it was so difficult eludes me. Many of the reasons are explained in "Sixty Minutes I and II."

I remember going into my study the day after I mailed off the piece. I was going in to work on a new article for my column, "Research Update," in *Language Arts*. Suddenly, I had the urge to tell the story about writing "A New Look at Writing Research." I thought that if I wrote about it, I might find out what had been troubling me all the time I was composing it. But I really needed to get on with the new column, so I set my kitchen timer for sixty minutes. Seldom have I felt such release and joy in writing. "Sixty Minutes I" is the first draft right off the top.

I thought that the full story had been told after I had written "Sixty Minutes I," but by noon and continuing throughout the day, a whole flood of new information began to bother me. I could hardly wait to get back to the typewriter again to see what I might discover. There is little chronology to either piece. "Sixty Minutes II" is just a fill-in of all the things I had forgotten in the first one.

The two pieces are part of this collection because I thought they would show what good first-draft writing can be like if the topic is an alive one. Although I call these first drafts on paper, in reality, I had been turning the information over in my head for at least six months. Painful thoughts can be great teachers and can lead to interesting advanced thinking. If you are used to writing on a regular basis and pain enters your life, you can't wait to get to the keyboard to find out what was going on during those painful moments. Most people like to forget pain, but I think writers are fascinated by any rich experience, be it great pain or great joy.

Neither of these pieces has ever been published before, but I have used them extensively in teaching and in addresses to groups of teachers and writers. They have been very well received, particularly by teachers who have taken courses or workshops where extensive writing has been expected of them. I could have edited the two selections for this collection, but I thought it best to share the first-draft raw material.

The last four months have been a nightmare. Since December, even November, I have been trying to "end" an article. I think I was trying to end it before it even started. For three years I have had an assignment to write a chapter about research in the teaching of writing in the elementary years. For many reasons I postponed the article. I had others to write. It was such an important article that it deserved more time than I could possibly give it at the moment. "Wait for a significant block of time," I said to myself. The time never came. But the deadline did. And I panicked. When I panicked I tried to end the article before it began.

You have just heard the simple explanation. I think a more important one was that I had actually gone about six months without writing. By writing I mean serious, day by day listening to a text that is going somewhere. There were many reasons for not writing. Family problems loomed with surgery, covering home base, cooking, keeping the house going, listening to the family, too much traveling, the pressing demands of keeping a full-time research project going.

One thing I didn't count on by not writing; my mind never ceased to build up the biggest pile of clutter about that article on research. My "in" basket was piled to the ceiling with hundreds of questions and issues that ought to be included in the xxxx chapter. Day after day the "out" basket was empty. To compensate I continued to think, to rehearse with one audience after another, to build grandiose castles of impact on teachers. First, the article would be about this, then about that. The rehearsal became a substitute for writing itself.

was like the person who bought xxxxxxxx four tickets to Los Angeles, New Orleans, Chicago, and Tucson, and was so excited at the prospect of taking a journey that I sat in the airport watching flight after flight take off without ever climbing aboard. I began to think that watching jets take off was better than the real thing.

Rhæxx

Rehearsal without xæguixxxx daily writing is a menace. The
cluttered "in" basket leads to the most convoluted prose imaginable.
I may pick up one idea from the "in" basket but ten others are stuck
to it. The problem is I can never choose just one. Everything seems
to be connected to everything else. A clinging kind of mold makes
those papers stick together. They have been there so long a kind
of ferment has taken place. Fermentation may make some ideas seem
sage-like. I doubt it. I think it makes them stink a little more.

Idid finishthe article. A few things helped along the way.
I quit trying to finish it. Myxxgxtt I had to spit in thexfxxx
that other face of mine that said, "You bastard, you're over due.
You are letting your friends down. You are the one person holding
thewhole book up./ Writers xxxxxxpppxxxx with a reputation are
supposed to meet deadlines. And you xxx have the gall to think that
you have a reputation." It took more than spit. Every day ixhxxx
for a week I had to belt that other face until I found that the
new way was working.

The new way meant writing every day but only writing about one
thing. I took a series of what seemed to be key topics within the
chapter and wrote about themas if they were going to be but one
article. Ixxxtxxixxxxx I sat down at the typewriter and found to my
xyx surprise that I could rip off four pages txxxx typed, double
space in about an hour and the writing wasn't all that bad. Best
of all when I put that idea to rest with all the other pages of
information stuck to it, I found the "in" basket start to go down.
The next day I'd take another xxx idea and write about it. Now the
xxxx information started to cluster and at last I could see the
one thing that cussed article was all about. Once I got the one
line, XRxxxXtxxxxxx "Writing research can never be done out of
the fullest of contexts in which it occurs," I was off and xxxxxxxx
writing.

I went back to the lead and xixppx wrote it again. The speed
picked up. Now I knew what to throw out and what to keep. /x/ As
more and more information found its place, lined up bxhixd in the
right places, the writing improved. I don't mean the rewriting.
Imean the first draft writing got better and better. I think the
best first-draft writing I did on the piece was the final two pages
f the article. The final two pages are about 400 words long. I
rote these in thxxxx three quarters of an hour. I took the last
our ideas in the "in" basket and made sense of them.xixhxuixxiix
hxixxixhxxxgxxbxgx When there arejust two left, how easy it is to
rite. Xxxxhx How joyous the writing! I don't mean because the
iece is finally completed. Ixhxxxxbxxxxxx At last the writing is
risp. You know xhxixxxxxxxx it is good.

John McPhee says he knows the last two lines or the ending of
is selection <u>before</u> he begins writing. For just an instant when
riting those last three paragraphs to the chapter I sensed in
he final hour what McPhee must know before he even begins. McPhee
as a place to put everything,writes so clearly from the start,
ecause everything is tied up to that last part.

From the moment McPhee begins to cluster information, rehearse
hile driving it all fits with the final statement. McPhee's
in-basket" is orderly, not a random mess of stuff piled in. Furthermore
cPhee writes regularly and bleeds the "in" pile off before it
ets in theway.

My story doesn't end here. The day after I finished I had to
ly to the University of Michigan for a talk. I don't hxxxxiixx
xxxxxpxxxixxxx find jets a good placeto write. I can write letters,
ut not xxxixxxxxixxfixxxxxxxxxxxxxxx articles. This time with my
in" basket empty I startedto write. In the space of twenty minutes
ight
xxxx articles, titles and all,came to mind. I wrote them down.

"Do We Leave Research Sites Better than
We Find Them?"

"Professors Ought to Teach Children Every
Week"

"Three Teachers Who Aren't Tired"

"The Ten Most Common Questions Teachers Ask About
Writing"

"One Day in the Life of A Teacher of Writing"

"The Two Best Pages I Have Every Written"

"Researchers Act as if Nothing Ever Affects Anything
Else"

"Type A Kids, With Type A Teachers, in a Type A
Curriculum"

On theway back to Boston from Michigan I continued to write
but this time listing chapters ðor a book I will be doing for Holt
Rinehart, Winston. I wondered if I would have anthing to put into
it. To my surprise I came up with twenty chapters that ought to
go into the book. I won't list these.

A final note. The release from all that clutter is still
going on. I can't wait to write these days. These five pages that
you have just read are about one thing, that painful trip, or
hðw to get free of clutter. They are a first ðx draftand took
just ðﾷﾷﾷ 601minutes by my timer to put down. The bell just went
off.

Next day
Sixty Minutes III

People helped. At my lowest point Donald Murray helped me
out of my research dilemma. Whenever I have to write something
vaguely resembling research the dissertation syndrome returns.
I don't want to write researchy research but it turns out that way
Such ðﾷﾷ words as variables,ðﾷﾷﾷﾷﾷﾷ nomathetic, phenomenology
creep in. My voice disappears. I become passive. The informatio
controls me but I don't control the linformation. I try so hard
to be responsive to all the possibilities in the data that the

reader gets **it** just **that:** all the possibilities in the data, chains
of information, charts. Material dumped on the readers dock with
the label:"you make sense out of it. Aren't you impressed with
the amount?"

XXXXXXXXXXXXXXXXXXXXXXXXXXXX

Murray sat in his chair, as he usually does, leaning slightly
back, glasses off as he flipped through my material. How painful
it is to give your writing to a professional when you know it is
poor writing, when it is garbage. I was desperate. I had tried
four different leads, working at least three to four days on each.
This time I had a table up front with an anecdote preceding it.
I explained the table in detail. The information was good but there
was no voice in it. Worse, I didn't know where to go from there.

Murray said, "Don, I think we fool around with the anecdotal
lead too much. And these rhetorical questions suck." The piece
was full of them. How hard I was trying to pull the reader along,
anticipating all the readers questions in advance. The rhetorical
questions were insulting. "I think you ought to get this good information up front. Hit the reader with facts. Right off. Think
of a lead like this. "Thebad news is . . ." The minute he said
that I knew what I had to do. It's amazing how one word helps.
That's the way it usually is with Murray. He give you the one word,
the one sentence, the one piece of advice thatshows what will help.
He doesn't load you up with advice. I walkaway wanting to get to
the typewriter just as fast as I can.

My lead turned out "First the bad news . . ."then two pages
later, XXXXXXXXXXXXXXX "Now for the good news . . ." I wrote
about eight pages from this and thexpxasexx for the first time the
prose was straight forward, the facts punched their way ahead.
XXXXXXXXXXXXXXXXX I had a voice but I still didn't have the
one thing the selection was about.

The largest sectin of the paper was about needed writing research for the 80's. It would take up about sixty-five percent of the paper. I had already written strings of questions that needed to be researched. Triple columns indicated the question, the discussion of the material, follbwed by procedures to carry out the questions. I had spent at least two weeks on this section, working every day with more and more detail on each question. But the deeper in I got the farthest I seemed to be from the lead. The lead was right, no question, but how would I ever get into a position where the last part would dock in space with the first part.

Thxkx The second major solution came when I realized what the piece was about. I remember standinglup in my study, no one else could hxxm hear me, and shouting, "It's about context. The whole thing is about context! Damn it all, why did it take so long to know it was about context?" Suddenly it was clear that the past research neglected context and the future must include it. The link was there between the first and the second part.

I abandoned the questions and columns, what was needed for the 80's, eventhough I had written about ten pages of material. I knew the material lacked voice and control because I hadn't yet known what the piece was xbxxkyxbxxxxxxx about. It didn't have the same voice as the lead because it wasn't linked with the lead. I went back and made minor changes in the seven page lead to make it agree with what it was all about, context.

Then I wrote toward the section, "Research for the 80's." Now when I came to the section on the 80's the questions and prose linked up to the start. I just wrote on through. The last twenty pages were done in about four days.

When I knew the research was about context, for the first time the writing bxxxxxxfxxx was enjoyable. Upxtxxtbxxixxmxxmxxixxxxxtx gaxtxxxxxxtxxly Before that day I would go to the study, xixixxxxixixg sit, wanting to run out the door, to go upstairs to see the news on T.V., readthe paper, talk to Betty, anything but write. I'd make a cup of coffee, some toast, and sit there letting the warmth trickle down,. hoping somehow that heat would kindle some kind of fire. It ꓲ didn't. ꓲ

I noticed that I'd still be sitting there in the study at 6:30 a. m., a half hour had gone by and the paper wasstill empty. XXꓫXꓭXꓭXꓭXXꓭXꓭXꓭXXXXꓭXXXXXꓭXXꓭXꓭꓭXXꓭXꓭXꓭXXꓭXXXꓭXX I came up with a solution for that. I set my timer for ten minutes the second I walked through the door of the study. Ten minutes for avoidance and crap. No more. After that I'd have to be writing words. Any words. Just words. It worked. Flow would come and by 7:00 a. m. I'd have at least two pages of material, typed, double-spaced.

Strangely, once I set my timer for ten minutes of crap I found I only needed about four minutes. Now I don't even set the timer any more. I even look forward to getting down to work. I know the words are there.

My friends continued to encourage me with the piece. Each day they would ask how it was coming. I could only say, "I'm still workXing on it." Do you know hard it is to say that when two months later the piece is still going? The piece is not ended. Of course, I would make such statements as, XXXꓫX "This weekend I am going to finsh the sonofabithc." I did work the whole weekend, but by Monday I could only say, "It isn't over and I'm still working on it. Progress. But it isn't done. In fact, I'm still a long ways away from being done." ꓮXXXXXꓭX I'd have some good sections. I'd read them outloud. Susan and Lucy were always encouraging.

Xꓫ Bꓭꓭ This chapter was hard on everyone around me. That makes the writing doubly difficult. It followed me to the office. It made me a poorlistener to colleagues. There was little joy in my life. There'd be a good day in Atkinson. Something new from the children.

I'd rejoice for a second and then the base of dread from the unfinished
piece would flood in.and kill the joy. Susan,and Lucy and Lois
knew this. That dread of thepiece filled so much of my life that
I was about fifteen percent functional. Iknew it and I guess that
made it worse. How hard it is when a writing selection comes between
you andthose you want to be responsive to most! I'd come in after
a morning of writing. They'd watch my face and say. "Those wrinkles
on your forehead show the writing didn't go well today." They were
right. They could tell.

It was worse at home. The pall of the article hung over
meals, conversations, evenings at the movies, with friends. It
wouldn't go away. There was a burnt odor that wouldn't go away.
The piece had a smell to it. Until the piece After a while the
smell got to be so much a part of the family woodwork the family
didn't asking question my lost head. I wouldn't be included in
plans. Betty Men would be asked all the questions, had to bear the brunt
of things. After a while they didn't want to know how the piece
wascoming. For their own pain, it would be best to learn to ignore
it.

After writing all of this about the piece, I still have the
feeling that something else was working that can't be touched.
Was this some kind of crossroads inlmy life as a writer? Was this
some kind of lifexplatienalxx plateau, one of Levinson's stages of
adult development? Was I writing the book befarexithex for Holt,
Rinehart, Winston before it wasto start? Perhaps a few years from
now I'll know what happened. Possibly the chapterrepresented some
major issue of information I had to come to terms with.

I remember being bothered by the productiveness of Lucy and
Susanaround me. Here I was, the leader thexof of the research expe
dition, and I couldn't even write. One piece was aabotaging our
research efforts.

The release isstill with me. I feel hot as a writer. Things aren't socomplicated any more. I intend to ride thislhigh right into the sunset. All that pain may be some kind of battery recharging, the more painful it was, the greater therelease. I hope so. I pray that I won't have to go that way again.

13. Questions for Teachers Who Wonder If Their Writers Change

Introduction

From September 1980 until June 1981, Mary Ellen Giacobbe, first-grade teacher in Atkinson, New Hampshire gathered data on her children's writing. Her study was done in conjunction with a study conducted by Lucy McCormick Calkins. The Calkins study was designed to see how teachers conducted research in their own classrooms. Giacobbe's data-gathering was designed to find out how children's concepts changed over the course of a year. Although Mary Ellen came up with specific questions to focus her data, her questions and the conduct of her study were all part of her normal approach to teaching writing with young children. Giacobbe had regular conferences with the children each day and throughout the year.

In May 1981, Mary Ellen and I began to work together formally on the data, which had been gathered on ten children and so were voluminous. We charted the data for each child for both December and June, and for each question asked in the study. Because we wished to report in as much detail as possible, it was clear from the outset that only data on two of the ten children could be reported. Actually, we started by trying to report on four of the children and later reduced the number to two. In each instance, we wished to have a boy and a girl, as well as a child representing higher and lower abilities. Thus, we would be able to show the dynamics of conferences as well as the differences in the growth patterns of the two children. Such an approach, we felt, would make the information more usable for classroom teachers, the main audience for this piece.

Another major problem was finding the categories around which the information clustered from the six questions Mary Ellen asked before and after the children wrote. It took several months of writing and analyzing before we arrived at the three final categories: information, process, and standards.

Writing in collaboration usually takes longer than writing alone since there is much shuttling back and forth of the manuscript and of information. Neither of us believed when we started that the manuscript would take seven months to complete. Even though we both reside in the same state, we live thirty-five miles apart, and much of the work had to be done by mail and over the telephone. I did most of the writing, while Mary Ellen did much of the data gathering and analysis, plus the editing. Mary Ellen had already published and was an accomplished writer, but we both agreed that it would be best to have one style and one writer for most of the text.

The best part about collaboration is that both writers are able to teach each other about the information. Since these were children from Mary Ellen's own classroom, she was able to give extensive explanations for many of the children's statements. For example, Mary Ellen was quickly able to point out the significance of Lauren's long dialogue about information on page 126. Because of my lack of involvement in the actual data-gathering, I was able to spot the children's growing sense of option in their conception of information, process, and standards. I suppose either of these findings could have been made by the other but the key thing is that we both helped each other to see new findings in the data.

Donald Graves and Mary Ellen Giacobbe

How hard it is for teachers to tell if their writers improve! The growth of young writers is often erratic: On Monday poor writing, improvement on Tuesday, an excellent day on Wednesday, an average day on Thursday, poor writing again on Friday. The teacher leaves school on Friday wondering if anything significant has happened during the week, even though such a pattern is a normal one for most writers. She wonders where to begin on Monday morning.

Since the growth of young writers in the short term is both uneven and erratic, new questions need to be asked that will give teachers a picture of child change in the long run. There are subtle changes of a more fundamental nature that can show teachers significant change, even in the midst of a child's struggle. Teachers who ask process questions, not only gather sound information about child growth, but also ask the very questions that contribute significantly to the growth of the children themselves.

A Teacher Who Found Out for Herself

Mary Ellen Giacobbe, a first grade teacher in Atkinson, New Hampshire, wanted to find out how her children's concepts of the writing process changed from December through the end of the school year. Underlying her interest in concepts were simple questions: "Are my children improving as writers? If so, how?" She formulated many of her interview questions with Lucy McCormick Calkins, who had a grant from the NCTE Research Foundation to help teachers conduct their own research.

Rationale for Questions

For three years Giacobbe met several times weekly with each of her children to discuss their progress as writers. She was aware her six year old children often made penetrating statements about their writing, even though the writing was not necessarily going well at the time. She noticed that as children broadened their ability to plan, solve problems, have a language to discuss their writing, and a sense of options for the writing process, their writing products ultimately changed for the better.

Giacobbe knew the products improved each year. This was easily documented in writing conferences and the children's writing folders. She needed information, however, that showed where the children were in the process of understanding, that she might have data to help them from day to day during writing conferences.

She framed a six month period of teaching with questions that were asked before and after children wrote in December and in June. Ten of her twenty-three children were interviewed about their writing process, transcripts made of interviews with copies of writing xeroxed to show the relationship between child concepts of writing and what happened in the writing itself. These ten children were distributed along low, middle, and high performance levels in writing. The following questions were asked of the children:

Before they wrote
1. What are you going to be writing about? (Children chose their own topics throughout the year.)
2. How are you going to put that down on paper?
3. How did you go about choosing your subject?

After they wrote
1. How did you go about writing this?
2. What are you going to do next with this piece of writing?
3. What do you think of this piece of writing?

Although these questions were asked in standard, formal fashion, Giacobbe didn't hesitate to ask further questions that promised additional information.

Two of the ten children are now reported to show more detailed profiles of child change in writing. The two children are chosen from the high and low groups to show contrast. Teachers will see the types of information questions elicit as well as changes within and between the two children. Each case is reported in the three most important sections to monitor child change through questions: information, process, and standard.

Although all the small changes between the two dates in December and May are not available, the information will be discussed in light of data from our study of children's composing from ages six through nine (see *Language Arts Research Update* 1978–1981).

Mark

Mark was chosen in December to represent the lower group of children. At that time he was barely able to read his invented spellings. It was not easy for him to talk about his work or writing; composing was a slow process where he struggled for the right letters to spell out his pieces.

Information

In December Mark is asked what he would be writing about. As in speech he goes directly to the subject:

"School ... writing and building and all that.
Math, science, art."

When Mark composes he has to lead into his subject from home base, a home to school narrative, a practice quite common in December with other children. Mark writes:

> I am in the house.
> We are going to school.
> Mrs. Young dropped off the other kids at the Academy.
> We are going to Rockwell. (His school, next stop on bus run from Academy.)
> We are getting off the bus.
> I am playing.
> The End.

Mark's entire text gets him *to the subject* discussed orally. It is difficult for any writer to get into a subject. Noting how writers get into their subjects is a fruitful way to view the change of writers at any age.

By June Mark's use of specifics has changed dramatically, both in his pre-conception of what will be contained in the writing, and in the writing itself. The same question asked in December about what will be contained in his writing brings a different harvest:

> Chicks . . . I might just write like what I know about chicks and I might write that one just hatched at about eleven past ten. I might write the day that it hatched. I might write that a chick just hatched a couple of days ago . . . that a chick hatched last night. I'll keep on thinking about it and I'll just think and I'll find out what I'm going to write.

Mark's sense of options changes from December to June. He is now familiar enough with both writing and his subject, "chicks," that he might exercise any of these options in writing: what he knows about chicks, the one that just hatched at eleven past ten, the day it hatched, or the chick that hatched last night. Any time children speak of different directions in content, process, or standards, there is evidence of a signficant growth unit. Once children realize there are options before them in information or process, they take on greater problem solving capacities, as well as greater access to the specifics that make their writing more detailed.

In June, with his sense of many options and rich information, Mark moves quickly to his subject when he writes:

> A chick hatched on Tuesday. The whole class was happy. I was happy the first chick hatched. I wanted to hold it but it was too small. You have to wait for two days when you can hold them. They will nibble at your finger. In two days they will nibble. It doesn't hurt when they nibble. One chick nibbled my finger until my finger got a cut. The cut didn't hurt. I was scared when he nibbled at my finger. We are trying to hatch eggs in our school but they hatched on yesterday, June 2, 1981. The chicks are wet when they hatch. If you wait for two days they will be grey. They will be fluffy too. That is when it is fun to hold them. I holded a chick. I had never holded a chick. It felt weird. It squiggled. It got out of my hands. I chased it all around John's house for a half hour. Finally he finally it stopped. It was too tired to run anymore. I finally got the chick. It tried to get away again and it almost did but it didn't get away. The End.

Mark's text follows in many directions with each sentence stimulating the next. His understanding of options doesn't mean he entertains one in the midst of four. Rather, Mark finds that each sentence mysteriously leads to the next; there is usually an option around the corner to be followed. Although Mark expresses what he will write as optional, in fact, he uses all of his options in the text. This is a necessary precursor to the child's stopping and making a decision about which option to entertain in the midst of composing. Thus, Mark's statement of options or "might" is really a statement of the suspected twists and turns in his piece about chicks.

Mark is able to show himself more in the June piece. His voice is present in feelings, surprise at what the chicks do: pecking, squiggling, running around the house. Mark has more access to himself in June than in December.

Process

The first element in Mark's process of writing is the process he uses to choose his subject. Note the difference from December to June:

December	*June*
I just wanted to write that. Cause I like school. It just came to my head.	I just thought about what we've done. I thought about dinosaurs first. And I thought about butterflies and chicks. We studied about food and shells. Then I decided the chick one.

In June Mark has chosen one of six options for his topic. He is used to the question, to having access to how he goes about choosing his topic. Children who have such options rarely see themselves as being without a writing subject. Best of all, they learn to exercise intelligent choice on subject limitation. They learn about what they know.

Giacobbe found out more about Mark's process by asking him about his composing before and after writing. Before writing, Mark said, in December:

> I'm just going to take the paper and write it down. And then I'll write the picture of it. I write the picture first and then I write about the picture because I like to write the picture first because if I mess up I can just make something out of it. If I mess up with crayons I already drawed on something I can make that part of it.

Mark already has a clear sense of process in December. He is aware that he draws (before he actually composes) and that he is able to transform drawing errors into sensible solutions. He also makes little distinction between the process of drawing and writing, a common understanding of many children Mark's age. He *writes* them both.

In June Mark's statements about process appear to be regressive. Now that he does little drawing to go with the writing, his language seems vague in comparison with December.

> *Before:* How he will write: "I don't know . . . in words. That's all I can think of for now."
>
> *After:* How he did write: "First I thought what I was going to write and I just thought and thought."

Children Mark's age consistently move from specifics about the process to such general statements as: "I thought and thought" as they develop greater internal language. It isn't long before the general statement "thinking" is replaced by more specifics about the process again. "Thinking" comes at the point when children use less speaking to accompany the writing process, yet they lack words to describe the internal process. They are just aware of a change that can only be expressed as "thinking." Later, they will see an external counterpart in what they actually do to describe their writing processes.

The future, however, is much more definite. When Mark is asked what he *will do* with his piece in June, there is great difference from his December statement: "Publish it." In short, the piece is done at the time of interview. In June, Mark has a *continuing* sense of what will be done with his writing:

> Probably get it published. I might sit down and work on it a little bit. Turn it over and erase the things on the back that I have and write some new stuff. Write new stuff about chicks. I might take this piece and just look through and see if it's chicks or ducks cause I had to chase one of John's ducks too. That even took more than an hour. I might change some of it to ducks.

The future is open. Mark will go back to rework his piece with some adjustments needed in the information. The piece still exists for more work.

Giacobbe has carefully developed a future for the children by asking them throughout the year, "And now what will you do with your piece?" But the question has come after continuing to have a conference about what the child still knows about the topic even though the child has "completed" the piece. It is the child's choice whether the information is used or not. Of course the child's time frame of working on the process changes as a result of such procedures. The piece about the classroom in December took one sitting whereas "Chicks" was carefully composed over three days. Even though the piece took longer in June, Mark still has more to say about what he will continue to do with his writing.

Standards

At the end of each interview, Mark is asked how he feels about his piece. Much of his standard in December is taken from the comments and help given by others:

> I think it's good. Because when I conferenced with Justin they said it's good. They thought it should be published too.

He gives few specifics of his own about why it is good. It is good enough to be published. (About one in four booklets composed by the children are published in hard cover in the room. This amounts to an average of one book every four weeks for each child in the school year.)

In June Mark had a much more elaborative statement about his thoughts on the quality of his writing:

> I think it's good. It's one of the best pieces I have. When I read it through it sounds good. When I read through all my pieces, they all sound good.

Mark had just completed a strong fantasy piece called "The Great Race." He is feeling that most of his selections are good after having two good ones in a row. Mark then goes on to make another statement about standards, one quite typical of children six through nine years of age, who are wrestling with issues of "real-unreal."

> This is better than "The Great Race" because it has more information. Anyways, that didn't really happen in "Great Race." I just imagined all of that. This is better because it is a real story. Real things really happened. Make-up things didn't really happen.

For children coming to terms with what is real, not real, true, untrue, the "real," the new realization, takes on greater importance and therefore greater merit as a written piece for Mark.

Lauren

Lauren was chosen as one of the subjects because in December she composed in the more advanced group in the class. She was articulate in speaking about writing and the writing process.

Information

In December Lauren tells far more than she writes. By June she has shifted to writing more than she tells. At first Lauren used the response to the question, "What will you write?" as a rehearsal for the text composed. In December there is little difference between Lauren's oral response and what she composed on the first page:

Oral: (December)	*Written:* (December)
Well, one time when we were coming home from our boat and Candace was going to sleep over my house we couldn't do it cause I was getting too crabby. Then my brother was allowed and he fell down the stairs with his tape recorder and his book and he broke his wrist.	Once when we were coming back from the boat Candace was going to sleep over my house but I was too crabby. Then Bobby fell down the stairs. He slept over anyways. He went to my house. Then he went to the doctor and got a cast on.

Lauren selects only the material *first* shared in telling about what will be in writing. Forty-eight of the seventy-three words written in the selection came from the first 75 words of the oral account of what would be written even though Lauren shared 246 total words of what would happen in her writing. Part of this is because Lauren, like many primary children, started out with great detail on the first page (47 words) but ran out of energy, and quickly closed in traditional fashion with simple subject, verb, object sentences:

> He can ride his bike.
> Bobby is better now.
> Bobby is at school.
> He came back from school.

Each of these sentences occupies only four or five words to the page. They form a similar pattern to Mark's lead from home to school and back again with only one sentence about school itself.

In June there is much less of Lauren's oral account in the writing. Like Mark, as will be shown in the process section, she is aware that she will discover new options in the composing; an oral rehearsal is much less needed. Table 13.1 shows the shift from oral to written:

Table 13.1—Percentage of oral in written December and June.

	No. words in oral account	Word information units in writing from oral	Word length of written account	% of writing made up from oral account
December	246	48	73	66
June	153	35	129	27

Even though Lauren's genre had changed from a narrative account to an informational "all about" writing, she takes the information and attempts to have small narratives within the article about her family boat. Each page has an illustration to go with it.

About my boat

p. 1—My boat is neat. I like my boat. Under a cushion there's a toilet under it.

p. 2—We go on my boat in the summer. Our boat isn't next to their boat. There's another boat between them.

p. 3—One time our friends came on our boat. Sometimes when they go out with us.

p. 4—We have a new marina. They put the docks out. My father is putting the boat into the water. I asked my mom if we could go on the boat tomorrow. She said maybe we could.

p. 5—I like my boat. Our boat has a hatch. Sometimes I stick my head out the hatch. But sometimes my father tells me to put my head back.

p. 6—There is a sink in our boat. We went on the boat yesterday.

There is an epi-narrative of her friends, the new dock and the hatch. There is no strong narrative or coherent approach to writing about her boat. Different features have their personal appeal, the toilet, the marina, friends, the hatch and the sink in the boat. The piece unfolds, and in a sense is less coherent than the December narrative. Working with a non-narrative account is much more difficult, however, especially when the writer tries to put in personal voice.

Process

Process statements give the strongest indications of Lauren's growth as a writer. Note the change from December to June in her two accounts of how she will compose:

December	June
Keep on adding pages. I might have a problem if I get mixed up. Yeah, I would. But I don't think I will. Maybe tomorrow I'll have time to do the whole thing, instead of doing other things like clay.	I might add or I just might take some out. I just might write the pages. If I ran into problems I would just think what we really did and erase that and put what we really did. Sometimes I get mixed up. I'm really not thinking.

In December Lauren chooses to complete all writing in one sitting. "Maybe tomorrow I'll have time to do the whole thing." This also shows why her big splurge of information on page one was followed by such simple sentences with data less relevant to her topic. She had exceeded her time limit set for writing. The only way out was to end the piece in simple sentences.

In June there are more specifics to Lauren's process. Lauren might "add, take out, erase, rewrite, (put what we really did")." In the developmental hierarchy of writing "taking out" information is an advanced concept. It is not unusual for children to cite addition of information; subtraction is another matter. This means that a child has decided something is irrelevant to the main idea. By June Lauren has a much richer problem statement, whereas in December "she might run into problems but probably won't." When children come up with options in information or process, they also come up with much richer statements about anticipated problems. The two must go together or the writer will be in great difficulty. There are too many children who are strong readers who can cite many problem options but are without the information and process options. That situation usually leads to a child who is very unhappy with writing.

Lauren's statement about how she actually composed in June shows even more about her understanding of process:

> I forgot to put in my mother. I forgot to put that so I had to erase for more room. I had more information but it was hard to put in. I put an arrow up here to say that. I saw you (Giacobbe) do that when you showed the boys and girls what you do when you leave something out of your writing.

Lauren has picked up on her teacher's strategies for inserting information and applied them to her own writing on a self-directed basis.

Lauren has also expanded the time-space dimensions of her process understandings. First, she composes over a longer period in June (three days as opposed to one day). Second, she returns to reexamine the text to insert new information. Third, even at the point of the interview for this study she still has designs on how she will continue to work with her piece: She still wants to check to see if it is "mixed up" in any way. To check this problem she will take the staple out of the corner of the papers, spread the papers on the floor, and look from page to page to put the information in the right order.

Standard

In December Lauren feels the piece is good because, "I like it. I really want to publish it because it's about the best so far. I like it. It's a good book. It's good because I just thought about it this minute and it's good." Like most children starting out, Lauren thinks it is good because she just "feels" it is the best. She is not yet conscious of criteria to apply to the piece. Teachers need to be cautious about children's understanding of what is good. Even though children cannot come up with specific criteria as to what is best, they usually do choose the best paper. Criteria *come after* they are able to choose best papers.

Lauren's standard in June has more specifics with some understanding of the effect of her place on the other children.

I like it a lot. It makes me feel good. That's what makes it a good piece but it may not be to other people. (Thinks it is important that it be good to other people.) It is good because it has a lot of information in it. I told a lot about my boat. I think I want to write even more.

Lauren has introduced feeling as a criteria but with feeling backed by information. She also has a sense of continuing standard since she wishes to keep working on her piece to make it better.

Final Reflection

Teachers ask questions to find out how children change. Questions about the writing process show how children change most because responses are rooted in the underpinings of child thinking and development. Children's perceptions of what they write and how they write it are data teachers can't do without.

The challenge to the teacher is making sense of the information the children give when responding to questions. Will the teacher know growth when it is present, even though the child may be struggling with his piece? Teachers should look for: the child's use of detail, ability to talk about the subject, sense of *option*, tentativeness of judgment, growing language to talk about the process of writing.

Questions themselves contribute to child growth if asked on a regular basis. Most of the questions, however, are asked because the teacher feels the child knows the answer. Although Giacobbe's question activity in writing conferences between December and June is not part of this study, the use of questions in conferences is a regular pattern in her teaching. Her records show regular conferences with children (about three per week). Conferences are spent in receiving, discussing and questioning the children about their work. The object is to help children teach her about their subjects and to discuss the process by which they compose. From our previous study (see *Language Arts*, Research Update, 1979–1981) it is clear that the conference, plus questions, produces reflection and a language of option and process in the children.

Children grow because they become aware of what they are doing, then forge on to tackle new issues in their composing. Questions make an important contribution to that awareness. Teachers become aware of where the child is from the questions and ask further stretching questions. Children, in turn, become more confident about where they are in the writing process, and take on more challenging issues in their composing.

14. Write with the Children

Introduction

This piece is a chapter from my book, *Writing: Teachers and Children at Work*. I wrote it just after my return from Scotland in 1981. It came at the end of a good string of writing for chapters 2 through 4 in the book. Although these chapters fall early in the book, they were actually written after the very difficult chapters on development, 21 to 26. These chapters were a terrible struggle. They were of a more theoretical nature and were based on our research with the children from the NIE study in Atkinson, New Hampshire. Chapter 21 took me about two months to write.

When I arrived stateside in June of 1981 I hadn't yet written any chapters on the teaching of writing. How surprised I was to find the writing running freely and easily! Chapter 2, "Survive Day One," was written in three days, from rough to final copy, a total investment of about six hours. Chapters 3 and 4 followed just as easily. This was a new experience for me as a writer, to be able to produce writing that just came off the top and needed little revision. I suspect that I had been rehearsing these chapters for about three years during our research in Atkinson as well as my year in Scotland. They were sitting there waiting for their moment to arrive on paper. All during the study at Atkinson we wrote mostly about the children and how they developed as writers; I had said nothing about teaching.

This chapter, "Write with the Children," was first named "Modeling for Children." I used an approach here that I continued to use for most of the book. An explanation of my approach may be helpful to readers and show how my writing was progressing at this stage of my writing career. I will use portions of my notes to show how the writing developed in composing this chapter.

BRAINSTORMING

The chapter began with a kind of brainstorming. I started by putting down ideas under categories. I didn't have the categories in mind before I started; they just emerged. I'd start a category and when it gave rise to another category, I would start the new one knowing I could come back to fill in the missing portions. I composed the following brainstorm list in about twenty minutes at my typewriter. The xxxs show where I crossed out.

PLANNING AHEAD:

1. Teachers don't have to be expert to model
2. Not a desire to show 1–1, or even show good writing.
3. Very simply the teacher talks and writes at the same time, choosing carefully one of two things for export and import.

FOUR WAYS TO MODEL WRITING:

1. Just sitting at your seat and writing. Not to be bothered.
2. Experience chart paper
3. Overhead projector
4. 3 x 5 card exercise of Don Murray's

SUBJECT TO CHOOSE—Choose the subject aloud:

1. A happening with a first, second, third, and fourth part to it. Something that builds and goes away.
   Much story content to it.
   Much motion and going about.
2. Something that happened to me when I was in school.
3. Not humor. That is difficult, involves careful choice of words.

SHOW A TRANSCRIPT:

Double column example

WHAT DO I MODEL?

Tone and process
Taking your time
Lining out
Looking for the possibility in something—
    reading over a piece, suspended judgment
Use an object when you write

INVOLVING THE CHILDREN AS YOU WRITE:

Tolstoy example
Choose a subject with them
    Something that has happened in the life of the class.
xxxxxxx And then it will happen
Better words
Forget anything here
Line you liked best   TEACHING THEM TO READ THE
    PAPER. TO XX READ WRITING
Have children interview you
    on object and include in the story

In the next planning stage I slotted the above information into a three-column format. The three columns give the general placement of where the information falls: Upfront (lead), Middle (guts) and End. Of course, new information would come to me as I slotted the information into the columns. Here is how the three-column format looked after I had composed it on the typewriter:

Upfront	Middle	End
Never see another person write	Overhead projector	What happens to you as teacher when you model?
Importance of children seeing another write	3 × 5 Card exercise of Don Murray	What happens to the children?

Upfront	Middle	End
One of the elements in acquiring a skill	Just sitting and writing What to Model Tone and process	See what the children adopt, remembering that the main reason you do this is that children may at least have concept that you and other adults write
Show another crafts-in the process	Taking your time Lining out Word choice Suspended judgment	
Other process subjects the teacher is highly visible.		Remember the tone is what you want most to come through
	CONSULT WITH THE CHILDREN ASK THEM TO HELP IN MODELING SESSION	
Don't have to be an expert to show.	Show a transcript of a modeling session, double column.	Process language in context See in another before you can see in self
Modeling is an exposure —no desire to make it a 1–1 experience	Story of Pat	Keep in perspective
	Choose only one thing, maybe two to highlight in the modeling session	
	Again, not to go 1–1 as I do	
	Choose your subject aloud	
	When experienced ask the children what you ought to write	
	Warts and all—talk aloud as you go	
	Easiest place to begin is just writing with them The five minutes you choose Have an object for children to see, even have them interview on it and then write	
	Process language in context	

After typing the three-column format I was ready to begin my lead. I think I started the lead on the day after this planning session. A look at the first few words in the lead column shows how I got into the lead that follows. And most of the words survive. I find that when planning has gone well, first drafts are much better:

DRAFT ONE

Think back. When was the last time you xxxxxxxxxxx observed how another person xxxxxxxxx wrote? You would be an unusual person if you could recall more than one or two in a lifetime. xxx It would be even more unusual if you could recall how they went about composing their writing. I'm not referring to professional composing. I am referring to anyone in the process of composing a list, xx letter . . . any piece of written prose.

There are many reasons for this lack of xxxxx recall. xxxxxxxxxxxxxxxxxx. When people write, they undress. They disclose so much of themselves that if you were to observe them composing, it would be xxxxxx akin to staring at a stripper. xxxxxx Instinctively we cover up when we feel undressed, bring an arm around to block our paper from the view of another. Somewhere along the line we have gotten the idea that our bodies, our writing bodies, are unacceptable, not for the viewing of others. It is only natural to want xxxxxxxx only our best to be seen.

DRAFT TWO

Think back. When was the last time you observed another person write? You would be unusual if you could recall more than one or two xxx in a lifetime. I'm not referring to professional writers. I am referring to anyone in the process of composing a list, letter. . .any piece of written prose.

There are reasons why we don't observe other writers. When people write, they undress. They disclose so much of themselves in the process they don't want others around. Instinctively they cover up and bring an arm around to block our view of the paper. xxxxxxxx In the course of learning to write they have taken on the idea their writing bodies were unacceptable, not for the viewing of others. It is only natural to want only the best seen.

DRAFT THREE

(The first paragraph remains the same right through to publication. In fact, the first paragraph in draft two is almost identical to the one published. The second paragraph was more of a struggle.)

Think of the children. They have seen even fewer writers composing. Ask children how adults write. Their replies blend concepts of witchcraft and alchemy. Children suggest that when adults write the words flow, arrive "Shazam!" on the page. Like the Tablets, words are dictated to us from on high; we only hold the pen and a mysterious force makes it move into stories, poems and letters. The better the writer, the less the struggle. They look sideways in their classrooms and note only the "poor" writer has to "do it over." Thus, the epitome of the good writer is one who gets it right the first time, has no struggle, and gets the bad task over with sooner than most. Children believe all this because they have xxxxxxx never seen adults write.

DRAFT FOUR (PARAGRAPH TWO)

Think of the children. They have seen even fewer writers compose. Ask children how adults write. Their replies blend concepts of witchcraft and alchemy. Children suggest that when adults write xxxxx the words flow, arrive "Shazam" on the page. Like the Tablets, words are dictated to us from on high; we only hold the pen and a mysterious force makes it move into stories, poems and letters. The better the writer, the less the struggle.

By draft four, the second paragraph is nearly in final form. The published version changed the text to "mysterious force dictates stories, poems and letters." The entire chapter incorporated many more changes but it was completed, drafts and all, in about five days or fifteen hours of total planning and writing.

This chapter is one example in this collection where the writing went more easily. And the language shows it. It is crisp, simple, and direct. Teaching procedures are much easier to write about than descriptions of human behaviors. Advice to others comes quickly, especially if the writer has been storing the advice for three years.

Think back. When was the last time you observed another person write? You would be unusual if you could recall more than two incidents in a lifetime. I'm not referring to professional writers. I am referring to anyone in the process of composing a list, letter . . . any piece of written prose.

Think of children; they have seen even fewer writers compose. Ask children how adults write. Their replies blend concepts of witchcraft and alchemy. Children suggest that when adults write, the words flow, arrive "Shazam!" on the page. Like the Tablets, words are dictated to us from on high; we only hold the pen and a mysterious force dictates stories, poems, and letters. The better the writer, the less the struggle.

We maintain their fictions by not writing ourselves. Worse, we lose out on one of the most valuable ways to teach the craft. If they see us write, they will see the middle of the process, the hidden ground—from the choice of topic to the final completion of the work.

Teachers don't have to be expert writers to "write" with the children. In fact, there may be an advantage in growing with them, learning together as both seek to find meaning in writing. However, it does take courage to show words to children who haven't seen an adult write before.

Pat's breakthrough as a teacher of writing came when she composed with the children. Before she tried it, she confessed that she felt she was getting set to bail out from a plane at 30,000 feet. Pat, ever forthright, strode to the front of the room and said, "I'm going to write and I need help." An hour later we met her in the hall. Her feet hardly touched the floor as she said, "You know, I said I needed help and they helped. They suggested words, asked questions, all the things that really helped."

When teachers compose before the children on an overhead projector or on large sheets of paper mounted on an easel, they speak as they write. Children need to hear the teacher speak aloud about the thinking that accompanies the process: topic choice, how to start the piece, lining out, looking for a better word, etc. Children merely select those elements from the teacher's composing that are relevant to their own writing. The teacher does not say, "Now

this is the way I write, you write this way," since the teacher cannot anticipate what is appropriate for each child. The following are three ways to model
writing.

Three Ways to Model Writing

The first and easiest way has already been mentioned in the previous chapter, merely sit down and write when the children do. In this instance, choose
the first five minutes of the beginning of the writing period to write yourself.
This is a time when the class is not to bother you as you compose. You might
tell the class *what* you are going to write about and *why* you chose the topic.
Telling the class in advance about your writing does two things: (1) It helps
them to realize there is a *process of choosing*. It is even better if you share two
other topics you decided not to write about today, and why you have chosen this
particular one. Also, tell the class how you even came up with the three. (2) It
takes the abstractness out of your activity. Children interrupt for many
reasons, but the chief reason is that they don't believe you are doing anything
significant when you are not working with them. The delay also gives them
time to find that *many of their problems can be solved without you.*

Large Sheets of Paper

Take large sheets of paper and clip them to an easel or bind them with clamps
mounted on a tripod. Large sheets of newsprint also work for this exercise.
You need paper large enough for the entire class to be able to read your
writing as you compose. The paper should be large enough to contain at least
four sentences on one side.

Overhead Projector

Write on an acetate roll, or single sheet of acetate clamped onto the overhead
projector. In this way the children can watch your words unfold on a screen or
wall where all can see it in the room. Some teachers find it easier to compose
on the overhead because they can "look down" on the flat acetate as opposed to
composing before the class on the vertical easel. It is easier to control the
writing on the overhead. Younger children, however, particularly those up
through age nine or ten, enjoy the more open composing on the large sheets of
paper. Having the full person in view, as opposed to sitting at the overhead,
provides a more intimate medium for some children. This is not a critical
issue, since what is most important is for children to observe the writing
process.

The Composing Session

The objective of composing before children is to make explicit what children
ordinarily can't see: how words go down on paper, and the thoughts that go
with the decisions made in the writing. Thus, the teacher writes so the
children can see the words, and gives a running monologue of the thinking
that goes with the writing. The following is an example of composing before
the class.

Choosing the Topic

This morning I've been wondering what to write about. Here are three topics that I've wanted to know more about. You see, when I write I find out things I didn't know before. The three topics are these:

"When I Got Mad When I Was in Sixth Grade"
"My First Air Raid"
"My First Fight"

The first topic is about a very embarrassing moment when I was in sixth grade. When I'm embarrassed I sometimes get angry. Did it ever happen to you that you were the only one in the room that something happened to? Well, that happened to me when I was in sixth grade.

The second topic also happened when I was in sixth grade. My, that must have been some year! When I was eleven years old the war broke out between the United States, Germany, and Japan. The third day of the war, unidentified planes were picked up off the coast of Canada. The military thought they might be German planes, so the principal closed the school right in the middle of the day. All the boys were excited because this was war, real war. I felt very brave until I got home and found that my mother wasn't there. I panicked.

The third topic happened when I was in third grade. A boy had pushed me around, and I was scared to death because he was a lot tougher than I was. I worried and worried and finally decided I couldn't let it pass by and would stand up to him on the way home from school. It didn't turn out to be much of a fight.

Now that I've told you about these topics, the one I've chosen to write about is the first one. Sometimes when I tell about what I'm going to write about, I can feel, just by talking, which is the one I want to write about most. Before I talk I don't necessarily know. The first thing I'm going to do is "brainstorm" a little bit. When I brainstorm I just write any old thing that comes into my head about what happened. I'll write these words or phrases down quickly up here now and come back and tell you about them afterwards:

Miss Fortin
Sixth Grade
Irish
Italians
"Raise you hands"
Social studies
French
Geography
Only one in the room
Watched as the hands went up
In the back of the room, second from end
Social studies books
Mother—shouting
"What's wrong with us."

Miss Fortin was our sixth grade teacher. I've had a surprise in writing down this list. It really isn't that important, I suppose, but I remember exactly where I sat in that sixth grade room. Can you ever remember things like that? I'll bet you can. I remembered, so I wrote it down. The details make you feel like you're right there, I think. Now I'm going to write:

Composing

(On the left side is the running commentary with the children; on the right side the actual words written before the class.)

Comment	*Writing*
When I write this I'm going to try to tell it in order, like what came first, second.	
	Miss Fortin, our sixth grade teacher, stood up at the front of the room. She had our social studies book in her hand. She said, "I wonder how many of you have relatives who come from another country. I'm going to name some countries and if someone from your family came from there, raise your hand."
When Miss Fortin said that I went blank. I remember feeling so funny inside. Do you think how I felt belongs here?	
(Usually the class wants very much to know how the teacher feels about something, especially if it has really happened.)	
	"Italy," said Miss Fortin. About seven children raised their hands. I was sitting in the back of the room, about the second seat from the end, and could see everyone and how they put their hands up. I felt horrible; I couldn't think of anyone from another country. "Ireland." This took another ten children with hands up. I took another look at the kids. Wasn't there someone who looked nervous? I desperately wanted someone to look afraid like me. "France," said Miss Fortin. As soon as she said that, she put up her own hand and about five other children joined her. There were three of us left. I felt so stupid. Why did our family have to be so dumb? Three other kids, Richard Costa and Elizabeth Lindberg and David Nichols hadn't raised their hands.

Writing

"England," said Miss Fortin. No one raised his hand. She looked at me when she said England. But I couldn't raise my hand. I didn't have anyone from England.

"Portugal," said Miss Fortin, and Richard Costa zoomed his hand into the air. I knew what was next, Elizabeth Lindberg and her cousin, David Nichols, were from Sweden. All was lost. I was the only one; I could feel the other kids looking at this stupid fool who wasn't from anywhere.

Comments After Composing

"Now that you've had a chance to read this, are there some other things you'd like to know, some things perhaps you feel ought to be included to make it more interesting?"

"Did the other kids laugh at you?"

"I'm not sure. I don't think they laughed, but I just had a funny feeling I thought they were. (To the group) Do you think I should include that?" A number in the group may say "Yes," others, "No." If there is a split opinion, I'd get the arguments from both sides. The children continue with questions.

"Well, what nationality were you then? Where did you come from?"

"Oh, thank you for the question. I didn't really say that, did I. The answer is that my ancestors came over on the Mayflower on both my mother's and father's sides. I knew that, but to me that didn't count as being an immigrant. I wanted to be the child of an immigrant family. You see, we were studying all about different nationalities who came to the United States from all over the world. I wanted to be part of those groups. I felt like just a common American. Do you think some of this belongs in the piece?"

"Yes, the part about you feeling you couldn't say England and you wanted to be from an immigrant family."

"All right, where would I put it? Perhaps two or three of you would come up and see if you can agree on where I should put it." Three of the children briefly discussed where it should go. This was an easier decision since the new material was merely added to the end of the piece.

In this instance, I have used choice of topic, general flow, and use of information to model with the children. On another occasion I might wrestle with word choice, lining out words, inserting information. I might leave out a main, unanswered situation that belongs in the middle, and then see if the children can determine where the information should go. Then I'd make a sign or number to indicate the insertion point and write the needed sentences in the margin.

When I compose on the overhead or on large paper, I write slowly, often saying the words a few ahead of what I might write to give the children an advance glimpse of what is coming. I might just stop and say, "I'm stuck. I don't know what to say next. I think I'll read this aloud to feel where I am." Sometimes when I read it aloud, I will stop and ask the children to ask me questions about *what they want to know next*. Thus, I am modeling questions they can ask each other when they are stuck in their writing.

Modeling opportunities are infinite. I don't expect children to immediately apply what has been shown. There is no one-to-one expectation: here it is in the modeling session, now do it. And some might argue that immediate reinforcement is necessary. I would argue that control, choice *over a long period of time* is the more lasting for the child. Modeling provides many opportunities for choice and for a wide range of development within the classroom. Note the range in the modeling session just completed:

Choice of topic
How the writing will go down: chronological order
Brainstorming
Surprises in the brainstorming
Putting feelings into writing
Writing about what you know
Process of recalling experiences
Can't remember everything the first time
Consult others for help
Where should new information go
There can be reasons for *not* putting in information
as well as *for* putting it in
Writers help each other.

Different conceptual levels are represented within each of these categories. Take *choice of topic*. The modeling may only show that there *can be* a process of choosing a topic. Sometimes there are several choices, at others, only one. The idea that speaking and voice help in topic selection is a little more advanced. Finally, the idea that you write to find out more about a topic is much more advanced. Each of these concepts is built into the modeling approach. I didn't *know* they were there. I only know them now as I review and compose this chapter. As long as children do not have to apply one-to-one content from the modeling, they will use elements from the modeling that the teacher may not have known were part of the demonstration. In short, there is a basic trust here that children *take what they need* within a classroom which is structured to help children teach what they know through their writing.

Leo Tolstoy, in his journal kept for the school he ran at Yasnaya Polyana, tells of a day when he asked the children to take out their paper to prepare to write. To his surprise the children said, "We're sick of writing, it's your turn." Tolstoy thought for a minute, then decided the children might have something in their request. He sat down at his desk and asked, "Well, what should I write about?" The children said, "Write about a boy who steals." Excitedly the children gathered round his desk while the don of the Russian intelligentsia, admired writer of *The Cossacks*, began to compose. Immediately, these peasant children corrected him saying, "No, a boy wouldn't do this; he'd do that." "You know," said Tolstoy, "they were right." Tolstoy was so astonished at the children's insights that he wrote his memorable essay, "Are We to Teach the Peasant Children to Write, or Are They to Teach Us?"

Children select skills in modeling more easily because they are shown within the context of natural predicaments. Modeling can never be a substitute for the solution to children's own predicaments. It can, however, be a referral point for confirming what children themselves go through. "Remember the other day when I was struggling for a topic? I noticed that you just read this aloud to see which one was right for you. Did it work?" The teacher does not use modeling to beat the child over the head with a new skill. Rather, the teacher uses the modeling to confirm the commonality of all writers, as well as to confirm new approaches by the child in the writing process.

Modeling helps teachers understand their own writing. Because they model various elements of the writing process, they will know what to observe in the children. They see differently because they have been through the writing process, composing the words before the children.

Modeling changes my relationship with a class. We become writers together when blocks become problems to be solved rather than sinful errors. Writing becomes a process of sharing what we know about our experiences. The class becomes a community because we possess a growing fund of facts about each other's experiences. Strangers don't work well alone. When a class becomes a community, its members learn to help and model for each other.

15. A Case Study Observing the Development of Primary Children's Composing, Spelling, and Motor Behaviors during the Writing Process

(National Institute of Education Report)

Introduction

In December 1981, I received a call from Marcia Farr, my program director at the National Institute of Education. Marcia had been a patient person all during our study on the composing processes of young children in Atkinson, New Hampshire. Now she was impatient. The final report had to be completed by February. Although I had been working on the final data for the study while on sabbatical in Scotland from August 1980 until May 1981, and on through the fall of 1981, I hadn't actually begun the formal writing of the final report. My book, *Writing: Teachers and Children at Work,* was still undergoing final work and it was important for that to stay on track. I remember Marcia's final statement, "I hope I won't ruin your Christmas." I knew that I had to put everything aside and go full tilt on the NIE report. I remember Don Murray's quip, "You'll easily finish this by the first of January."

"Like Hell," I said to myself. "That's if Murray were writing it that it would be done by the first of January." I knew there were many "out there" who were eagerly awaiting the final report from our study. "Yes, " I said to myself, "what the Hell did we find, anyway?" We had already written some twenty-three articles and given innumerable workshops and addresses around the world, and now I had to say what we finally found. How hard it was to make the final judgment about our findings. Furthermore, I wanted to write the report in simple, direct prose for a wide readership. I knew that it would make for a better report, but it would also make the writing much more difficult.

On December 29, I started a daily journal for the next year. I don't have entries for the early part of the report-writing during Christmas vacation in 1981, and by December 30 I had only gotten as far as the section on findings, the most difficult part of the entire report. These entries are from my journal:

December 30, 1981
To work at 6:00 a.m. Determined to complete a good lick on the NIE report. Worked at home most of the day and stayed at it. Very hard going, but I have some very concentrated stuff on paper. Discovered for me the obvious—the writing process is made up of many other processes, not components in a unit sense, but each of these is a process:

Topic Choice	Speech to print
Rehearsal	Speak

Spelling   Listen
Handwriting
Selection—finding access to the information
Word choice   Rereading
Organization
Revising

Each of these solves a sequence of problems—each has its own discrepancy depending on the writer's level of development; of course, level only determines the *potential* problem-solving level of the child. *Actual* performing level is so dependent on the *challenge* within the environment; challenge has to be within the perceptual and interest range of the child. This is why teachers need some sense of both the ingredients, the process of ingredients, and the axes of development. Many know this instinctively.

Got up through the section on egocentric—sociocentric in NIE report. This was exceptional progress for me.

January 1, 1982
After a slow start I wrote three and one half pages of very tough stuff on revision. *I am pleased!*

January 4, 1982
1:00 p.m. Three hours in on concept and some *good headway*. Will be time well spent because the writing can also count for my chapter on the book. I will work some more this p.m. as I had some *good momentum* when I stopped. Later, I will write for an hour and see what is still there.

Seven and one half pages in on concept and some pretty good stuff in it.

January 8, 1982
Well, it's to work on NIE at 8. I won't even take time to write what I need to do; I'll just do it!! I did it. Pretty well finished the section on "scaffolding." Well condensed and I'm fairly secure both on the data and the way I got it down. Of course, it is all based on Susan Sowers's work. It is one of the most important findings in the study. A good feeling to be back on track with the report. Bodes well for Saturday. Tomorrow I'll do a schedule for finishing.

January 9, 1982—Saturday
Today I have high hopes for NIE (4 hours). What else? But I also have three other projects: 1) My 880 course. 2) Job descriptions for the church. 3) Outlining three talks for the University of Michigan.

A good sequence done on transition from oral to written discourse. As always, new data arrangements emerge whenever I try to classify them. *But*, I didn't get as far as I needed to.

January 11, 1982
Met my first objective. Finished the section on spelling.

January 15, 1982
Only got an hour in on NIE material on punctuation but made good headway. Just shows how much can be done with good focus. A lesson that shows how *important* it is to just get even fifteen minutes in on something but not to break the rhythm of writing every day.

January 16, 1982—Saturday
Worked on Becky's and Virginia's findings—got stuck without exact quotes. Now that I've gone over Becky's data, I don't know how she reached her conclusions. I'll have to meet with her to find out. Virginia's data are strong and I know her process. There is good data here but relating Becky's section with Virginia's is just a bit mystifying. Got to rethink it. Anyway, I feel pretty discouraged about it all tonight. There are times when you feel so much like a fraud. How hard it is to be true to data.

January 17, 1982—Sunday

I'm finally at work on revising the NIE report—got through to page 30 by 8:30 p.m. Didn't really roll until about 4:00 p.m.

January 21, 1982

I keep thinking I'll feel better when this NIE report goes off. Laura has finished typing it now. Well, a good morning. I wrote a long letter of transmittal to Marcia (Farr) and then worked on the appendix. I know how it will be handled. I also spoke with Marcia and she is delighted to know how the study is going and that she will have a summary of our findings to use in her report. I felt a great release from all of the burdens connected with this NIE report. It has been so *long* since I have felt *any kind* of release! It is what it must be like to get out of jail.

February 6, 1982

Hard to get going this morning. Edited the summary of findings again. Not as much for Laura to retype as I had expected. Then I turned to writing the implications of findings for teachers. This is a most important section for teachers . . . and for me. I worked for about three hours on it. The words came slowly—got down about 1,000 words but with much revision to go. I must finish this cuss by tomorrow. If I can get some more in motion for tonight that will be a big help and get me going first thing in the morning. Yes, a good idea. Still, some good insights are coming to me about the essentials.

February 7, 1982

Writing went well. Three pages in an hour and a quarter. The words were rolling and I think the content good. I'll go over what I've done and smooth it out later. Much rewriting to do on this very important section.

February 10, 1982

Worked hard on data implications—wrote and rewrote two pages and it is just tough going. Jane and I chatted about data and implications, similarities and differences in data and the problems research presents to teachers—the very thing I was working on with my implications section this morning.

The section that I discussed with Jane Hansen was for me one of the most important findings about research. One of the depressing things about looking over our data to this point had been the incredible range of exceptions that each child presented in the study. In short, the more I focused on each child's data, the more exceptions the child presented. Somewhere around February 10 (and I didn't notice any entry about this in my journal) I suddenly realized the purpose of research. Heretofore, I had always thought that the purpose of research was to show similarities in human beings. That is, if I saw something in John, I would look to see if the same was true in Alison and Henry. After all, isn't the purpose of research to generalize? Well, it is, but that is only half the contribution of research. My big insight at this point was that research enables us to see similarities in human beings, but only as a first step to seeing the true differences that are present in every person. My hunch is that this finding is anathema to statisticians and experimentalists. Such findings (in the line of exceptions) are only seen when human beings are observed over long periods of time. I am sure that many will debate this, and the debate could be very healthy. To this point, however, this single finding about research itself is shaping more of my future views of research than any other.

What Did This Study Set Out to Do and Why?

This study set out to document *what* primary children did when they wrote.*
Data were gathered over a two-year period, following the same children, ir
order to show how they changed what they did in the course of writing. The
research task was to be present when the children wrote in their classrooms
and to record, describe, identify, and sequence the order of their behaviors
during the composing process.

The study was done because children simply haven't been observed while
writing. Most research about children's composing has been retrospective
Extensive analyses have been made of children's written products, and inter
views have been given to children asking them to recall how they wrote, but
such data only provide partial information about what might happen in the
writing process.

Worse, school curricula across the country are often based on suppositions
about what children do when they write. Teaching is an active process where
teacher behaviors meet child behaviors, yet why children behave as they do
when composing is anyone's guess if there hasn't been systematic observa
tion over time. Teachers need a forward and backward perspective when they
deal with a child's paper; they need to know where the child will be going and
where the child has been developmentally in order to understand the behav
iors of the present moment.

It would be unheard of in child development research to explain child
behavior solely on an interventive or retrospective basis. There is no substi
tute for *being there*, for extensive periods of observation to record data wher
children play, interact with parents, materials, and their entire environ
ment.

How Did We Go About Doing It?

Sixteen children in five different classrooms in the same, small, rural
suburban school in New Hampshire were observed for two years. Eight of the
children were observed from age six through seven, and eight from age eight
through nine. The children were chosen because of their differences along
pre-selected criteria of language, composing, spelling, and motor perfor
mance. The intent was to have children from both grade levels with low
middle, and high writing abilities in order to see if behaviors from one level to
another were repeated as the children changed over two years of writing.

Three researchers were on-site in classrooms four days out of five for the
two year project. Data were gathered through child and teacher interviews
direct observation of children through specific protocols, video recordings o
children while composing, conversing with other children, and in conference
as well as through all of the children's written products.

Although case-study data were gathered primarily on the sixteen selected

---

*What is contained here is the introduction covering the main findings of the study
The full report, including articles and appendices, may be purchased from the Writin
Process Lab., University of New Hampshire, Durham NH 03824.

children, there were many intervals over the two year period when these children were not writing. Researchers then collected data on other children who were writing at that time. There were also all-class data gathered in punctuation and spelling to serve as back-up information to process data from the case studies.

The data were analyzed through a variety of procedures depending on the type of information collected.

1. *Video Data*: Language and behavior analysis in relation to evolving text was done by set protocol. Charts were made of shifting balances over a two year period. Utterances were assessed in context for concept level and change.
2. *Child Utterance Data*: These came from video-audio recordings, observations of teacher conferences, and discussions with other children. Data were analyzed according to 26 concepts. Definitions of concepts came from children's utterances. Extensive work with inter-rater reliability was done at *several points* in the assessment of concepts.
3. *Direct Observation*: Through set protocols, all sixteen children were observed before, during, and after composing. Behaviors were charted to show shifts in:
   A. Overt to covert activity
   B. Growth in time and space
   C. Uses of revision
   D. Problem solving
4. *Product Data*: All written work from the children was xeroxed. This included all copies of drafts. Product data have been charted to show changes in use of:
   A. Punctuation
   B. Handwriting
   C. Spelling
   D. Topic
   E. Patterns of writing quality
   F. Prosodics
   G. Person and territory
   H. Information
5. *Interview-Conference Data*: Interventions along standard, informal question formats were asked of the children before, during, and after composing by researchers and teachers. Questions and responses have been placed on computer and analyzed for complexity, sequence, and function along the 26 concept lines.

Substantial analysis of the above data is complete, but because of the amount gathered, there is virtually an inexhaustible supply of new variables yet to be examined, as well as possible interrelationships between those variables already investigated.

What Did We Find?

The Writing Process

The writing process in this study was defined as a series of operations leading to the solution of a problem. The process begins when the writer consciously or unconsciously starts a topic and is finished when the written piece is published. Many professionals would argue that the process continues to throb even after publication.

Children show us what is involved in the writing process through the many sub-processes that contribute to a finished product. Significant sub-processes include topic selection, rehearsing, information access, spelling, handwriting, reading, organizing, editing, and revising. These ingredients for writing are much the same for six-year-olds as they are for more advanced ten-year-olds. Six-year-olds, because of overt behaviors, show the underpinnings of ingredients before they go underground and become implicit. The following defines several important ingredients:

1. *Topic Choice* – There is a process to topic selection, again, conscious or unconscious. Choice can be limited to a topic on the board given by the teacher, or it may be embedded in a previous piece. The child may go on a search through interviews with other children, or through reviewing a list in a folder labeled "future topics." When topics are self-selected, part of the process seems to be "voice-matching" with what feels right today; the child measures intentions against his audience, which may be his classmates, teacher, or even parents. Choice may also involve weeks, months, or it may be a snap judgment based on a whim. More needs to be studied about topic choice because it probably has much more to do with subsequent behaviors in writing than we know.

2. *Rehearsal* – Rehearsal refers to the conscious or unconscious preparation writers make for what is to follow. It may take the form of daydreaming, reading, sketching, working with blocks, journal entries, or discussion of events. A discovery draft can be spoken of as a rehearsal for the next draft.

3. *Composing* – Composing includes selection of information, mechanics, the part in relation to the whole. The part may be letter formation, sound-symbol correspondence, the final stage of Vygotsky's process of symbolization, or reading for orientation.

4. *Reading* – The function of reading the writer's own text varies according to the developmental level of the writer and differs significantly from the reading of another person's text. The writer can read to reorient, search for errors in conventions, and check appropriateness of information, organization, or language.

5. *Revision* – Revision, or "seeing again" ranges from simple adjustments in spelling and letter formation, to major additions, deletions, and reorganizations of information. At the lowest level it could be called proofreading.

There is no set order to the writing process. It cannot be construed as simply a matter of topic choice, rehearsal, reading, composing, and revising. It is highly idiosyncratic and varies within the writer from day to day. A person may discover a new topic in the midst of writing another. The end of a piece may be rehearsed while eating breakfast, especially if the writer knows she will be writing that day in school. Thus, the unearthing of process ingredients and their recurrent appearance is an important finding in this study.

Development of writers

The development of writing ability among the children appeared to fall into sequences. These sequences were useful to trace, but great care had to be taken to view several simultaneously before making any decisions about the child's writing development. The following are among the most significant sequences used to trace changes in writers' behaviors.

Time and Space: This was the most fruitful combination of factors by which to assess the development of young writers. Three factors were viewed in relation to each other.

1. *The Page*: At first children must discover the use of space, or how to relate their bodies and small muscles to a regular sequencing (time) across the page. Letter follows letter, ranging from indiscriminate chains to vertical and reverse orders. Later, when children see writing as a temporary process, as in a draft, they begin to break down the sides, placing extra symbols as direction markers for the next draft.

2. *The Process*: The parameters of process define space, while the events from start to finish represent time markers filling that space. When the process parameters are narrow, writing has a tenuous connection to preceding events; the decision to compose may have been spontaneous, but of very short duration, perhaps as little as two or three minutes. In this case, process resembles spontaneous play. Process broadens when the writer rehearses when not composing, contemplates a piece for weeks or months, and composes many drafts prior to publication. This writer can transcend the constraints of the present draft; he can move back and forth between past, present, and possible future products.

3. *Information*: Early information has tenuous logic (time) and occupies little space (the subject or event). The simplicity of the choices connects highly disparate events and fills the subject space with only a few lines.

External to Internal: Writing is a highly external event in the beginning. Children draw, and talk with other children. They need to see and hear what they mean. Later external language becomes inner language. The child has put mechanical conventions (spelling, motor) behind him. Problem-solving shifts to topic and information and is particularly done with the absence of overt behaviors.

Egocentric to Sociocentric: Early writing closely resembles play. The child writes for the sake of writing. The opinions of others about the quality of his work are not heard. He feels his pieces are basically good and he experiments fearlessly. Seldom does the teacher hear, "I'm stuck. I don't know what to do." The child sees little discrepancy between intention and performance.

Gradually, however, the child begins to hear questions and concerns of others. Mechanics are placed behind him and his own critical reading level is raised. He perceives discrepancies between his message and what is understood.

Explicit to Implicit: When children first write, they bring their papers to the teacher and before she can read them, they tell her what the papers say. The child makes the message explicit through conversation and also through accompanying drawings. They supply what they think may be missing in print.

In transition from oral to written discourse, children include many oral features (prosodics) in their pieces. In later stages they put everything into the message (bed to bed story) with little selection or valuing given to the narrative.

Children eventually create more meaning through heightening certain pieces of information and excluding others. They raise the level of reader participation by implying meanings, suspending action, and using words with greater precision and economy.

At first then, the pieces were shorter with logical gaps, then expanded to an overtold level. As writing became more implicit, the pieces were contracted to a level of greater meaning.

The Process of Development and Revision

Children show us what they see when they change something. The child notices a discrepancy between intention and a letter, word, or sentence, and makes a change depending on what he thinks is important in the writing process. Thus children's writing development can be monitored by recording the changes they make while composing.

In our study, problem-solving was broken into five categories: spelling, motor/aesthetic (appearance on the page), convention, (marking off meaning units with spaces, punctuation), topic/information, and revision. These categories are common to any act of writing, and when the children first began to write, they functioned in all of them. The children were unaware of most of the problems they solved, especially those placed in the "automatic" category. A child who revised extensively, for instance, was hardly aware of spelling unless he found a particular word difficult to spell. Problem-solving became a conscious act when the child spoke out loud of his intention to make a change in his piece.

The following figure shows the sequence of problem-solving categories and the relationship of unconscious to conscious activity. The diagonal lines indicate when a category was dominant, or part of the child's consciousness. The white areas show when that activity was "underground" or unconscious. There are no ages assigned to these categories because they are irrelevant. There is evidence that some six-year-olds may go as far as category V in one year, while, on the other hand, some writers because of development or teaching emphasis, may never get beyond the first three categories in four years. The self-diagnosed poor speller or handwriter may go for a lifetime wrestling with the same difficulties.

Figure 15.1.   The Sequence of Problem Solving During the Writing Process

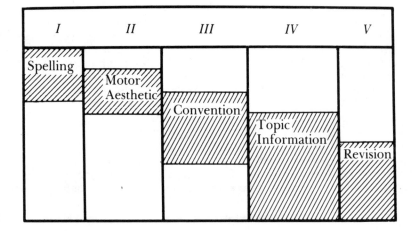

The order of problem-solving follows the above five categories. Children first changed spelling, almost simultaneously letter formation and aesthetics, conventions, then topic and information. Problem-solving takes on greater significance when in topic and information.

One way children show us general trends in development is by where they place information when adding to a draft. The easiest place to add information is at the end. It is the most visible, most recently completed and there is room at the bottom of the page. The beginning of the piece is the next choice. It is a recapping of a personal narrative and there may also be room at the top of the page. How a piece starts is clearer than after it gets underway. The interior of the narrative, however, is the most difficult place to add information. Adding information in the middle demands a strong sense of chronology and logic. The child must understand what has come before and after the information being inserted into the text.

Calkins has shown us in our study of revision with eight-year-old children that revision begins with the addition of information at the end of a child's piece. From this data four categories of eight-year-old revisors emerged:

  I. Writes successive drafts without looking back to earlier drafts. Does not reread, or reconsider what has been written and therefore does not weigh options. Much of the writing is left unfinished. New information can only be added at the end.
 II. Can refine an early draft but refinement is of minor consequence with some changes in spelling or punctuation. Content and structure of piece remain unchanged. Will at least reread piece and come up with new information, but cannot insert it into text.
III. Keeps shifting between refining and abandoning and beginning new drafts, as in category II. Is extemely restless; reading level leaves the child dissatisfied with his text but he seems powerless to move to a level of personal satisfaction. The child can add information into the interior of text. This child is in transition to category IV.
 IV. Revision results from interaction between writer and draft, internalized audience, and the evolving subject. Does reread to see what he has said and to discover what he wants to say. There is a constant vying between intended meaning and discovered meaning, between the forward motion of making and the backward motion of assessing. Can insert any information into text, make major reorganizations, line out, use symbols to manipulate information, and can see information as temporary, moving *toward meaning*.

Some advanced writers scarcely revised at all. They had such a well-developed inner language, had internalized so many thinking schemes, and were so strongly oriented in the process and information components of time and space, that their revisions occurred internally. How extensive these internal revisions were remains unknown. One eight-year-old, for example, wrote, "A cheetah would make a sports car look like a turtle," as her lead to a piece on cheetahs. At the time of the writing, the researcher could perceive no external language, drawing, or assistance of any kind. Later, in the second year of the study, this same child was advanced enough to articulate some of her thinking processes to Calkins.

Further evidence of internalization of the revision process was seen in the category IV children in the second year of the study. Their drafts were fewer, their first drafts were of higher quality, and decisions about changes were made earlier, at the point of topic selection or lead composition. As will be seen in the concept data, these same children became much more articulate about their composing processes. Their ability to explain the writing process increased as they externalized less in their drafts.

Concepts

All of the children's utterances over the two-year period were classified by concept with the exception of .029 that were too ambiguous to classify. Ambiguity was greatly reduced because the utterances fell in the midst of other data gathered during the writing process or conferences with teacher or researcher.

The following concepts were identified:

Standard	*Audience interest (self)
Process	Audience interest (others)
Information	Audience—clarify
Information selection	Audience—clarify—others
Information addition	*Audience—no need to consider
Information deletion	*Neatness
Experience	Mechanics
Experience verification	Drawing
Audience	Feelings
Motivation	Topic
*Action	Language
Action—sequence of	Length
Action—frequency of	*Length—needs to be shorter
Organization	*Length—needs to be longer

Although many years' work on the concept data is still needed, several categories of concept research emerged from this study:

1. Definitions of concepts
2. Which concepts are used
3. General orders of concept use
4. Changes in concept density
5. Profile of one concept: topic
6. Interrelationships of concepts

*These concepts did not provide enough information to make statements across the children. They did, however, provide enough to begin a concept profile. For example, "No need to consider audience" was thin in data across the children, but polarized at one end of the spectrum to show that just six and seven-year-olds cited it.

Concept Definitions

A major finding was simply the definitions of concepts. Because of their slippery nature, six months work went into the defining phase. The stability of definitions was then checked on several inter-rater reliability assessments.

Several of the concepts still need to be broken down into other concepts because their definitions need further delineation.* I particularly refer to the five concepts used most frequently and listed below. The number in parentheses indicates the percentage of total utterances which use the concept:

Process–21% (136)	Topic–7% (445)
Standard–15% (601)	Organization–5% (345)
Information–9% (601)	

What Concepts are Used

What concepts the children attended to as well as ignored gave an interesting picture of where they were in the understanding of the writing process. Susie, age 8-9, made very many statements about feelings, standards and organization, but she made very few about drawing or the need for greater length. On the other hand, she uses just about all of the 27 concepts. Six-year-old John talks about information, topic, and drawing, but he doesn't make any statements about audience or language. Thus, although some generalizations can be made across children, the more significant data lies *within* children. More work needs to be done in this area. Each concept needs to be broken down into hierarchies. The higher level utterances will show more clearly if they are placed in chronological order.

General Order of Concept Use

If all data on concepts across six, seven, eight and nine-year-old children are combined, a number of trends are apparent:

1. The heaviest use of *drawing* concept is with six-year-olds and it decreases with each successive year.
2. Statements about *organization* increase with each year from six through nine.
3. Six and seven-year-olds use very few statements about *language*. Eight and nine-year-olds, especially those into revision, speak about language and its more precise use.
4. Eight and nine-year-olds make many more statements proportionately about *feelings* than six and seven-year-old children. As the characters become more developed in writing, or as they recall more details of personal experience, more feelings are cited.

*For example, process could be broken down into concepts of various phases of the writing process. When does the child use rehearsal, specific problem-solving strategies?

5. The sequencing of *action* is much more important to six and seven-year-olds than eight and nine-year-olds. The early development of narrative would require this, whereas with older children their pieces have become more selective, indeed, some of the chronologies changed by the advanced writers.

Concept Density

Children seldom make utterances with only one concept involved. Those who do are generally six years of age, as in the simple process statement, "I'm going to finish this today." A more advanced nine-year-old writer, on the other hand, will make statements that are much more dense with writing concepts as in this spontaneous statement by Andrea:

I thought the first (lead) was good but I think   (SD)
this was even better and now I'm going to keep   (SD)
going until I find one I really like and I may
take parts of each one but after my Dad takes a   (P) (IS)
shower, my mother does and she wears a flowered   (O)
robe—but I don't know if that is important to   (T)
my story. I'll put lots of different things for
how I could put my father on the sofa and after   (IS)
I'll choose.

Andrea's statement contained the following concepts: standard (SD), information selection (IS), organization (O), topic (T), process (P), and information selection again (IS). There is also much overlap; in the same breath, Andrea expressed information selection within the writing process. The more advanced children became, the more they expressed reasons for their choices and the more concepts became embedded in each other. Notice how Brian's concepts changed over two years:

Percentage of Concepts per Utterance
by Semester

	Fall '78	n	Spring '79	n	Fall '79	n	Spring '80	n
1 concept or more	100	11	100	15	100	76	100	105
2 concepts or more	82	9	87	13	88	67	88	92
3 concepts or more	27	3	33	5	56	43	67	70
4 concepts or more	0	0	20	3	31	24	31	23
5 concepts or more	0	0	7	1	1	1	3	4
6 concepts or more	0	0	7	1	1	1	3	4
7 concepts	0	0	0	0	1	1	3	3

Although Brian was not speaking nearly as much in the first year of the study, perhaps it is all the more significant that with a higher volume of statements about writing, his percentages of concept embeddings increased during the second year.

Profile of a Concept—Topic

One of the 27 concepts, topic, was examined in the context of utterances to determine a profile of high and low limits of the concept, and to come up with categories that differentiated the levels of concept use. The 445 statements were ordered according to rough criteria for determining hierarchies. Ultimately all of the concepts will be ordered chronologically as well as by level, to produce a clearer profile of concept use.

The following are characteristic of four levels of topic concepts:

I. The topic is the story. The child must relate the entire story if asked what his piece is about. The child cannot identify the topic separate from the story. Q.: "What is your piece about?" A.: "The cowboy will climb on his horse and ride the road to town and . . ."

II. The topic is what the story is about. The child specifies topic/title and goes on to recite the story. The child can name a topic. Q.: "What is your piece about?" A.: "It's going to be about a cowboy. He'll climb on his horse and ride the road to town and . . ." The topic occurs to the child and the story follows.

III. The topic controls the story. The child selects information to fit the topic. The child uses concept of topic with one other writing concept. Q.: "What's your piece going to be about?" A.: "It's going to be only about Cowboy Sam and his riding adventures, not about what he does on the ranch . . ." Child selects topic, and the story follows, but the child expresses beginnings of options.

IV. The story controls the topic. The child selects the topic based on a writing logic. The child integrates concept of topic with other writing concepts. Q.: "What are you going to write about?" A.: "I'm going to write about Cowboy Sam's riding adventures because I can put some action with good details in . . . but part way through I might find out some new stuff and I'll have to revise things." The topic evolves, twists and turns as the child is responsive to the dictates of the information.

Scaffolding

The term scaffolding was first used by Jerome Bruner to explain temporary structures placed around children's language to assist their development. Susan Sowers, research associate on the NIE study team, took teacher-child conference data and examined them in light of the following characteristics deemed important in scaffolding:

1. Response should be predictable.
2. Limit the focus.
3. Allow for reversible role relationships.
4. Demonstrate solutions.
5. Limit and "make familiar the semantic domain."
6. Maintain a playful atmosphere.

The conference in our study refers to the discussion-review of a child's paper with the teacher, researcher, or other child in the room. From hundreds of conference transcripts, and the printouts of concept data from language interactions, the following hypotheses have been formulated about successful conferences based on the scaffolding concept:

1. Writing conferences follow *predictable sequences*: content discussion is followed by a discussion of mechanics. Often readers ask the writer for an evaluation of the piece, "Which is the best part?" "How does it compare with others you have written?" As part of our data gathering, children were asked to tell what happened in conference or simulate the conference with another child. Children of both high and low developmental levels from six through ten were able to relate the basic elements contained in conference.

2. Teachers *limit the focus* and mark critical features in the conference. It is rare when more than one skill or one major aspect of the child's information are chosen for discussion.

3. Conferences allow for *reversible role relationships* between speaker and hearer. Because conference structures are predictable, the child knows how to reverse roles. He asks questions of the teacher and makes comments about content or skills in anticipation of teacher practice. Children are also able to conduct conferences with each other, independently of the teacher. There are as well instances where children have conducted conferences with themselves, "Let's see now, this beginning doesn't have enough action in it. What do I want it to be about?"

4. *Demonstrate solutions*: Through the oral conference with child, teacher and paper present, it was possible to show within the limited focus how to solve problems. Most of the teachers waited for the child to encounter voice or a problem before moving into solution demonstrations. Frequently the children were able to invent solutions without teacher demonstration.

5. *Limit and Make Familiar the Semantic Domain*. Children chose about 90% of their own topics, thus making it easier for teachers to control the semantic domain. The language of process was introduced slowly and within the context of the child's paper. This is probably why the concept-semantic densities of childrens' statements about writing changed so rapidly.

6. *Playful atmosphere*. A high degree of humor persists in conferences. The playful, humor-filled atmosphere prevails because of predictability, role-reversals, limited focus, and the highly familiar semantic domain.

Transitions from Oral to Written Discourse

Every child and possibly many professional writers, makes the transition at his level from oral to written discourse. Four stages of transition were apparent in the study and are listed below. Transition factors are closely allied with what writers call "voice," the writer's individual imprint on the piece.

I – Overt and Early Manifestations of Speech

1. *Speaking simultaneous to the writing*. For every grapheme, children will use about 20 phonemic units, plus eight other language functions.

2. *Para-language and the paper*. Children continue to use a wide repertoire of kinesics, haptics, and proxemics in relation to the paper. These are usually accompanied by sound effects, particularly with boys.

3. *Drawing*. The child supplies visual context (as in speech) through drawing. The child draws before writing.

4. *Letters and words run together.* There are fewer breaks for meaning and thus resembles oral discourse.
5. *Prosodics in capitalization and blackened letters, mixture of upper and lower case letters.* These become much more sophisticated in Stage II, then are significantly reduced in Stage III.

II – Page Explicit Transitions

1. *Speaking simultaneous to the writing.* There is far less overtness of a speaking or sounding nature as in Stage I. Transition factors are shown in what happens on the page.
2. *Drawing.* The child may draw *after* writing. The drawing now is more of an illustration than a rehearsal, thus losing the speech transition factor.
3. *Prosodics.* Many more capitalizations for speech meaning function, use of blackened letters, stress words written two lines high, sometimes underlined. Particular use of interjections, exclamation and quotation marks. The child wants sound to be read from the page.
4. *Para-language.* Less overt than Stage I but at times writes very closely to the paper (nose an inch from the point of the moving pen). I think it is an unusual use of a proxemic but am not sure yet.
5. *Frequent conversations with companions.* A write, converse, write rhythm suggestive of switching in conversation. This is sometimes seen in Stage I but is particularly pronounced at this time.

III – Speech Features Implicit in Text

1. *Less overt sound off the page.* Interjections, exclamation marks all but disappear.
2. *Early drafts contain prosodics.* Capitalization of important words (but not those capitalized according to convention).
3. *Use of information now contains a high degree of selectivity* that makes text flow like speech but selection is of high quality.
4. *Little conversation* with neighbors of a "play-by-play" nature. Conversation is more related to the writing process itself—"How did you solve that one?" "Do you think this is a good lead?"
5. *Use of adjectives and adverbs:* Some writers move through a stage of excessive use of adjectives and adverbs, a kind of noun and verb propping. The noun or verb may be poorly chosen or the writer just feels that they cannot stand on their own, or that the extensive use of adjectives constitutes good writing. This is a characteristic of some writers in this stage, but just where it fits into the total scheme I do not yet know.

Handwriting

The original study design called for the tracing of handwriting variables for their influence on composing. After a short time, this aspect of the study was abandoned, even though data continued to be gathered on handwriting itself. A more meticulous approach to data gathering may have unearthed more.

Two children who were diagnosed as writers with handwriting problems were included in the original study design. Both children saw themselves as people with handwriting problems. As soon as the children wrote daily, controlled the choice of their topics, and had specific responses to the content of their pieces by teachers and other children, the handwriting barrier disappeared. Other than handwriting speed, there was little connection that could be made between composing and the handwriting variable.

Nevertheless, it was fruitful to observe how children changed in their use of handwriting, since it became a very important area in which to monitor the writer's use of time and space, views of information and the process itself. Stages of handwriting development could be traced in general terms and are reported below:

1. *Get it down phase.* Letters follow each other in sequence, the ingredients are present as words (not necessarily separated) move in columns, circle, or run together across a page. These are the child's first explorations of ordering a message. Letters may be in both upper and lower case with upper case in domination.

2. *First aesthetics.* Overlaps a little with "get-it-down." Soon erasures start, presenting other kinds of control problems. Children are more systematic in left-to-right composing, with more spaces inserted between words. Less use of upper case letters, smaller size to letters overall. Pressure is more evenly distributed in letters composed.

3. *Growing conventions.* More focus on "the right way" to shape, layout letters on the page. Concern for conventions in spelling, punctuation also accompanies the event. Concerned about appearance of page to others.

4. *Stage of breaking conventions.* This stage is quite dependent on teaching. If teachers ask questions that make children want to add information, then conventions associated with "first draft" writing only have to be broken. Words and sentences are lined out; children erase very little. Arrows, symbols, appear with information written up margins, across top and bottom of the page.

5. *Later aesthetics.* Children who have acquired greater ownership of their writing through additional information, have written several drafts, can be fussier about final copy. An interest in calligraphy, appearance of published piece, can reach a refinement not seen in earlier stages.

Handwriting speed seems to be an important variable in the quality of writing produced. Children who wrote at a speed beyond eight words per minute had better products. It appeared that they had internalized more of the process elements (handwriting, spelling, other conventions) and had a better understanding of part-whole relationships of information. But there are many exceptions both on the high and low side of handwriting speed. It is merely one factor among others to observe.

Spelling

Data on spelling come from two principle sources: early acquisition of spelling in grade one, and the use of spelling in drafts at the third and fourth grade level. Spelling data were probably influenced by the particular methods of instruction and therefore need description.

All of the children in first grade were permitted to use spelling inventions as a means to composing their pieces. Most of the children who had a strong ear for sounds used this method, with the exception of a few who already knew how to spell very well. This means that the children were allowed to spell words the way that they sounded, and to use words as accurately as they could at the time. During conferences, the teacher would help by focusing on sound-symbol correspondences within the context of the child's piece.

Preliminary hypotheses on childrens' spelling are listed as follows:

1. Children use very different application of spelling under different assessment conditions.

   A. *Isolated sounds*: When tested on knowledge of consonants in initial, medial, and final positions, long and short vowels, blends and digraphs, the children exhibited 90% accuracy.

   B. *Isolated words*: When tested on ability to spell 20 isolated words, applying the above same skills, children exhibited 50% accuracy.

   C. *During Composing*: When tested under composing conditions, using the same words, children exhibited 30% accuracy.

   In short, the more spelling was assessed in isolation from the composing process, the more accurately the child spelled. The only true assessment of spelling, however, is during the writing process, because the child has to attend to many things simultaneously. The other assessments, A and B, are useful in that they may show how a child is changing before spelling words while composing, but studies of these shifts from A to B to C have not yet been done.

2. Children who invent may use several spellings of the same word within the same writing. Until the word is stabilized in a set invention, the child will continue to invent.

3. Spelling is in a constant state of evolution during the invented spelling phase. The spiral, however, is toward more and more accurate spelling with many regressions along the way when other composing variables take precedence.

4. Invented spelling relies heavily on "ear for sound," consistent use of 1–1 sound-symbol correspondences. As children "complete" fuller spellings of words, they become more sensitive to the visual memory elements containing irregular correspondence—e.g. kiss. Children's reading of their published material where their invented spellings were in traditional spellings, plus reading of other books, contributed to final spellings.

5. Children write in order to read their messages at another time. But early inventions, either because of too few cues (bc = book) or words run together (Ilcthsbc = I liked his book) cannot be read back. It would appear that words have commerce when there are three cues in initial, medial, and final positions, and the context provides enough help (I lct hs buk) to be read back.

6. Children who have difficulty with spelling and who draft, change their spellings from draft to draft until more accurate spellings are reached in final draft form. In the case of Brian, although nine years of age, he used spelling inventions in early drafts, then brought in more visual features when arriving at the final draft. This is not necessarily a developmental phenomenon since the teacher permitted, even encouraged, an emphasis on content in early drafts, with surface features to be cared for in the final draft.

Punctuation

Punctuation data was gathered from an intervention study between one classroom that stressed punctuation rules outside of the writing process context, and another classroom that emphasized punctuation within the context of children's pieces. The definitions that each group gave are typified in the following responses to the question, "What do periods do?"

Rule Group—   "They tell you when the sentence
ends."
Context Group—"They let you know where the sentence
ends, so otherwise one minute you'd be
sledding down the hill and the next
minute you'd be inside the house, without even stopping."

From this data, it was apparent that children's understanding of punctuation depended on the context in which it was taught. The use of punctuation,
consequently, also varied, as the four categories listed below indicate:

1. *Usage preceded nomenclature* when children used punctuation forms in the
   context of their own pieces. They used such forms as commas, quotation marks,
   and colons, without knowing their names.
2. *Nomenclature preceded usage* when taught in the isolation of the child's paper.
3. *Children needed many more punctuation forms when they were revising drafts.*
   As information moved toward clarity, punctuation demands increased in relation to heightened understandings about the intentions of the text.
4. *Punctuation was more difficult to choose when the writer searched for meaning in
   an early draft.*

The challenge in assessing punctuation data is to separate the teacher
variable from the child's own development or order of perceptions. One
measure, the child's actual performance in relation to his statements about
punctuation, was not carried out. A major project remains to be done in
monitoring statements in relation to use.

Seven Hypotheses on Implications of Findings

Data from child behavior during the writing process together with data
from teacher practices led to hypotheses about what teachers can do to help
children write. The seven hypotheses that follow were selected because
they represent broad, fundamental issues in the teaching of writing. Specifics
about day-to-day practices are available in sixteen chapters of *Writing:
Teachers and Children at Work*, by Donald H. Graves, published by Heinemann Educational Books, 1983.

Behaviors of Writers Are Idiosyncratic and Highly Variable

The teaching of writing is a response to what a writer shows either in oral
or written statements. Until a child writes or speaks, it is difficult for the
teacher to know what to do because of the inherent idiosyncracies or vari-
abilities of each writer. Just as quarterbacks don't make a move until the
defense is read, teachers don't respond until the child shows where he is in
both information and process on that particular day.

The purpose of research is to note similarities in order to make generalizations. Many similarities were seen among the children when they wrote, but
as the study progressed, individual exceptions to the data increased in domi-
nance. In short, every child had behavioral characteristics in the writing
process that applied to that child alone. It is our contention, based on this
information, that such variability *demands* a waiting, responsive type of
teaching.

Calkins' data on stages of revision highlighted the similarities and differences issue. For example, Calkins identified an "interacter" type composer, a child who saw writing as clay-like and manipulable, the information as temporary and evolving. Children in this category shared this perception, yet functioned differently in its application. Amy made internal revisions, "thinking through" several drafts without making many changes on the paper. Andrew made progressively fewer revisions, while Brian wrote more and more drafts.

The ability to sense idiosyncracies will determine the success or failure of the writing process. One teacher may see revision as worthy of a classroom mandate, and remain unaware that Amy revises internally. Another teacher may not realize that although Brian revises extensively on most drafts, today may not be a good day to ask him to revise. Teachers who *respond*, who follow what children say and do, will be able to see differences among writers and to help the individual child write.

Observe Clusters of Behaviors Before Making Decisions About Writers

Teacher assistance cannot be based on one variable because of the variable nature of the writer. A teacher should therefore look at a cluster of behaviors during the writing process such as the child's use of the page, process, and information, before she makes a judgment on how to help the child. Even then, the teacher should suspend judgment until she has listened carefully to the child's intentions.

Case studies can help teachers see clusters of behaviors because the full context of composing and discussion is reported, as opposed to the discussion of isolated variables. Teachers can then transfer clusters of information to their own classrooms.

Scope and Sequence Curricula Have Little Relevance to How Writers Develop

In scope and sequence curricula, all the skills needed in writing are assigned various levels at which each is to be taught. I suggested in my proposal for this study that this approach was not based on developmental evidence, and promised to make inroads on the problem. My promise was a false one. There *is* evidence for behavior sequences of skills acquisition, but it is too closely connected with the *context* in which it is taught to make specific conclusions. For example, one-fifth of the first graders used quotations marks accurately because the children were given the skill when conversation appeared in their writing. Some first grade children were capable of making several revisions and a few top fourth grade children revised a selection over a three-week period. Some children in first grade used colons, commas in a series, and question and exclamation marks.

If scope and sequence are not used because of child variability, then teacher responsibility increases. Teachers can provide individual curricular responses only if they know the writing process and the development of the children who use it. The curriculum content is *within* the children; only the teacher who knows the full range of writing tools can make it manifest. She will know those tools if she uses them in her own writing.

Scaffolding—Conference Approach Is the Best Response to the Variable Writer

The conference process was the heart of the writing program in our study. Our data on conferences, concept changes, and improvements in writing, document the importance of such an approach. It is the best answer to date on dealing with writer variability and idiosyncrasies.

Because of writer variability, the conference structure should be highly predictable, almost ritualistic in order and setting. Predictability creates consistency and a comfortable, familiar environment. Within this setting, the teacher can introduce appropriate imbalances—unpredictable statements and questions—that will stimulate child growth and learning.

When conferences go well, the child does most of the talking, teaching his teacher about a subject he knows. The teacher follows the child, reflects the information to keep the child on track. She is *observing* the child's understanding of the writing process.

Conferences do not usually occur at every step of a single paper, but over several papers, as various steps surface in conferences and the child discusses different process components. The learning is cumulative and the effect remarkable. Study children who had two years of conferences developed a noticeable responsibility for their writing.

Teachers Should Let Their Writers Write Daily, Sustain Selections Longer, and at Predictable Times

Children do not rehearse their writing when both time and subject are unpredictable. Observe a child after a holiday, protracted illness, or three-day interruption from school activities, and note the struggle to find a subject or get back on track. Writing demands a daily, ritualistic set time (always at 9:00 a.m. or 1:00 p.m., etc.). There can be no writing program unless time is provided.

When writing is regular and at predictable times, the child controls the subject and can rehearse. He thinks and plans the writing when he is not directly on task. The approach becomes the baseline for children to sustain a piece over a *longer period of time*. Children who sustain their pieces over several weeks acquire a different understanding of their subject and what it means to know it well. They have had time to read, take notes, listen to their information, and plan changes with other children. Teachers can also scaffold a piece at different points in the writing process.

Completion times are highly variable when writing is sustained at the child's own ability. Some children could handle two days on a piece, while others worked their way up to three weeks of drafts because they were able to maintain a clear understanding of information parts and wholes. In most classrooms, children began their next piece several minutes after finishing another. Learning to use time for planning, rehearsal, discovering new information, or for publishing, was not only a clear indication of child growth, but a strong predictor of the quality of the piece.

Teachers Should Let Children Choose About 80% of Their Topics Because It Assists Them With Voice, Heightens Semantic Domain, Skill of Narrowing Topic, and Basic Decision-Making

When children choose their topics, several other sub-processes are helped. Children begin the process of revision: "I won't write about this topic, I'll write about that one." They also learn to match their voices and intentions with what appears in the text. If the writing program relies on assigned topics, then children tend to produce voices that sound like their teacher's voice.

Choosing a topic is a learning process. Inexperienced choices are often global, bizarre, or reflect stereotypes of teacher-chosen "good subjects." Teachers who provide little time for writing instinctively try to avoid these poor choices by assigning topics. But by making decisions for children, they deny voice, intercept revision, and rob the child of ownership.

Children will choose topics more wisely as they develop an understanding of the writing process. They will show a richer semantic domain in both their pieces and their discussion of content and process. Preliminary data on three case studies over a three-year period suggested a strong relationship between topic choice, writing quality, and the emergence of new writing concepts.

Skills Are Best Taught Within the Context of the Child's Own Writing

The child can better understand a skill when it is taught within the context of the writing process. He can learn quotation marks in first grade if there is conversation in his piece. As he struggles with clarity, he learns skills are tools to enhance meaning and they become his allies. For this reason, skills should be taught in the midst of the scaffolding process, usually one at a time.

Calkins' preliminary data show that children who received punctuation in context used over twice as many punctuation forms in their texts as children who received them in isolated exercises. Children also gave articulate definitions for skills usage by giving examples from their own texts. Although the data refer primarily to punctuation, other skills such as use of leads, following a single subject, verifying experience with specifics, etc. followed the same pattern in writing and in descriptions of what the children did when they wrote.

Since the completion of this study, these hypotheses have been shared in many workshops and writing courses around the country. Even though the formal data gathering and work with the Atkinson teachers ended in June 1980, the findings continue to be refined and their validity assessed in classrooms with other children. Far more systematic study is needed on both teachers and children within the same setting to understand the changes of each in relation to the other. Only then will the interaction of child development with environment be started. As in any research study, many more questions have been raised than answers provided.

Annotated Bibliography

Calkins, Lucy McCormick. "Andrea Learns to Make Writing Hard." Research Update, *Language Arts*, 56 (May 1979): 567–76. Presents a case study of how one child changes her approaches to revision during the first year of the study.

Calkins, Lucy McCormick, "Case Study of a Nine Year Old Writer." Unpublished manuscript, written May 1979. Calkins reviews research procedures, Andrea's change in revision, search for a lead sentence, uses of symbols to manipulate material, changes in chronology and uses of information, and then the disappearance of external strategies viewed by the researcher.

Calkins, Lucy McCormick, "Children Learn the Writer's Craft." Research Update, *Language Arts*, 57 (February 1980): 207–13. Shows how children move from play to craft in writing process.

Calkins, Lucy McCormick. "Punctuate? Punctuate. Punctuate!" *Learning Magazine* (February 1980): 86-89. A first cousin of Calkins' other articles in research section on punctuation. This piece gives more specific recommendations for what teachers ought to do to help children within the context of their own composing.

Calkins, Lucy McCormick. "When Children Want to Punctuate: Basic Skills Belong in Context." *Language Arts* 57 (May 1980): 567–73. This article shows children's concepts of punctuation when it is taught from a meaning base within the writing process. Contrast is given to a room where punctuation is taught in isolation from writing itself.

Calkins, Lucy McCormick. "One School's Writing Program." *National Elementary Principal* 59 (June 1980): 34–38. Calkins describes the overall writing program at Atkinson Academy, the building in which the NIE study was conducted. Examples of the teaching of writing from grade one through five are given with further specifics of child and teacher cases. Recommendations for teaching, based on the NIE data are given.

Calkins, Lucy McCormick. "The Craft of Writing." *Teacher Magazine* (October 1980): 41–44. Shows a class engaged in the writing process. Specific suggestions made to teachers about how to help children take ownership of their pieces, with special focus on learning how to revise.

Calkins, Lucy McCormick. "Children's Rewriting Strategies." *Research in the Teaching of English* (December 1980): 331–41. Through interviews, observation, and examination of children's products, Calkins defines four kinds of revisers in young children.

Egan, Judith. "After All, They have Writing In Common." *Insights into Open Education* 14, No. 3 (November, 1981) Center for Teaching and Learning, University of North Dakota. Egan, second grade teacher in the study, describes how she integrates literature into her writing program. Because children write, they see common elements between their writing and the writing of professionals. Their critical levels in reading the work of others are raised.

Giacobbe, Mary Ellen. "Kids Can Write the First Week of School." *Learning Magazine* (September 1981): 132–33. Giacobbe, first grade teacher in the study, describes her approach to helping children write their first week of school. Giacobbe also shares a spelling assessment given to the children to help her understand their abilities. This article has been reprinted by the New Zealand Council of Teachers, as well as the Primary English Teaching Association in Australia.

Graves, Donald H. "Research Doesn't Have to be Boring" *Language Arts* 56 (January 1979): 76–80. First piece written to introduce seven subsequent columns on the study to teachers. The study design and variables to be examined are discussed.

Graves, Donald H. "Let Children Show Us How to Help Them Write." *Visible Language* 13 (March 1979): 16–28. This article describes how children give us clues in their handwriting about their understanding of the writing process. The child's use of the page, prosodics, and the breaking of handwriting conventions all show various aspects of the writer's development.

Graves, Donald H. "What Children Show Us About Revision." *Language Arts* 56 (March 1979): 312–19. First articles on revision giving preliminary data on six and eight-year-old practices in revision. Revision was already becoming one of the most important foci in the study as it showed, from the start, what children perceived in the writing process.

Graves, Donald H. "The Growth and Development of First Grade Writers," in *Learning to Write: First Language/Second Language* ed. A. Freedman, I. Pringle and J. Yalden (Longmans Ltd.) 1983. Written early in the study, 3/4 of the way through the first year, composite developmental profiles are given of three six-year-old writers at low, middle, and high levels.

Graves, Donald H. and Murray, Donald M. "Revision: In the Writer's Workshop and in the Classroom." *Boston University Journal of Education* (Spring 1980): 39–56. Comparisons are made between the writing process of a professional writer and those of six to ten year old children in the NIE study.

Graves, Donald H. "A New Look at Writing Research." *Language Arts* 57 (November/December 1980): 913–19. In light of what has been discovered thus far in the NIE-New Hampshire Study, an evaluation is given of 25 years of research in writing in the elementary years, reviewing changing methods, topics evaluated, and the need for studies that consider the context in which they are conducted.

Graves, Donald H. and Giacobbe, Mary Ellen. "Questions for Teachers Who Wonder if Their Writers Change." *Language Arts* 59 (May 1982): 495–503. An article not connected directly with the study but based on questions raised by the study at Atkinson. Study was done as a follow-up to the first, under Lucy Calkins grant from NCTE. Giacobbe was a teacher involved in the NIE study.

Graves, Donald H. "Break the Welfare Cycle: Let Writers Choose Their Topics." *Fforum* (March 1983). Students' dependency on teacher topics are described, with recommendations from NIE data given on ways to help students take more responsibility for their writing.

Graves, Donald H. "Where Have All the Teachers Gone?" *Language Arts* (April 1981): 492–96. A plea is given for teachers to become involved in research for themselves or at least in collaboration with NIE studies. Examples of how a teacher in the Atkinson study conducted her own research and how other teachers published their findings are also provided.

Graves, Donald H. "Writing Research for the Eighties: What is Needed." *Language Arts* (February 1981): 197–206. Specific research studies are suggested in three areas: the writing process, background information about other processes to understanding writing, and the ethnographic context of children's composing. Some suggestions are given for research designs.

Kamler, Barbara. "One Child, One Teacher, One Classroom: The Story of One Piece of Writing," *Language Arts* 57 (September 1980): 680–93. All of the variables connected with the development of one piece of writing by a seven year old child over three weeks time are recorded. Influences of other children, the teacher, on the child's revisions are reported.

Rule, Rebecca. "The Spelling Process: A Look at Strategies." *Language Arts*, Vol. 59, Number 4, April, 1982. Rule takes an older writer with spelling problems and shows how spelling changes from draft to draft.

Sowers, Susan. "A Six-Year-Old's Writing Process: The First Half of First Grade." *Language Arts* (October 1979): 829–35. Sarah, one of the cases in Grade One, has her changing writing processes described during rehearsing, composing, and adjusting her text.

Sowers, Susan. "Kds Cn Rit." *Learning Magazine* (October 1980): 14–15. Sowers shows how teachers, in particular, Giacobbe, works with young children's invented spelling to help them become better writers. Background to work in invented spelling from Chomsky, Bissex, and Montessori is given.

Sowers, Susan. "The Researcher Who Watches Children Write." in *Children Want to Write (Donald Graves in Australia)* ed. R.D. Walshe (Exeter, NH: Heinemann Educational Books) 1981, 29–35. This article shows how data were gathered during the NIE study. This is a non-technical, human interest type approach to showing how Graves and others gathered data at Atkinson.

Sowers, Susan. "Young Writer's Preference for Non-Narrative Modes of Composition." Shows how children changed from non-narrative to narrative writing during the first year of school. A number of pre-narrative forms are discussed.

Articles Related to the Study

These related articles are not attempting to report research. On the other hand, most of the articles contain recommendations for classroom practice based on the study.

Calkins, Lucy M. "One School's Writing Program." *National Elementary Principal*, Vol. 59, No. 2 (June, 1980) pp. 34–38. Calkins describes the overall writing program at Atkinson Academy, the building in which the NIE study was conducted. Examples of the teaching of writing from grade one through five are given with further specifics of child and teacher cases. Recommendations for teaching based on the NIE data are given.

Calkins, Lucy M. "Punctuate? Punctuate. Punctuate!" *Learning* (February, 1980) pp. 86–88. A first cousin of Calkins' other articles in research section on punctuation. This piece gives more specific recommendations for what teachers ought to do to help children within the context of their own composing.

Calkins, Lucy M. "The Craft of Writing." *Teacher* (Nov./Dec., 1980) pp. 41–44. Shows a class engaged in the writing process. Specific suggestions made to teachers about how to help children take ownership of their pieces, with special focus on learning how to revise.

Caroselli, Marion. "Romance Precedes Precision: Recommended Classroom Teaching Practices." in *Perspectives on Writing in Grades 1-8*, Haley-James, S. (Ed.), Urbana, Ill., NCTE, 1981, pp. 60–67. In this chapter on recommended teaching practices, four of the Atkinson teachers practices in the teaching of writing have been chosen for publication in this NCTE book on the teaching of writing in the U.S.. Brackets are placed around the material written by the Atkinson teachers.

Egan, Judith. "After All, They Have Writing in Common." *Insights into Open Education* 14, No. 3 (November, 1981) Center for Teaching and Learning, University of North Dakota. Egan, second grade teacher in the study, describes how she integrates literature into her writing program. Because children write, they see common elements between their writing and the writing of professionals. Their critical levels of reading the work of others is raised.

Giacobbe, Mary Ellen. "Kids Can Write the First Week of School." *Learning* (September 1981) pp. 131–132. Giacobbe, first grade teacher in the study, describes her approach to helping children write their first week of school. Giacobbe also shares a spelling assessment given to the children to help her understand their abilities. This article has been reprinted by the New Zealand Council of Teachers, as well as the Primary English Teaching Association in Australia.

Graves, Donald H. "Break the Welfare Cycle: Let Writers Choose Their Topics." *Fforum* (March 1983). Students dependency on teacher topics are described, with recommendations from NIE data given on ways to help students take more responsibility for their writing.

Graves, Donald H. and Giacobbe, Mary Ellen. "Questions for Teachers Who Wonder if their Writers Change." *Language Arts* 59 (May, 1982): 495–503. An article not connected directly with the study but based on questions raised by the study at Atkinson. This study was done as a follow-up to the first, under Lucy Calkins' grant from NCTE. Giacobbe was a teacher involved in the NIE study.

Sowers, Susan. "Kds Cn Rit." *Learning* (October, 1980) pp. 14–15. Sowers shows how teachers, in particular, Giacobbe, works with young children's invented spelling to help them become better writers. Background to work on invented spelling from Chomsky, Bissex, and Montessori is given.

Sowers, Susan. "The Researcher Who Watches Children Write," in *Children Want to Write* (Exeter, NH: Heinemann Educational Books) 1981, pp. 29–35. This article shows how data were gathered during the NIE study. This is a non-technical, human interest type approach to showing how Graves and others gathered data at Atkinson.

16. Don't Underestimate What Children Can Write

Introduction

On March 30, 1982, I received a call from Ramsey Selden at the National Institute of Education office in Washington asking me to give a talk to the National Commission on Excellence in Education hearings in Houston, Texas. He said I would have fifteen minutes to give the talk and two weeks to write it. I made the following entry in my journal: "How difficult it will be to write such a piece on such short notice. I'll have to blast away with time I don't have. Oh, how I wish I had a word processor to just get the stuff moving and to be able to revise it!" The journal entries continued to show my efforts on the Houston talk.

6 April (Tues.)—I wrote for an hour and a half on the Houston talk.
6 April (Eve.)—Brainstormed each section of the report.
7 April (Weds.)—Did some work on the NIE piece—got my licks on two good sections. A good feeling with some shift occurring in what the piece may be about. Will write again today on the "what is needed" section. I'm overwriting in order to cut back on what I have—make the information more concentrated. This is sort of a mini-Ford report. I want to be able to give it to Don [Murray] for a look on Friday afternoon.
7 April (p.m.)—Worked on section on how our NIE data has been used—went well, I think. Now need to do section on "what needs to be done?"
7 April (later)—Wrote 2.5 more pages before going to bed.
8 April (Thurs.)—Worked on the NIE report—especially the section by Lewis Thomas.
10 April (Sat.)—This is the day when I get a write-through on my Houston report.
April 10 (afternoon)—Worked hard all afternoon on a lead for the piece. I felt reasonably satisfied but still uneasy.
April 10 (later, p.m.)—Went to see Don Murray—He didn't care for the lead— embraced too much—is too general. I'll go to work on it again. I know what I need to do.
11 April (Sunday)—Up at 6:30—feeling a bit heavy—kind of discouraged. Maybe it's the legacy of the piece not going well. Don Murray's advice, as always, on target, but the thought of being so far behind is difficult.
Worked on a new lead and it went well. Things are looking up. It just pieced together with the right information, voice, etc. Now if I can make a voice go through the part on what we found in the study, I'll be all set.
Worked late evening on the next section of the report for Houston. Too tired to write well.
12 April (Mon.)—Worked on the Houston talk for two and a half hours solid. At least I got a bunch of stuff down, though I am not very pleased with it. The voice isn't right. I am reporting the research and it is very difficult not to lapse into a research tone.
14 April (Weds.)—Up at 5:45. I'm very wakeful in the morning lately. That is, I'm aware of the light outside. I thrive on light and want to get to work too soon. I went straight to work on the NIE talk for Houston. I rewrote from the beginning. I find this helpful as I get the feel for the piece by revising early sections and coming upon the part I am writing for that day. Today I am rewriting the section on "Why did we do it?" "What did we find?" The writing went

well. It isn't as good as the lead but it is better than what I had before. Wrote all morning until about 10:30.

15 April (Thurs.)—Up at 5:45—Big day ahead. Worked on and finished income tax by 7:30, then wrote an ending to my presentation in Houston that I really liked. I suggested that kids wanted excellence even more than we did. It just seemed right. Headed into office to give materials to Laura. Need to get everything typed to have good copy for Houston. Read the ending to Don Murray and he really liked it. He also helped me with the title by deleting three words:

Don't Underestimate What Children Can Do When They Write

How obvious it is that those three words don't belong.

Children want to write. They want to write the first day they attend school. This is no accident. Before they went to school they marked up walls, pavements, newspapers with crayons, chalk, pens or pencils . . . anything that made a mark.

Mark has just finished a draft about some chickens he has been raising. His teacher, Mary Ellen Giacobbe, asks him what he will do next with his piece:

Possibly get it published. I might sit down and work on it a bit. Turn it over and erase the things on the back that I have and write some new stuff. Write new stuff about chicks. I might take this piece and just look through and see if it's chicks or ducks cause I had to chase some of John's ducks too. That even took more than an hour. I might change some of it to ducks.

Mark is six years old and learning to write. He is also learning to think. He takes a subject, examines the facts, suspends judgment, and keeps on writing until he is satisfied. He has that sense of confidence about the writing because in his first week of school his teacher let him write and kept on asking questions about what he was doing.

Before the year was out, the children in Mark's first grade class composed 1300 five to six page booklets and published 450 of the best in hard cover for their classmates to read. Half revised their work, with a fifth using quotation marks accurately.

This information is the by-product of our New Hampshire study of what children do when they write. The study, funded by the National Institute of Education, made it possible for three researchers to take two years to record the details of what children do when they write. This was not an experimental design. Rather, it was a detailed study of how writers developed. As fast as we gathered the information, we shared it with the teachers. The teachers used what made sense to them. Because teachers used this new information to help children write better, we found out more about children's development.

Children improved so rapidly that before the study was completed mor than 2000 visitors observed the teachers and children at work. The deman for the story of these children and teachers didn't stop. Twenty-five articles in professional journals, three books, with coverage in *Time*, *Psychology Today*, *Better Homes and Gardens*, and *Family Circle*, as well as eighty-four work shops in schools from the Bronx to Stowe, Vermont to Sydney, Australia, an seminars in thirty-seven universities in the U.S. and abroad give som perspective of the travels of our data from this 400 pupil elementary schoo constructed in 1798 in Atkinson, New Hampshire.

Today I would like to share some of what we learned about children an their writing. I think our findings will show what children can do, and the important contribution writing makes to the development of the learner Finally, I will list some of the needs for the continued study of writing an what those studies can do to help young writers in America.

What Did We Do?

Three researchers lived in five classrooms, grades one through four, over a two-year period, following sixteen particular children and their classmates The research task was to be present when the children wrote in their class rooms, and to record, describe, identify and sequence the order of what the did when they wrote. We gathered the facts about what the children did by hand recorded observations, video recordings, interviews, and analyses o everything they wrote for two years.

Why Did We Do the Study?

We did the study because children simply haven't been observed while the have been writing, especially in classrooms. Past research about what chil dren did during the writing was based on guesswork. The researcher looke at the paper, analyzed it, interviewed the child, and speculated on wha problems were solved during the writing. After all the facts were in, re searchers and teachers were still left wondering what children actually did from the time they chose their subjects, wrote, and finally put down thei pens.

Teaching patterns have followed research patterns. Most writers in ou classrooms get help only *after* the paper is passed in. The help is usually too late. The writer probably needed help in choosing the subject, in the middle o the first draft, or in finding a voice in the second draft. Teachers have avoide giving early help because from the outside the process looked like a tangle jungle. Our research tries to make sense of that jungle by showing what the writing process is, what problems children solve when they write, and the rough orders of the writer's development.

We wanted our information to aid teachers to give more timely help at al stages of the writing process. The Atkinson teachers used the information to challenge the children during the writing, not just after it was done. We also hoped that our mapping expedition of writer's development and the writing process would help school curricula designers and publishers.

What Did We Find?

Six-year-olds choose topics on their own, rehearse information, write, re-read what they have written, and revise. They can even work on several pieces simultaneously. The writing process involves drawing, talking, reading, accessing information, rereading, spelling, handwriting, organizing, editing, and revising. The writing process is made up of many sub-processes that don't necessarily fall in any set order. A child could be rehearsing the next piece in the midst of composing another. The *ingredients* of the writing process were the same for all ages. Their use was another matter.

We found many rough orders of development that could help teachers see what children were doing when they wrote. We saw how children learned to use a page, then temporarily abandon old conventions of neatness, in order to line out, draw arrows up the margin to point to new information found in reading. We observed six-year-old children speaking aloud as they wrote while they made the switch from speaking to writing without sound.

Next we saw children go through the first shocks of audience awareness. Children didn't necessarily understand the content of a classmate's writing the way the writer did. Children surprised us with the way they changed the time frame in using the writing process. Some six-year-olds apparently chose a topic in the space of ten seconds, drew, then composed the message in three minutes, and speculated about the next topic while writing the last two words of the first. But within two years this same child would observe an occurrence on a weekend, talk about it for three days, then write through eight drafts over a two week period until the piece was the way he wanted it.

Our most fruitful area of data gathering was in the area of revision. When children changed something they showed us what was important to them. We watched revision move from erasures of letter formation and spelling corrections, to the addition and deletion of information. We observed children who at first couldn't deal with two drafts simultaneously, move through revisions from minor changes in spelling and punctuation to a transition phase marked by restlessness, even anger, because their reading skills outweighed their ability to make their writing do what the critical eye demanded. Finally, we observed the writer write to discover meaning, where he saw the words as temporary, where there was a constant vying between intended meaning and discovered meaning, between writing ahead then looking back to see where the present line fits into the whole.

Lest you think our sequences, these chains of development, were fixed and inviolable, let me set the record straight. The purpose of research is to make generalizations, to find something in one human being that can be used with another. We did come up with information that would help teachers know generally where they were with the children in the midst of the process. But as the study progressed, individual exceptions within the data increased. In short, every child had behavioral characteristics that applied to that child alone.

At first I was discouraged until I realized that the deeper the data got, the more the differences would be highlighted. Every child had similarities with others, but the differences were very important. Just a moment ago I mentioned a stage in which children regularly wrote four to ten drafts of a single piece. But let's look at three children within that same category. Amy wrote: "A cheetah would make a sports car look like a turtle," at the age of eight, yet made no changes. Later we found she made extensive revisions *internally*. Andrew made progressively fewer revisions while Brian wrote more and more drafts as his writing improved.

The teacher knew what to do with this information before we did. She was successful because she sensed how each of them revised differently. If she had seen revision as a legislated requirement, then she would have violated Amy's way of handling revision. She knew that although Brian revised extensively on most drafts, today wasn't the best day to raise expectations for another draft. Teachers who understand the process and the similarities of writers, can also deal with the most important part, how writers differ. Teachers who respond and follow what children say and do, will be able to see differences among writers, and be better able to help individual children write.

The teachers took our information about the children and used it to confer with them at all stages of their writing. The conference is a discussion-review of a child's paper. When conferences go well, the child does most of the talking, teaching his teacher about a subject he knows. The teacher follows the child, picking up valuable information about just where the writer is in his understanding of what he is doing. This enables the teacher to be timely with the tough questions the writer needs to consider in the draft.

Although we knew conferences helped writers in draft, we didn't realize until after the study just how much they contributed to changes in the writer. From all transcripts over two years we traced how children learned to talk about their subject, the way they wrote, and the effects the conferences had on their writing. The transcripts also carried a printed record of how children changed their thinking. The children sounded like writers when they spoke, and, in fact, wrote like them. Listen to some nine-year-old children talk about their subjects and their writing:

> Sometimes when I write a sentence and I realize it doesn't make sense, so I'll cross out part of it and make like a circle and up on a space that is blank I'll write what I wanted to write if I didn't have room on my paper. Like here I put, "more and more snow falls. After a long time something amazing happens." But I didn't like the word happens, so I put a little sign and I put the same sign up at the top of the paper and I wrote "starts to form."

Another child was asked, "Why do you write?"

> You learn about yourself. You can learn that—maybe you've had a really tough day and everything—and nothing seems to be going right. And you think, "I can't do anything," you know. "Nothing's mine." Well, your writing is, you know. It's up to you whether you want to do it or not, really.

What Is Needed?

The National Institute of Education has only been funding research on the writing process since 1977. We are just beginning to find out what children do in the writing process. Based on these early findings we have some inkling of how to help them. But on this Lewis and Clark expedition into understanding more about writing, we are only twenty miles west of St. Louis.

What then is needed? We need more research gathered in schools, over sufficient time to report children's patterns of development. Although not every study can have immediate effect on schools, much more of our research ought to leave sites better than we found them.

The translation of research into actual classroom use has taken too long, partly because of the way in which we have gathered the information, the arcane language used to report it, as well as a lack of researchers who know how to function in a school setting. Basic researchers need to know more about teaching and teachers need to know much more about basic research. Thus, future funding ought to consider the means by which the researcher will relate to the research site much more carefully than it has in the past.

I would like to make eight recommendations for the committee regarding the role of research in the teaching of writing as a contributor to excellence in education in America.

1. Conduct more research in schools, over sufficient length of time, for more detailed work on how writers make decisions in the midst of writing. Consider the use of satellite classrooms where preliminary findings can be quickly replicated.
2. Conduct more basic classroom research on writing in urban sites with different language and ethnic backgrounds.
3. Study the changing conference patterns of both children and teachers, and the effects of those patterns on writing.
4. Conduct research that examines the relationship between writing and reading. Language and thinking bases underlying the processes of each need to be studied so that teachers may use the two together more effectively.
5. Encourage more collaborative research between teachers and researchers with either joint or separate publication of research findings.
6. Conduct research on the reading and writing of teachers, so that they may understand their own processes and those of the readers and writers they teach.
7. Conduct research on the ethnography of microcomputer literacy as they are introduced into school systems. How do concepts of literacy change through their introduction? The computer has brought us to a time as radically new as the first use of the alphabet or the Gutenberg press. We need to understand the effects of microcomputers as much as we need to assist their use in schools.
8. Conduct more studies on the types of writing problems solved by persons using microcomputers.

In the past, we have focused on children's errors. For this reason we have grossly underestimated children's ability to write and to think. They have perspectives about what they are doing that we miss from day to day because we don't let them write or speak. Listen to eight-year-old Wendy's perception of writing:

> The more you do in life the harder it is to write because you are growing older and do harder things. When you do harder things, the writing gets harder.

Children want to do harder things. They want to be challenged. They want to think. Our job in both research and teaching is to make possible the excellence they may want even more than we do.

17. Back to School

Introduction

In June 1982, while working at a meeting of editors and university professors, I was asked if I would like to write a guest editorial for our state newspaper, *The Concord Monitor*. It seemed to be a very good idea in June, but acceptances in June come due in August. I wrote most of the editorial while vacationing in Maine. The hard part about an editorial is that it has to be short and written directly to the public. As in the Ford report, I have always found this to be the best discipline for any other writing that I do. I was trying to interpret in practical terms for teachers, children, parents, and the public in five hundred words, the meaning of our Atkinson research.

My first approach to the editorial was to campaign to do something about the terrible things we are doing to classroom teachers. I wanted to let a public that had been extremely critical of teachers see what teachers had to put up with from the inside. The lead to this editorial draft went as follows:

In a few weeks school will start. It takes me all the way back to my fifth grade teacher, Miss Adams. I mark the contrast between her classroom and the ones children will enter this fall. They weren't the good old days, but there are some things that need to be kept, some forgotten. If Miss Adams were teaching today, she might have quit within a week.

There is no point in setting the clock back but we'd better take a strong look at today's classrooms. They are the subject of one raid after another. A sequence of instruction is hardly known. The teacher barely gets a lesson started when the interruptions begin. Question is not followed by question. Rather interruption is followed by interruption. Interruption becomes the main event, teaching the sideshow. I challenge any parent or administrator to sit in a classroom to observe the number of times a teacher's day is changed without plan, to say nothing of the numbers of specialists who trip in and out for speech, reading, learning disability, handicapped work, psychological help. Then there are the announcements, carried over the loudspeaker, carried notes, rescheduling of TV, motion pictures, art, physical education, music. Into the interruptions is a school curriculum so detailed in syllabus, curriculum guide that lessons are broken down into seven and eight minute compartments, punctuated by further interruptions.

Although I liked this first draft of the lead, I felt uneasy. Something was missing. After a few days of avoiding writing, I realized that the children were not in the piece. If I was to have any impact on parents—and I realized that my audience had to be parents—more had to be said about children.

I tried another lead for the editorial, working along the lines of being more positive about children. I tried to get at the problem by showing what we were doing to children in the old days and today. I then wrote the following:

Children have always had their reasons for not liking school. Lest we think this is something new, few of us in middle age can forget children who repeated three years in the same grade or stood in humiliation while stumbling over words they could not read. Each age has its own way of causing problems. Two come to mind. The first is the sickness approach to learning. In more subtle ways we have shown children how they are sick by attending to what they can't do. We do it through psychological testing, reading assessments, normed tests, or a dozen other therapies. There is no denying that there are children with acute learning problems. But the main issue is that we haven't communicated to either parents or children what the children can do, in light of the problem at hand. The second

I never finished the line, "The second. . . ." Once again, the tone wasn't right. I spent too much time on what was wrong, rather than focusing on what we are to do about it. I began to realize how easily I could run off at the mouth on major problems and write an entire editorial about them. Actually, I had written two leads that probably belonged in an article somewhere, but a five-hundred-word editorial wasn't the place to do it.

I started again. This time I could tell that I was on the way to conveying the tone and the information I wanted. The first two lines are very close to the final text: "In a few weeks children return to school. Many are delighted to be back with their friends and to have the renewed chance to learn." Although I had a number of rewrites consisting of overwriting and trimming of several sections, I knew I had found the way to get to my main objective, namely, "there are things that we can do, both at school and at home, to help children" and these approaches are based on research showing how children learn.

Back to school

By DONALD H. GRAVES

Some children will be delighted to return to school in a few weeks, but a growing number of American children hate the prospect. They will be reminded daily that they are failures, hopelessly behind, and make little contribution to the school community. Ask these children what they know or can do well and they answer, "Nothing . . . Never could learn and never will." Many become behavior problems or lapse into indifference.

All children can learn, and there are specific things that teachers and parents can do together to help them. Lately help has come from a source few people expected, writing. Recent research in writing, begun at the University of New Hampshire and taking place across the United States, Britain, Australia and New Zealand, has given children from all ability levels a new lease on life and learning.

The research shows that when children discover what they know in their own experience, whether it be fashion, lasers or space stories, then write and defend their topics, they learn to think and speak with authority. They become aggressive learners, and their new-found strengths spread to other subjects.

Ten-year-old Mark was beginning to hate school. His teacher caught him just in time when she helped him realize how much he knew about the white-tailed deer. Normally Mark would dislike the prospect of writing, but his teacher helped him to speak, read, write and finally publish his subject in hard cover for the other children. They too are afraid to affirm what they know on a personal basis or to defend their information before others.

Mark's teacher did what more and more teachers and parents have found helps children learn. They deliberately look for what children can do and call their attention to it. For example, a child may have placed a period correctly only two times in four. The teacher asks the child, "You got two right here; how did you know how to do that?"

Children are expected to know how they do things. At home I notice that my son retracks a bicycle chain. I ask, "'How did you know how to do that?" I want him to teach me. I want him to know what he knows. Then I can ask the tough questions that challenge him even more.

We rightfully worry about the decline in national scores and the pursuit of excellence. Excellence, however, is not achieved by decree, testing or new curricula. The new research in writing has shown that excellence is achieved by helping children learn what they know, then by asking the tough questions that help them know even more. Make no mistake: Children want to be challenged, but challenged about what they know and can defend. The child who hates to go to school today may want to pursue excellence even more than we do.

18. The Author's Chair

Introduction

Titles don't often precede the writing of an article. In this instance we had a title looking for an article. Jane Hansen, my colleague in the Education Department at the University of New Hampshire, and I were conducting a two-year study on the relationship between reading and writing in Somersworth, New Hampshire. Halfway through the first year of research it dawned on us that Ellen Blackburn, the first-grade teacher in whose room we were conducting research, had a chair that symbolized the crossroads of our research as well as the natural meeting point of the children's understanding of reading and writing. Thus, the term *author's chair* emerged in Ellen's room long before we started our article.

Usually when titles emerge early in the writing process the writing goes easily. This was true in the article "Let's Get Rid of the Welfare Mess in the Teaching of Writing" and "Back to School." But the "Author's Chair" piece was an attempt to synthesize the first year's findings in one article. We had hundreds of pages of handwritten data, plus videotapes, from which to extract our data. The natural impulse, unfortunately, was to try to stuff too much into one article. I suspect that when two people write an article together, the ambition factor is doubled. We started the article early in June 1982, but didn't finish it until late October of the same year. The article was on both of our minds during this entire period.

We both agreed that we needed to have one voice and one style in the writing. Although we were quite close in style and writing philosophy from the outset, the final style turned out to be more Jane's than mine. A look at the evolution of our content and style may be useful to those persons who collaborate on writing articles together.

Jane first wrote a quick draft on her word processor. The title was "Authorship." This was early in June. There were many good illustrations in the piece but I didn't feel that it had a direction that would enable us to post data plus stories under the various components that would make up the article. I took what Jane had written and went to work.

I wrote up a four-page brainstorm list, single-spaced and typed (I compose on the typewriter; Jane composes on a word processor.) The brainstorm list was a combination of questions, single words, and more extended comments. Here is an example of a brainstorm list:

At first the components of becoming an author oneself are very much in the mechanical realm. It is when the writer moves to content, and the self is distinguished from the act, that something happens. Daniel signs his piece—first time he puts his name to a piece.

The piece is over there and I am over here. I am a craftsperson.

How does the teacher follows the leads of the children and thus foster authorship?

What does the author's chair do?

At first they thought the writing was easier than the reading. Now they think the reading is easier than the writing.

Read authors
    Choose their own topics
    Publish
    Write daily
Egocentric to sociocentric
External to internal
Children see authors:
    Self as authors
    Other children as authors
    Published authors as authors
    Teacher as author
    Mr. Graves as author
    Jane as author

At no point did Jane and I have difficulty brainstorming, planning, or composing. Words, ideas, and formats came quickly. But we were working with such a deluge of information that everything applied to everything else. It was very difficult to find a format that would work.

I worked through much of August from an outline that first discussed how writing and then reading affected the child's concept of authorship. Each of these sections was followed by a listing of hypotheses. I wrote all the way through the writing section and three-quarters of the way through the reading section. The words came quickly but I had an uneasy feeling throughout. There was something false about keeping the sections separate; our study was trying to show the relationship between the two. My approach would not **place** the findings in their proper context: reading and writing together.

Jane and I had another meeting. She attempted to work with my draft, even to the point of smoothing out the language. But we both agreed that the article, in its present format, simply didn't do the job although the information was good and some major insights came from the drafting.

My approach also failed to show how children developed as writers. There was development in subsections but no overall approach to a child's development in reading and writing that carried the reader through the entire article. We both went to work during several meetings to see if there were any distinctive periods in a child's growth in the authorship concept. There were. We found three distinctive phases and easily reclassified much of our data and my early draft under the three headings. Outlining moved quickly as did the final writing.

Most writers (myself included) don't recommend outlines for children or writers of any age. But this article seemed to lend itself to numerous outlines. I count at least eight in my attempt to shift data around to some manageable form. I suspect that the outline was also an attempt to kid myself that the article was proceeding in orderly fashion. It wasn't. The only outline that worked was the one that evolved from that last meeting with Jane, in which we decided that reading and writing data should be reported under the three child-growth stages.

Jane did the final draft of the paper using the three-stage approach. We both

'orked very closely on the formulation of the hypotheses, so closely that it is
npossible to say where Jane's language begins and mine ends.

As I look back over the written material excluded from this article, I realize how
many other articles are embedded in "The Author's Chair."

Donald Graves and Jane Hansen

he Author's Chair is where the reader sits. Randy, a first-grade author,
eads a page from one of his published books: *I Went Bottle Digging*. Then he
urns the book to show the pictures to the class assembled on the carpet in
ont of him. When he finishes the book he places it on his lap, "Now."

The acceptance begins, "I liked the part where you get dirty. I liked the part
here you found the pottery."

The questions follow, "What do you do with the money when you sell
tem?" "Why did you choose this topic?" "How do you feel about being an
uthor?"

Each day in Randy's classroom the children take their turns reading from
te Author's Chair. They read their own published books and trade books.
he teacher also reads the children's published books and trade books from
te same chair. Of the four situations, in only one case is the real author on
te chair. But, it is always the Author's Chair.

Whether the story is about Anatole, or Jeremy's new piece on his dirt bike,
te process of responding to each work is the same. First, the children receive
te work by stating what they think it contains; then they ask questions of
te author. When the child-author is present, the child answers the ques-
ons. For the authors of trade books, the teacher and children together
)eculate on answers the author might give. The prestige of the chair grows
roughout the year.

The author's chair is in the first-grade classroom of Ellen Blackburn in
reat Falls School, Somersworth, New Hampshire, a working-class com-
unity. The two of us intereacted with the children in Ellen's classroom at
ast twice each week throughout 1981−82 and will continue during 1982−
3. Our intent is to formulate hypotheses about the development of the
ildren's understanding of the relationship between reading and writing.
'e started by giving the same definition to both reading and writing: They
·e composing acts.

Then, because no study had ever been done with beginning writers and
·aders on the two composing processes simultaneously, we used case study
; the principal method of investigation. We studied three children who

represented low, middle, and high achievement levels. This meant biweekl
data collection through video, audio, and hand recordings of the childre
composing and conferencing in reading and writing. Also, we asked th
children questions from ten different protocol sheets. When the case stud
children were not composing, we gathered data on the other twenty childre
in the classroom. The Author's Chair became an important point to examin
children's concepts of authorship as well as the relationship between readin
and writing.

The Classroom

The children read and wrote every day. They lived in a community of author
who were constantly reading and writing. They viewed other children con
posing books, and reading the words of Freddie, Jennifer, Ezra Jack Keats
Dr. Seuss, or Holt, Rinehart and Winston. They were both audiences an
writers.

They kept all their writing in their writing folders and published in har
cover about one out of every four pieces. These published books are placed o
the bookshelves in the classroom library along with the published books o
professional authors. Each published book has a biographical statemer
about the author at the end. This writing, in both its invented spelling forr
and published form, is the center of instruction for reading.

Most of the children's writing is done at one time of the day with readin
handled at another time. But the distinction is misleading; much reading i
done during the writing, or writing during the reading time. For example
one day when Charley came to the writing table to illustrate his newly type
book waiting for publication, he spontaneously reread his book before colo
ing. Joey, seated next to him, asked, "Will you teach me to read it?" Soo
Robbie, seated on the other side of the table, got up, walked over and askec
"Will you teach me too?" When Charley finished teaching, Robbie said, "No
do you want to learn how to read mine?"

Each week a child is chosen as Author of the Week. This means the child
photo is placed on a bulletin board along with a list of the child's publishe
book titles. The books are in pockets and other children post comments abou
the author's books. The author chooses his or her own published, favorit
book and the teacher makes five copies for the other children to read durin
reading time. During this week the child reads his or her own books, basal
and/or trade books to the class.

Whenever anyone reads a trade book to the class the children are inte
ested in the authors. When Ellen reads to the children she first gives back
ground about the author, including other books composed. She doesn't sepa
rate the person from the work—the same procedure used for the children's ow
books. Soon children become known for the books they have written, for th
territory they have established, and are capable of defending it under th
questions of the other children.

The prestige of the Author's Chair led to satellite chairs during the readin
time. Children would gather their own copies of books, readers, trade book
and read to clusters of children. Reading was a time for sharing, receiving th

content of the selections and asking questions of the reader. During this reading time the teacher moved about listening, questioning the work of children, working with reading tools in phonics, and meeting with groups, but above all, focusing on the meaning of what the children were doing.

Development of the Author Concept

Three phases marked the children's growing understanding of the author concept: 1) Replication, 2) Transition, and 3) Sense of Option. We will give background for changes in the author concept in light of the children's composing in both reading and writing.

Phase I: Replication Phase: "Authors Write Books"

"Authors write books," answered most of the children when asked, "What do authors do?" We asked Ellen's students this question during September 1982 as part of a series of questions about their concepts of reading and writing. We followed it with, "Well, if authors write books, how do they do that? What do they do?" The answers followed no pattern; they varied from, "I don't know," to "Make a cover, then pages in there then they typewrite it, staple it together," to "Probably print up words." The author's process is invisible to the beginning first-grade child.

Earlier in this same interview we asked, "Can you write?" All the children answered, "Yes," and showed what they meant by drawing, making numbers, writing their names, writing letters or, for a few, even writing sentences. But after each child had written and we asked, "Are you an author?" few of the children felt they were authors. They knew their own ability to write was different from that of an author.

We also asked, "Can you read?" Several of the children surprised us by answering, "Yes," and showed what they meant by telling stories as they paged through familiar books, by mixing in repetitive words as they told a story, or by reading from early basals.

The children "play" their way into an understanding of reading and writing. They both invent and imitate their way into reading and writing. They observe and interact with the other children and Ellen as they read and write. They borrow certain conventions but demonstrate their own renditions of how to compose in each process.

They invent and imitate versions of writing through drawing, spelling, and various uses of the page. Their words change from erratic placement on blank spaces and around drawings to more orderly lines reserved for the print. Children also share their versions of oral reading by imitating the intonation of others. They hold their book, "read," and share the pictures from a pseudo-author's chair when they are reading alone and they take part in impromptu sharing sessions during the reading period.

They imitate the appearance of writing when they invent the spellings for the words they want on the pages they write about their personal experiences. They imitate the appearance of reading when they invent their re-telling of a story they have heard. They imitate the general processes and invent their own renditions.

In this phase the concept of authorship is a vague one. But they begin the long process of advancing toward a richer understanding of the concept by doing what writers and readers do: As writers they struggle to put their thoughts on paper and they talk about these thoughts with other writers. As readers they compose messages and ask questions about published stories. They play, they invent, they mimic when they compose in reading and writing and sitting on the Author's Chair.

Phase II: Transition Phase: "I Am an Author"

The author concept follows the publishing cycle in the classroom. The first published book appears during the first week of school and by October many of the children have had their first writing published in hard cover. Whenever a child publishes a book he or she reads it to the class. Their books are displayed alongside those of the professional authors read to the class. The author concept begins to become real as more and more children publish books.

As the children take part in the publishing cycle from drawing, to writing, to the making of the book, and sharing it with the class, they begin to understand the chain of events that leads to authorship: "Cindy is an author. She just got her book published."

The children start to identify with professional authors when they become aware of the prominence of topic choice. They think about what they know and make a decision. Usually they write about personal experiences. Professional writers choose their own topics and these children do likewise. They look at the content of trade books with the assumption the author is relating personal experiences. After reading a book to the class, Ellen frequently asks, "How do you suppose the author chose this topic?" One day she had read a factual book about barber shops and the answer to her question was by now predictable, "Rockwell must have just been to the barber shop."

The children project more than experience to the professional writer. One day Don Graves was not at the research site and one of the children asked, "Where is Mr. Graves today?" Jane Hansen replied, "He is at home writing his book." "He's doing the same thing we are," the child said casually.

The children think they know authors as persons. For example, Bill Martin becomes an early favorite because of his collection at the listening center. His books are some of the first ones they learn to read: "I can read my own book and Bill Martin Junior's book about the brown bear."

During this phase the children gradually show greater precision in their use of print. Although art work in reading and drawings in writing are still important, the transition phase is marked by more interest in print. Their decoding and encoding skills mature so they view the information in the illustrations as an extension of the text, whereas in the inventive phase the drawing was of primary importance. Now the children see the print as a necessary adjunct to the drawing. Whereas the drawing (when writing) and the illustrations (when reading) were dominant in the inventive phase, now there is a more complementary connection between the two. In their published books they draw a picture for every thought they express in words. The child sees pictures and print as an organic whole, a necessary precursor to seeing the distinctive functions of each.

The reading and writing in this phase take on different forms. The writing becomes more internalized. There is less oral composing during writing; they can write some words without producing every sound orally. The reading process evidences itself in just the opposite way. More and more sounding is heard. When we ask the children what they do when they read and write in this phase the response is the same as in the inventive phase, "Sound out the letters," even though it is less true of what they do when they write and more true of what they do when they read. A further query produces a glimmer of their process awareness, "Some kids still memorize their books, but I sound out when I read."

Gradually, more of their attention shifts to broader units of involvement in the composing processes. Rereading may go back several words and even several sentences in order to decide which word comes next. When they write, they reread before almost each new word. When they read, they reread when the message is interrupted by sounding out a word. The children do an abundance of rereading as they strive to make meaning.

This context broadens because of the events around the Author's Chair. As they receive and question books their questions involve the information in the stories. They ask, "Why didn't you tell why you still love your sister? Why didn't the author explain the way the goat felt?" In short, as the time-space units expand with the process moving back and forth between current word and broader text, the child begins to develop a sense of option. And as the child develops a sense of option, the authorship concept for self, other children, and professional becomes more distinctive.

Phase III: Option-Awareness Phase: "If I Wrote This Published Book Now, I Wouldn't Write It This Way"

The children's books no longer end with, "I feel sad," or "I feel happy." They can understand stories when authors write implied messages. Although they still expect most information to be explicit they now portray the mood of a story in their overall message. They expect their readers to compose a message when they read. They start to do this on purpose. One day Susan was reading a draft to us, "Do you like gym?" As she read she inserted, "Yes," and explained to us, "I won't put 'yes' in the published book. The kids will have to say that when I read it."

And one day when Steven read a new published book to the class someone asked him why he hadn't included a certain piece of information, "I thought you could figure it out." It is unlikely Steven had made this conscious decision as he was composing, but he does know that this is an acceptable assumption. Authors have the option of leaving some of the composing up to the reader.

In time they also learn how to handle the option of fictitious information. Jessica has sat in the Author's Chair both as a reader of her own books and trade books. She has heard different points of view about content and author's intentions from the other children. One day when she read her piece about the death of her grandfather, her book sounded like a first person account. Richie asked, "Is this a true story?" Jessica replied, "Some of it is not. Most of it is true." Richie continued, "Which parts are fake?" Jessica replied, "The part where I said I went to the funeral." At this point the teacher asked Jessica about her options, "Why did you put it in if it's not true?" Jessica asserted, "I thought it made the story better." The teacher wants to reveal Jessica's option, the right of any writer.

At this phase the children are wrestling with such polar issues as true-untrue, imaginary-real, and explicit-implicit. As each becomes more distinctive, children develop a sense of option in interchanging them in their writing and reading. They learn that child authors and professional authors have options.

Children also discover that authors publish different versions of one story. "Hey, look, here's the same story but the words are different. I wonder why the author published it both ways."

The sense of option becomes real to the children because of the changes in their own reading and writing processes and because of the Author's Chair. Children both exercise and experience the effects of audience. When they share their own pieces and view the reception of the works of both classmates and professionals, they recognize the variance of opinion. Ellen encourages children to provide information to back their opinions. "Why do you suppose the Author rewrote this book and published it again?" "Because the first one was sad." As children experiment, adapt, change their opinions they become open to options during the reading and writing process.

In the previous phase children read more for fluency. They read in order to share their accurate reading of words. The effects of the story on the listener were not as important as an accurate rendition of the print and the sharing of illustrations. The children read the book or rewrote the piece until it was "just right." The children already knew what the message was going to be because in reading they almost always chose stories they had heard before and in writing they related incidents that had happened to them. They didn't read and write to find out the product. They read and wrote because the process of putting together an already known message intrigued them. Now, the children reread and rewrite for layered meanings.

The children reread not with the conscious view of going after different levels of comprehension. Rather, the children reread to reenjoy characters, plots, and actions. But in doing so the child gathers a sense of option about the interaction of various components of the story. New meanings appear in successive readings. In short, the child "revises" the content of the piece read.

The actual reading performance changes as well. The children go back and forth within the paragraph or story in order to juxtapose part-whole relationships in the whole piece.

The writing process also involves an exercise of option. The children reread with more than a view of reorienting themselves in their emerging texts. Now they reread with a view to making the part under construction consistent with the overall intention in the piece. The child discovers inconsistencies and will choose to cut and paste for reorganization, choose to organize a story by chapter in order to make it more clear, or write a complete second draft that includes, "a lot more information." The child rewrites with a sense of what the class will ask when he or she reads the piece from the Author's Chair.

When children are asked about how they read and write, their answers now show more separation between the two processes, "When I write I choose a topic. That's the hard part. Then I write drafts. Then I might publish it. When I read I choose a story, sometimes I can read it without lots of practice, then I might read it to the class." In both reading and writing, the children have a sense of process and are especially free of the "sounding out" component so dominant in earlier statements. Such freedom lifts the children into more thinking about information and the content and organization of what authors actually do in writing.

The children do have options. They do make decisions. They decide whether to put information in their pieces or not. They defend their pieces when the class asks questions. They question published authors. They respond to a story by accepting it and asking questions. Their responsibility as writers is to anticipate questions from readers. Their responsibility as readers is to ask questions of authors. They become assertive readers who expect authors to defend the choices they made when they wrote.

Hypotheses About Authorship

We did not know where the 1981 – 82 year would take us. We certainly did not know the Author's Chair would come to symbolize the relationship between reading and writing. Somehow, readers who are also writers develop a sense of authorship that helps them in either composing process. The above observations lead us to the following hypotheses about the relationship between reading and writing as it develops in beginning readers.

1. Children's concept of author changes from a vague notion about some other person who writes books to the additional perception of themselves as authors to the realization that they have choices and decisions to make as authors.
2. Children's concept of authorship becomes more pronounced as their concepts of reading and writing become more differentiated.
3. Authorship concepts become more differentiated because children actively compose in both reading and writing. Composing in each of these processes consists of imitating and inventing during encoding, decoding, and the making of meaning.
4. Children change from imposing their own understandings of process and content upon authors, to realizing various authors can use process and content differently.
5. Children realize authors have options because they do the following in both the reading and writing processes: exercise topic choice, revise by choice, observe different types of composing, and become exposed to variant interpretations.
6. Children who learn to exercise options become more assertive in dealing with other authors. At first an author is distant, then an author is self, finally the self-author questions all authors and assertive readers emerge.

The data for this article came from the first year of our investigation of the relationship between reading and writing. We could not have gathered these data if we had not been in a classroom in which the children had ample opportunity to both read and write. Our recognition of the importance of the author concept came because of the uniqueness of our field site. Since the significance of the author concept did not emerge until the second half of the year, we have started a new year-long study with a new group of children to examine the author concept in greater depth.

19. The Enemy Is Orthodoxy

Introduction

Talks don't always live up to their advance titles. In August 1982, Mary Maguire, program chair of the Canadian Council of Teachers of English, asked me to be one of the speakers at their annual meeting in Montreal in May 1983. Later she asked me for a title over the phone, and I gave her "Everyone Has a Story to Tell." I was interested in narrative at the time and wanted to use the speech to further develop my thinking. As the date for the speech got closer I began to make outlines for the address.

But I felt uneasy. I had received a critique in the mail, from David Dillon, of our earlier work, which was written by Myra Barrs. In a number of workshops I had found some orthodoxies creeping into supervisors' and teachers' interpretation of our work. These orthodoxies were stated as maxims or problems: "Children should only write in personal narrative." "All work should be revised. Tell me, how do you get children to revise?" "This publishing is too much." "I don't have time to listen to the children anymore." Also, letters from around the world were hinting that reactions to old orthodoxies were spawning new ones. These new orthodoxies would result in less listening to children. I also had to face the fact that I was responsible for some of the misunderstandings.

I asked my secretary, Dori, to sit at the word processor. "I'll dictate for an hour and let's see what we have on a new topic." The title, "The Enemy is Orthodoxy" came immediately. I felt good about the title—a good omen. This time, contrary to my experience with "The Author's Chair" piece, the text flowed and stayed with the title. My dictated first paragraph went as follows:

The enemy is orthodoxy. In both research on the writing process and in the writing process movement, there are many danger signs that would only serve to imprison children. With any new approach to the teaching of anything, there is a constant danger that sensitive edges to child writing and thinking will be lopped off in the guise of making the approach to teaching children more simplified. Right now, there is a danger that with the high attention given to the writing process movement, that for those of us involved in it a kind of complacency will move in that will lull us and interested parties into a stiffening orthodoxy. There is a high danger to researchers, teachers, and children. This morning, I would like to outline some specific approaches to the teaching of writing that would insure safeguards against the dangers of orthodoxy.

I felt good about the voice and content. I then dictated another 2,500 words on the subject. I guess I had been rehearsing the issue for some time. All eight orthodoxies were in the original dictation, with the exception of the ninth, which was added in a later draft.

I gave the talk twice in Montreal and it was very well received. Three issues emerged in my first talk that I adopted for the second address: limit the talk to orthodoxy in teaching; include some information on why teachers embrace orthodoxies; develop the section on phasing into conference work more fully. The first two were changed in the talk, the third took many revisions during the summer of 1983 before I felt comfortable with the content. I suspect that the whole process of phasing from traditional corrections on each revision to one teaching focus had to be sorted out. I guess the same is true of every issue spelled out in this piece. There is always the issue of when to intervene and when not to intervene in a writer's work. I lean toward *not* intervening, to giving the writer more responsibility, more credit for knowing more about the subject, but I am restless about my role as a professional. If the subject or topic is a good one, I want my imprint, my fingerprints, to be part of the writer's success.

At this writing, I believe the "Orthodoxy" piece to be one of my most important ones. It gets at an issue that will always plague me. When I finished my talk in Montreal, my colleague, Don Murray, joshed me, "You have a new orthodoxy, you know. Beware of orthodoxies!"

The Writing Process Movement has been responsible for a new vitality in both writing and education. But orthodoxies are creeping in that may lead to premature old age. They are a natural part of any aging process. Some are the result of early problems in research (my own included); others come from people who try to take shortcuts with very complex processes. These orthodoxies are substitutes for thinking. They clog our ears. We cease to listen to each other, clouding the issues with jargon in place of simple, direct prose about actual children.

Orthodoxies have to be called by name. I've traveled around the United States, Canada, Australia, and New Zealand over the last two years and have gradually built up a list of the ones that bother me most. Here is my list, recording the most extreme forms:

1. Children ought to revise everything they compose.
2. Children should only write in personal narrative; imaginative writing ought to be discouraged.
3. Children should have several conferences for each piece of writing.
4. Children should publish each piece of writing.
5. Children should make each piece of writing last four days.
6. Children should share each piece with the entire class.
7. Children should own their own writing and never be directed to do anything with their writing.
8. Children should choose all their topics.
9. Spelling, grammar, and punctuation are unimportant.

I will now discuss each orthodoxy and offer solutions for dealing with the problems inherent in each.

1. Revision

Six-year olds change little of their writing. Just the miracle of putting down information in words is sufficient to fulfill their intentions. Children often write on the same subject three or four times with each subsequent composing an unconscious revision of the one before.

As children become better readers and more sensitive to how other children and the teacher interpret their pieces, they begin to want to change their writing, especially when they care about their topic. The child notes a discrepancy between his text and his intended meaning. The teacher helps the child to deal with the information and the mechanics of making changes.

The following examples call for practically no revision at all in a piece:

1. The child has made a poor choice of topic. The child may choose the topic on a whim, to impress another child or parent, or simply be too ambitious. After a good effort, the piece is abandoned and placed in the folder.
2. The child has already made revisions in another way. The piece may be an extension of several other pieces written on the same subject and little change is needed. Or the topic may be so hot, the information so rich and deep, that little change is needed.
3. The teacher has asked a child to do "quick burst" writing. This type of writing is often assigned to help a child get into a draft, experiment with advanced thinking about a subject, or write a quick impression of a chapter or conversation. Such writing is not thrown away; it is merely used to get temporary impressions for the child or the teacher.

Both teachers and children need to learn when the time is right to revise. Teachers understand this best when they write themselves, and especially when they write with and for their children. A review of influences on revision show, in fact, that children revise in the long run more because of indirect influences than through direct conferences:

1. Literature. The children are surrounded with literature. They hear and respond and delight in reading a wide range of literature.
2. Sharing of writing. They share their writing at all draft stages with a wide variety of well-prepared audiences. If children have access to each other, and the teacher has prepared children to help intelligently, this is probably the most important influence on revision.
3. Use of time. If teachers provide a process approach across the curriculum where error is opportunity for learning and rediscovering meaning, then revision, or rethinking, becomes a way of life. This requires a different pace and use of time.
4. Expectation. When children know that the teacher believes they know things and that their learning needs to be shared with others, then children are not afraid to rethink their way to excellence.
5. Publication. When children are able to share their best in more durable form, and that piece will be shared with their friends, other classrooms, and relatives, their intentions are raised and their expectations along with them.

2. Personal Narrative and Imaginative Writing

Most children find it easier to compose in personal narrative. It is easier for them to recall what has happened in their own lives than to compose new and imaginative material. Nevertheless, what children bring to the writing experience ought to be taken seriously. If a child is composing an imaginative piece about last night's TV mystery, I treat the piece in the same way I would a personal narrative. That is, I listen to the text, and ask questions that will help the writer. I treat the writer as a serious author who intends to communicate with others.

It *is* important for children to be able to compose good fiction. Many truths can be better expressed in fiction than in personal narrative. Children and teachers need to discover this for themselves, but a number of issues surrounding the personal narrative-fiction debate need to be clarified.

Teachers should help children compose fiction but they ought to be aware of the "American" problem that pervades the composing of imaginative pieces. Fiction in America seems to imply the bizarre. Teachers and children believe fiction allows only tales from outer space, high body counts, monsters who destroy, or a different set of rules for using information. Events ought not to be plausible or the result of human frailty. Rather, they just happen. Fiction may demand even more detail, more command of the reader's experience if the reader is to participate in the story.

I label the fiction problem as an American one because we seldom surround our children with good fiction through regular reading, or even demonstrate the composing of fiction. Good fiction must be plausible even though the story may be centered in outer space; readers need to meet multi-dimensional characters who are ambitious, impatient, tempted, or aware of feelings. Most fiction written by children stresses an action line with mono-dimensional characters reminiscent of TV plots. Children want things to happen, to have excitement in all genres. Children want to be authors. One child said, "Being a real author means writing fiction."

3. Writing Conferences

The conference is the heart of teaching the writing process. The common orthodoxy that surrounds conferences, however, is that teachers need to confer with the young writer at every stage of the writing process. Teachers have seen themselves "correcting" children's work to prevent the proliferation of mistakes. It is only natural for teachers to feel withdrawal pangs from such practices and to become over-involved in conferences. They complain, "If I am to really correct the way I need to, conferences should last about fifteen minutes. Now with twenty-eight kids in my room, that's impossible. Conferences don't work."

For teachers who have been thorough in correcting, or for teachers who are wondering how to start conferences, I suggest a phasing-in process that enables the teacher to grow into conference work along with the children. As much as a teacher can simplify teaching writing and writing conferences, the more children will be able to take responsibility for their learning. Teachers will find the following four-phase approach to conferences helpful:

Stage One: Circulation:

Have the children push their desks together in clusters of four. The children won't be working together at this point but it will enable them to overhear your conferences as you circulate around the room. Move from one cluster of four to another, but only receive the work of one child. "Oh, I see you are writing a space wars episode; they are just preparing for a launching from the satellite. Yes, I can see that." The children in the cluster hear your emphasis on the flow of information in early drafts. There may be handwriting, spelling, punctuation and grammar problems staring you in the face, but these can be temporarily ignored while the writer struggles with the information in his piece. The teacher moves about the room encouraging, listening, but first attending to children who may need her most. For the first week, possibly longer, the teacher—for her sake and the children's—just circulates with one focus, that of receiving the children's information. Receiving takes about forty-five seconds to a minute per child.

Stage Two: Questions:

During a second week, the teacher receives the children's work, but adds a question. The question is one designed to help the child teach the teacher about his subject. "They are just leaving the main satellite, Mark. What is going to happen next?" or "Do they live on the satellite, Mark, or is this just a temporary launching site? Could you tell me about that?" Try just one question, no more. Keep it simple.

Stage Three: Clusters of Concern:

As children get into their subjects, choose their topics more wisely, observe the teacher composing with the class, or hear responses to their writing from other children, their pieces lengthen in words and in the time spent in composing. In stages one and two, teachers have worked very hard to help young writers gain fluency and discover that they can command their subjects. Because the children are more fluent, teachers have more opportunities to teach them in the midst of their drafts. As long as an entire class completes their writing in two-day bursts, the teacher has very little opportunity to help them in-process.

As writers gain fluency, teachers can also gather clusters of children together to work on common problems. Some children have trouble choosing topics; others are stuck on early revising, how to insert information in a draft, or how to deal with conventions going into final draft. Clusters may be groups of children who meet once a week to share their writing and to learn how to help each other with the teacher's help. The teacher can divide the number of children in class by five for Monday, Tuesday, Wednesday groups, etc. Other cluster types follow common skills needs: work on commas, proofreading, writing titles or leads, sentence sense, etc. Clusters are brought together when the teacher notes that the rest of the children are able to work quite well on their own.

Stage Four: Mutual Aid:

As children learn more and more about how to help each other on an informal basis and as the teacher is able to refer children to each other for certain help, there is less formal group activity. Once in a while the teacher will stop the class for a special all-class workshop or bring in a cluster on leads, but this phase is marked by children's intelligent help of each other.

This comes later in the year and is the result of much work by the teacher in helping children to take responsibility for their own writing, and of the teacher's teaching the children how to learn to listen to and question the pieces of their classmates. The teacher now has more time for trouble-shooting; some conferences can be longer and more detailed with a specific challenge given to children who need to be brought through particular crises in drafts.

The basic principle in these four stages of phasing into conferences is to give high focus to various components of teaching and of the writing process. It is easier for both teachers and children not to deal with the entire process initially. It is particularly helpful for teachers who are trying to move away from taking responsibility from children through overcorrecting of papers.

4. Publication

Publishing is important to children. Sometimes it is even more important to teachers. Publishing is concrete evidence that the children are making progress. Mary Ellen Giacobbe, first-grade teacher in the Atkinson study, published 440 books in her first year with the writing process, and freely admitted that she needed the hardcover books more than the children did. In the next two years she reduced the numbers of books published, which she could do because she sensed the best timing for publication.

Publishing creeps in as a dangerous orthodoxy in several forms. The first type includes the teacher who publishes everything, the "everything" being all of two books composed in the entire year. The supervisor proudly exhibits them to adminstrators and parents. In the second type, the publishing becomes such a burden that teachers are unable to respond to the children. It would be better for teachers to *delay* the publishing step for several months until the "bugs" of finding better ways to respond to children through conferences can be ironed out. Children need personal response more than they need to publish.

5. Length of Composing

The old orthodoxy was the three-day assignment. Put the topic on the board on Monday; the children write in class; work on the piece at home Monday night; pass it in for correction on Tuesday. The papers are passed back on Wednesday, the red marks taken out and cleaned up in a second "draft" and passed back for a grade. In reaction to the first orthodoxy, the new one creeping in does not consider a paper good unless the writer has been working on it for three weeks and sustained it through three to four drafts. There *is* a need for children to learn to listen to a topic and sustain composing over longer periods of time on topics of their own choosing. But there is also a need to reexamine the children's entire composing diet.

Children need a wide range of composing experience involving different uses of time. Note some of the uses of writing in these assignments:

- "Just write for five minutes on what you think this chapter will be about."
- "Write a three-sentence precis on what this chapter will be about."

- "You say you are stuck, don't know what to say next because you have too many ideas. Well, just write for ten minutes on *one* of those ideas; then try another one. Don't change anything, you are just exploring."
- "I want you to read over your piece so far; tell your partner about it, then write in one sentence what your piece is about. Your partner can do the same."

Such rapid, short-term composing, involving little revising is as useful to long-term composing, as long-term composing is to the precis. Children then learn to compress thinking in order to expand it and learn to expand in order to compress it.

6. Sharing Writing

Writing is a public act. It exists to influence others or provide thinking for oneself at another place and time. Too much writing is composed for just one person, the teacher. Young writers don't grow without the expanded horizons of other children's reactions; they possess too limited a concept of the effects of their text. Sharing becomes an orthodoxy when writers are required to share, regardless of where they are in a draft, or at times when they simply do not need help. This is particularly true for older writers beyond the age of eight or nine. Six-year olds have the built-in immunity of self-centeredness to protect them from the effects of audiences. Here are some guidelines to help protect both children and teachers from sharing that is poorly timed:

1. Provide a place in the room where writers can work and *not be disturbed* by teacher or other students. Six to eight seats, or more, depending on reasonable demand, is usually enough. Writers are in these seats because they are discovering their subjects or the writing is going well and they do not want any interruptions. It is useful to both teachers and children to know who is taking advantage of this situation.
2. Provide some self-select audience situations in the room. Help children to learn more about *when* response is helpful. Work hard to help *children to learn* how to respond to each other's writing.
3. Realize that writers are more vulnerable when discovering their subjects in early drafts.
4. *Sharing is negotiated.* If writers are asked to share, first *be specific* about what is good in their pieces. Be specific on how you think sharing will help either the writer or the class. The writer still has the right to veto the sharing.
5. *Limit response to sharing:* Audiences cease to provide help when help is too extensive. Too much advice is worse than none at all. The teacher needs to know the writer and the process well enough to end a shared response at the right time.

7. Teachers Shouldn't Be Directive

"The trouble with process teaching," complains the teacher, "is that you never get to tell the kid to just plain *do something*. I get nervous about just hanging back, waiting for something to happen." Another expression of the same orthodoxy comes from the teacher who says, "I'm afraid that I will hurt the child if I say that he ought to reread his piece to see where he might have some problems with information." One teacher is itching to move in, the other is afraid that an intervention will hurt the child. Both are reacting to the orthodoxy, "Don't direct the child, follow."

A large proportion of teaching writing in process does follow the child. Following means keeping in touch with the writer's intentions and helping writers to see how they are living up to what they intended to do in the first place. Following means listening to writers talk about what they know, then asking questions that reveal more about information and process to both writer and teacher. But it takes time to know both how to follow and how to observe writers. At first, teachers don't know the child or the process well enough to know what they are seeing. It is hard to trust such uncertain ground; it is hard not to be directive. I find that I become directive in my own teaching at two distinct points: when I am *completely unsure* of my ground, or when I am *secure* in my knowledge of process and of the writer with whom I am working. I meddle when I want pieces to go my way, when I want to save the writer's product from my own embarrassment as a teacher. If I don't know the writer's subject or those early problems in grammar, punctuation, and spelling, I move in to solve some unsightly problems.

Directives work better when children and teachers write together and they are several months into process work. The teacher says, "John, your piece is due tomorrow." Sometimes a child needs to try a new genre. "John, try writing this as if you were the driver of that racing car. Just take twenty minutes and see what it is like to write from that point of view." John knows the teacher is giving him time to try something new. He knows the teacher has a history of wanting writers to learn more about writing and to discover something new about their subjects and themselves. The more writers and teachers understand each other, the more directive writing conferences can become. A simple directive, "Do it," or "Get busy," is clearly understood by each. Children do the same with teachers. "Mr. Thomas, I don't know what you are talking about. How come I have to do this?" Jennifer isn't being insolent. Mr. Thomas knows she is asking because she doesn't want to sit in confusion for the next forty-five minutes. Because Mr. Thomas is consistent in his response to children and they know that he wants them to gain control of their writing, they are not afraid to challenge or ask questions about essential information. The important fact in the writing studio is that neither teacher nor child is afraid of the other. Still, there is no mistaking the situation: the teacher is the person in charge, the professional responsible for the direction and the success of the classroom.

8. The Writing Assignment

The new orthodoxy contends that all writing should be unassigned; the teacher never intervenes by placing the topic on the board. This orthodoxy is a reaction to the tradition that teachers always choose subjects and topics for children.

Writers do need to learn to choose a topic, limit it, learn what they know and present it to other audiences. The personal base is the base of voice. But how difficult it is for teachers to know where the voices of individual students may lie. As Donald Murray says, "You can't write about nothing." Yet every day students in thousands of classrooms are asked to write about nothing. They are asked to write about experiences that are not theirs, or if they are, to write about experiences long since sterile. Still, there is an important place for the assigned topic; it belongs in the writer's diet.

About twenty percent of a writer's diet ought to be assigned. But an assigned topic requires preparation; it requires the writer to read, interview, find the voice of opinion and concern in wrestling with the facts.

Assigned topics mean that the teacher participates in the process of gathering data. Students see the teacher go through the process of doing the assignment with them. Modeling is never more important than in assigned writing, particularly writing in the content areas. Modeling means that the teacher demonstrates topic discovery, brainstorming, reading and note-taking, drafting, and final copy.

Assigned topics can also be the short ten or twenty minute discovery of a new area in reading, or a precis as mentioned in the section on different uses of time for writing. Teachers may also assign genre: "You have two lines of a poem here. Take another piece of paper and just see if there is a poem there. Have fun with it." Teachers are not afraid to assign topics as long as they understand the need of the writer to discover the material demanded by it.

9. Spelling, Grammar, and Punctuation

A new orthodoxy holds that grammar, punctuation, spelling and handwriting are unimportant as long as the information is good. Not so. These skills, or surface features, are very important . . . in their place.

Once the information has been developed and organized then the final touches that will enhance the meaning need to be applied. If a sentence is not punctuated properly, is illegible or convoluted, the reader has to struggle unnecessarily. Worse, it appears writers care little for their information or their audience. Then there are traditionalists who simply dismiss an entire piece, good content and all, because the writer hasn't done the final job with surface features. Teachers must continue to help writers through the final work. The full job of teaching is not completed until the teacher has helped the children to handle surface features on their own.

Here are some guidelines for successful work with surface features:

1. **Timing.**   Work with grammar, punctuation, and spelling should come after information has been clarified.
2. **Writer Responsibility.**   Writers need to make their own estimates of where they think they might have errors in spelling, punctuation, grammar, or precise choice of words in their next–to–final draft. The writer's estimate shows the teacher what needs to be taught.
3. **Teaching Skills.**   Only one or two skills can be taught at a time, and taught within the context of the writer's piece. Teaching means *showing* a writer how to place quotation marks and commas, or work with spelling problems. Correcting is not the same as teaching.
4. **Choosing Papers.**   Not every piece goes through to final draft stage. Some pieces ought to be abandoned for a variety of reasons: the topic was poorly chosen, the writer cared little for the subject, or the child just wanted to experiment with a new approach to writing. When the writer believes the piece is going somewhere then the teacher pushes it through to final audit, edit, and teaching.

Final Reflection

All of us have orthodoxies in our teaching that prevent us from being sensitive to writers. Some of these orthodoxies, or maxims for teaching, are necessary for temporary sanity as coping mechanisms for our teaching situations, or our personal need to overuse something in order to understand it. Often, something like publishing meets our own needs as teachers at the expense of what is best for children. Publishing is visible evidence that "I am a productive teacher."

There are ways to protect against the establishment of orthodoxies. The *first* requires us to let children teach us about what they know. As long as we work hard to place the initiative in the child's corner, observe what the child is doing and telling us, and adjust our teaching to fit child growth, then orthodoxies shift. "Gosh, my way of publishing doesn't fit. I've been publishing too soon." Or: "John is changing too much. This time I'll ask him to write the entire piece and change nothing. Then we'll look at it together."

All of the orthodoxies I challenge in this article arose out of real needs in the teaching of writing. In the past, writers seldom revised, seldom had teachers listen to them, or wrote only fiction; they seldom listened to their pieces beyond two days, or were directed by the teacher, without learning to take responsibility for their work. Now that one phase of the writing process movement, the early correction of past problems, is over it is time to re-examine the new orthodoxies, lest we cease to listen to children.

The *second* check against orthodoxy is to keep writing ourselves, to learn more and more how we write, to discover firsthand the nature of our own writing in order to understand what children are doing when they compose. The process must always be fresh to us and to the children. The exciting thing about having the children teach us and having us teach ourselves in our own writing, is that teaching becomes a process of discovery in its own right. Orthodoxies continually make us use old data, without today's fresh evidence. Orthodoxies make us tell *old stories* about children at the expense of the new stories that children are telling us today.